The Alienated

Reader

The Alienated Reader

WOMEN AND ROMANTIC LITERATURE IN THE TWENTIETH CENTURY

Bridget Fowler

Department of Sociology
University of Glasgow

HARVESTER WHEATSHEAF

New York London Toronto Sydney Tokyo Singapore

First published 1991 by
Harvester Wheatsheaf
66 Wood Lane End, Hemel Hempstead
Hertfordshire HP2 4RG
A division of
Simon & Schuster International Group

© Bridget Fowler, 1991

Typeset in Bembo 10½/12 pt. by Columns Design
and Production Services Ltd, Reading

Printed and bound in Great Britain by
BPCC Wheatons Ltd, Exeter

British Library Cataloguing in Publication Data

Fowler, Bridget 1943–
    The alienated reader: women and popular romantic literature in
    the twentieth century.
    1. Romantic fiction in English. Women writers – Critical studies
    I. Title
    823.085099287
    ISBN 0–7450–0249–8
    ISBN 0–7450–0250–1 pbk

1 2 3 4 5 95 94 93 92 91

Contents

Acknowledgements

Many people have helped with this book, on various fronts: as readers of fiction, with whom enjoyable hours of interview were passed, as academics who have contributed theoretical ideas and as childminders in the domestic arena.

I am particularly grateful to Mike Gonzalez and Bert Moorhouse, whose acute and pithy comments on the manuscript have sustained me throughout. My thanks also to Seithi Chagage, Anne Crowther, Harvie Ferguson, Eleanor Gordon, Barbara Littlewood, Terry Lovell, Herminio Martins, Mick Scott and Michel Lowy, all of whom have offered invaluable criticism, advice and references but none of whom can be held responsible for the remaining weaknesses. Without them, there would have been many more.

My children, Meg, Daniel, Ben and Luke, have kept up my spirits in the preparation period and provided technical assistance with the word processor. John Fowler has consistently held the view that an empirical study of popular literature and its readers might be illuminating and has cheerfully accepted extra family obligations so that it could be undertaken. Finally, the book would not have been finished were it not for the generous cooperation with typing from Sandra Matti and Avril Johnstone.

Glasgow, 1990

Introduction

This book has as its subject the popular culture of women. It explores literature as a form of consciousness shaped by changing social relations. In particular, popular literature is the arena of class and gender conflicts over symbolic representation. I shall dissect one such genre, the 'domestic romance', and seek to display its structure, origins and appeal. Romantic fiction is so stigmatised at present that it has received very little academic attention. However, if archeologists can discover valuable materials for reconstructing entire societies from the contents of prehistoric middens, even the most formulaic romance may reveal important clues to both human needs and the existing social relations within which they are expressed.

I suggest that we need to move beyond the traditional dichotomy between realism and ideology to focus on the demand for *magical fictions*. The specific use-value of the romance lies in its interweaving of images of 'civilisation' and women's discontents, with the miraculous suspension of these alienating conditions. Enjoyment of the genre depends on an acceptance – however brief – of its conventions, hence the abandonment of the disenchanted, secularised perspective of modernity in the pursuit of a 'magical garden'. Yet the transformations of these fantastic escapes also require elaboration: not just in the centrality of the erotic encounter in the 1980s in comparison with the silence in the 1930s about female sexuality, but in the new regulation of the private sphere and the permanent commitment to work on the part of the heroines.

I have found the most imaginative and fruitful theories of the world of genre literature in Ernst Bloch, particularly in his division between day-dreams and night-dreams, conceived as distinct structures of feeling which illuminate cultural consumption. His unravelling of the various meanings of escapism is introduced in

1

Chapter 1 but his influence on looking at literature in terms of ideology and utopia has shaped the book as a whole.

This book is organised around three main objectives. The first is to elucidate the ideological structure of the romance and to explain the social and literary conditions for the cultural production of this popular form. The second task is to dissect representative popular texts in order to show both continuities and structural transformations within the genre. The third task is to assess cultural consumption. By passing from texts to readers, I show how the reception of literature varies with social experience. Since the mass romance has become the monstrous 'other' of Western high culture and since women have been its bearers, I investigate, in particular, what social reality now sustains its tranquillising dreams.

In the first chapter I introduce a model of the domestic romance, Samuel Richardson's *Pamela*, which not only contains desire within marriage, but is the characteristic expression of the world's first bourgeois class, the modernising landed gentry. I then assess the conditions under which this form took off as a popular, cross-class genre. The modern Western romance is *not* universal but is grounded in three historical preconditions, the transition to capitalism, Protestantism and patriarchal relations. In turn, cheap mass romances emerged after the 'domestication' of working women, that is, after married women had withdrawn from partnerships in production into economic dependence on men, from 1842 onwards.

I then sketch recent changes in the economics of publishing, which have led to the aggressive marketing of a highly formulaic product. This has reinforced the tenacity of the genre in its place on the market while reducing the availability of other types of literature to lower-class women. Yet despite its commodified form, the popular romance responds to certain social needs. I look at how this issue has been broached in cultural theory. In particular, the current debate about 'high' and 'low' culture is reappraised, partly to contest the neo-Althusserian approach in which canonised literature is approached as ideology.

Chapters 3, 4 and 5 show how different types of writing have competed for lower-class women readers since the 1840s. First, I consider the classical patriarchal form of popular literature in the magazines of the 1930s. This is a highly regressive fiction of social integration: however, the authors' concern for a wide circulation still sets some limits on the types of dominant perspective that can be incorporated in the cheapest narratives. Moreover, as I shall show, there is a 'popular canon' in which certain writers are esteemed highly by lower-class readers. It is this choice which is examined in Chapter 4, with the work of the highly successful regional writer, Catherine Cookson. The roots of her story-telling lie in using the conservative romance with a 'labourist' or social democratic inflexion, evident both in the lower-class perspective and her alternating strands of realism with redemptive utopia. This is not a 'dominant ideology', since its appeal lies in its reworking of popular history with a renovated form of the 'condition of England' industrial novel. Rather, her novels preserve what Benjamin called 'dialectical images'. Within these gaudy and dog-eared covers can be found 'correspondences': 'an experience which seeks to establish itself in crisis-proof form . . . the data of remembrance'.[1]

Chapter 5 shows how the romantic story has developed historically from the 1930s to the 1980s, with respect to the decline of Madonna/whore figures, the lessened intensity of the work ethic for heroes and the reduced salience of questions of class injustice. In the best sellers and short stories of the 1980s, there is fresh growth developing beyond the withered ideological branches of Mills and Boon, which suggests the questioning of the old patriarchal paradigm. A new genre of romantic story has emerged, extending the vocabulary of individual 'natural' rights to women, but combining it with a vision of their heroic progress in the free market economy. Barbara Taylor Bradford is the Horatio Alger or Samuel Smiles of the 1980s and the female entrepreneur is the most fashionable style in which the bourgeoisie presents itself! Chapter 5 also shows the continued significance of the gentry within this fiction; here I follow Roger Bromley's analysis of this class as the bearer of social unity within the romance universe.

The sixth chapter asks: 'How do women decode literature?' I examine critically the work of Pierre Bourdieu on cultural consumption, in the light of interviews with a sample of 115 women in the West of Scotland and conclude that Bourdieu's contrast between popular and cultivated taste in terms of the opposition between social 'function' and 'form' is too limited a perspective on artistic perception. While agreeing with Bourdieu that late capitalism has not severed the old stratified connections between class and culture, I argue that he has focused too narrowly on the 'aristocracy of taste' at the expense of understanding the role of art in movements of social change and the emergence of different, indeed competing, types of popular culture. Using readership groups based on Bourdieu's categories, I contend that the multiple uses of popular literature – including support for folk political philosophies – is too condensed in his account. My interpretation of the interviews elaborates the meaning of popular women's fictions for their readers mainly in terms of Bloch's perspective: by bouncing Bourdieu off Bloch, so to speak, a clarification of the uses and ideological status of romances can emerge.

In concluding, I argue against the recent plea for an 'end to ideology' in social theory. My interviews provide grounds for the view that the type of literature women read is linked to their wider world-view, thus giving a new significance to struggles within the cultural sphere. I suggest that the traditional gentry–bourgeois romance embodies a highly *regressive utopian consciousness*, which legitimates the world of the dominant classes. Nevertheless, some popular writers are shown to be the bearers of working-class and plebeian experience, possessing a limited capacity to interrogate social contradictions, whilst also bestowing the imaginary solutions to women's needs. The expression of hopes and wish fulfilments *are* important. For many working-class and petty-bourgeois readers particularly, a 'happy ending, seen through but still defended' is a literary imperative.[2]

Part I
CULTURAL
PRODUCTION

1 *Understanding the Romance: the Origins and Structure of a Major Mass Cultural Genre*

THE ORIGINS OF THE MODERN DOMESTIC ROMANCE

Throughout its long history, the romance has both legitimated female subordination and spoken of the needs of women – hence its lack of appeal for men and, to a lesser extent for 'emancipated' women. Its origins lie in patriarchal relations and in the feudal mode of production. However, in the feudal period, the popular romance also possessed critical elements which became more attenuated as bourgeois society developed. Consequently, the formulaic romance of the twentieth century lacks the rebelliousness of some other popular genres.

This chapter will situate the genre in terms of its social and literary coordinates. It is argued, first, that the ideological form of the romance is conditional upon the dependence, propertylessness and vassalage of women *vis-à-vis* men in feudalism. Secondly, the subsequent development of capitalism from the seventeenth century has left its indelible traces on the romance, fusing a restless individualism, upward mobility and erotically charged marriage with the paternalist pastoral idyll of the agrarian bourgeoisie.[1] Thirdly, its primary concern with the private rather than the public sphere is conditioned by the double exclusion of women, both from the contractual rights of bourgeois (male) individuals and the arena of production entered via wage-labour. Finally, the literary preconditions of the popular domestic romance are traced through the lines of lower-class descent, and specifically through the feudal fairy-tale, the peasant novella and the eighteenth-century novel with its formal realism of time, space and psyche.

What, then, are the defining characteristics of the romance?[2] The popular romantic story today has two major forms, either the quest of the lovers to overcome obstacles to marriage, or the restoration of marital and family harmony after the threat of disintegration. In both forms, social unity, ethically correct action and individual happiness are simultaneously guaranteed. In particular, the romantic narrative is about troubles which disturb the proper mapping of the 'machinery of sexuality' onto the 'machinery of alliance'. The circulation of wealth and family names through legitimate channels has to be engineered in these texts so as to coincide with love and sexuality. Romances explore conflicts over both the subordination of women in patriarchal relations and the modern channelling of intense emotional ties into the confined, privatised sphere of the family. They celebrate heterosexual monogamous relations. For this reason, the female folk-devils of the traditional romance are 'masterless women', just as the tramps, beggars and rogues, who were the folk-devils of the seventeenth century, were also 'masterless men'. This is so even though the perspective of the stories is that of the dominated woman herself. Such fictions depict both the alienation experienced as a result of dependency and the supercession of such alienation. The 'wisdom' achieved at the end of the stories speaks of a patriarchal order that is natural and necessary, hence typically invoking an idealised model of existing social reality.

The traditional romance presents women's dependence as service which is 'perfect freedom', not unlike that of the Christian's devotion to his or her lord, Christ. However, its mechanics also operate through the tensions between women and men, similar to those described in the fraught dichotomy of male master and slave analysed by Hegel:

> For recognition proper the moment is lacking . . . the object in which the lord has achieved his lordship has in reality turned out to be something quite different from an independent consciousness. What now really confronts him is not an independent consciousness, but a dependent one. He is therefore not certain of being-for-self as the truth of himself . . . [But] just as lordship showed that its essential nature is the reverse of what it wants to be, so too servitude in its consummation will really turn into the opposite of what it really is; as a consciousness forced back into itself, it will withdraw into itself and be transformed into a truly independent consciousness . . . .[3]

It will be objected that modern popular romances do not operate with an exactly analogous model of *gender* inequality at their core. It *is* true that images of 'reformed patriarchy' and formal equality pervade much of this fiction and that this change corresponds to the historical restructuring of relations between men and women around the bourgeois ideals of freedom and equality. Indeed, the twentieth-century development of egalitarian perceptions of gender has perhaps now removed the conditions under which great romances, such as Jane Austen's *Persuasion*, can be written. Nevertheless, the persistence today of marked social differences between the destinies of men and women, in part linked to the utility of women to capital as a source of cheap labour, and in part to the survival of a legal double standard, continues to give some contemporary credibility to the traditional world of the romance.[4] Thus to understand fully the ethos of the story in which the man is the woman's lord, it is necessary to trace its roots to the distinctive patriarchal mode of feudalism. For if feudalism was grounded on a set of production relations based on the extra-economic, coercive extraction of a peasant surplus by a class of lords, it was also accompanied by a set of social bonds in which labour service, marriage, homage and protection were expressed through the model of an idealised family, both in vassalage and its linked hierarchical forms.

Production relations and patriarchy in feudalism and the transition to capitalism

Gender relations in feudalism were organised minutely around the inheritance of property, the main mechanism for the reproduction of class. The descent of property after death increasingly benefited males in the long period from 1066 to the seventeenth century.[5] In particular, primogeniture favouring men spread from the nobility to the gentry in the early sixteenth century and to the yeomanry by the eighteenth century. It resulted in the consolidation of landed estates, a policy which was premissed on the control of women. Such control was initiated in the power structure of the aristocracy, and later extended to the agrarian bourgeoisie.[6] Marriages were arranged to maximise the secular interests pursued by the families of the great: paradoxically, the smaller the property, the greater the scope for individual choice in marriage. Arranged marriages between individual houses were thus axiomatic in the aristocracy, were limited to endogamy within a broad band of families within the peasantry, but were non-existent in propertyless groups such as vagrants.[7] Women's dependence on men had at its fulcrum their inability to subsist independently of fathers or husbands, especially in the classes living off rent or profits: they were permitted in their own right only clothes and personal jewellery.[8] Thus, even if there was no rigorous expectation of monogamous sexual relations until the Reformation, the entailing of estates to legitimate male heirs made the life of bastards precarious and consequently deterred women from sexual freedom.[9]

Peasant women in the feudal mode of production were much less confined to 'feminine' tasks than was to be the case in capitalism, though even at this stage a gender division of labour was detectable.[10] Whole families acquired part of their subsistence from occupations subsequently thought of as 'male' – such as brick manufacture or iron construction.[11] Despite this, married women were permitted exemption from the performance of servile labour for the landlord since this conflicted with duties to their own 'lords', their husbands, whose needs had precedence.[12] Furthermore, in feudalism as in capitalism, the more impoverished was the peasant family, the more often were heavy agricultural tasks shared by both sexes.[13]

Rape, like adultery, was punishable legally, rank being inscribed in law by varying the punishment according to the class of the violated woman.[14] Punishments of this type represented merely the defilement of another man's property – in which the raped possession became 'damaged goods' – rather than a recognition of any offence to the woman herself.[15] In these cases, as in the loss of virginity, the family honour was besmirched and had to be symbolically restored.

The whole edifice of punishment was constructed around double standards, not least of which was the husband's right to chastise his wife physically (with a stick up to a thumb's breadth).[16] Such hierarchical inequality appeared most vividly in the ultimate sanction, for murder of spouses. If a man killed his wife, he was merely a murderer, whereas a woman who killed her husband was, until 1828, guilty of petty treason.[17]

Resistance nevertheless occurred, as can be seen from technological and linguistic relics: the chastity belts and nags' bridles, 'shrews' and 'hen-pecked' husbands, as well as from the records of contingents of women in the medieval heretical movements, Albigensians, Beguines and Franciscan Spirituals.[18] It was perhaps to frustrate this resistance and to quell a threatened disruption to sexual, as well as class, power, that the 1543 Council of Trent banned Bible-reading not just by servants, apprentices and artisans but also by women.[19]

The structure of feeling which associates men alone with productive and professional activity derives from two waves of female exclusion. The first, in the twelfth century, swept over women in the universities.[20] The second, in the seventeenth century, separated women in the merchant and artisan classes from equal partnership in the family workshop or office by installing them in separate homes. The ebbing tide of women out of industrial work was also strengthened at this period by the spread of capitalist merchants' control, dooming many artisans to remain perpetual journeymen.[21] The earlier specialisation of young women in menial housework and mature women in productive activity was thus overturned in these developments.[22] Where women had once been active members of autonomous guilds, they now became relegated to the purely domestic sphere.[23] Moreover, as the seventeenth- and eighteenth-century apprenticeships became more expensive and formalised, women were increasingly bereft of training, leaving the better-paid skilled work to become the province of males.[24] In the country, the consolidation of estates and weakening of the peasantry were pushing men and women into wage-labour, the effect of which can be gauged by the increasing disparities between agricultural wage-earners, with an average of 2.7 children, and the gentry, with average families of 16 children.[25]

The seventeenth-century growth of contracts both reflected this new expansion of markets and further marginalised the position of women.[26] Women were legally unable to sign any contracts, being shielded from full financial independence by their husbands as *femmes couvertes*.[27] From this time until the first Married Women's Property Act in 1870,[28] women had neither legal rights to their own earnings, nor control of any property brought to the marriage.[29] The effective absence of equal rights to divorce until 1923 and the male monopolisation of legitimate custody of children until 1839, further confined women to marriage, independent of their will.[30]

Literary forms: folk-tale, fairy-tale and peasant novel

I now turn to the oral and literary development of the popular romance in Feudal Europe and the Transition in order to contrast the modern form with earlier 'ancestral' versions. Although there are important genealogical links between the modern stories and earlier epics of courtly and noble love, I shall restrict my scope to the art forms of the common people.

Modern romances are fairy-tales sieved through a net of realism. All pre-capitalist societies have produced fairy-tales. Although told by story-tellers who have imparted to the tale their own distinctive vision, the stories exist as collective products.[31] They have been approached in two main ways. First, under the influence of Ferdinand de Saussure's linguistics, fairy-tales were collected and classified by the Soviet formalist, Vladimir Propp. He noted the remarkable uniformity of structure within the Russian tales and proceeded to uncover the unity of the narrative action, or 'functions', which remained unvarying beneath the often dazzling colour of character and setting contributed by each story-teller.[32]

However, as Claude Lévi-Strauss noted, to reduce the tales to *actions* of the dramatis personae was to be limited by a 'bloodless grammar'.[33] For him, narratives had to be seen in the context of the culture's cosmology, which ordered the oppositions and uniformities of the stories in accordance with an underlying ethical and political logic, emblematic of the group itself. While Lévi-Strauss did not himself explore feudal fairy-tales, this was undertaken by E.M. Meletinsky, who approached the stories in terms of their coded correspondences and oppositions to feudal reality, thus preparing the ground for Mikhail Bakhtin later.[34]

The second approach to fairy-tales has been that of Jack Zipes.[35] Zipes, following Ernst Bloch, contrasted the rebellious character of folk-tales in pre-capitalist Europe with their modern versions, in which are embodied an underlying perspective of social harmony. The medieval stories collected by Antti Aarne or the Grimms represented the struggles of 'little people', peasants and artisans, against the 'great', their seigneurial superiors.[36] However – and this was frequently a limit in the consciousness of the peasantry – they could not conceive of a world radically different from their own. Hence the hero and heroine transcended their initial class positions only as individuals, by marriage to a prince, manipulation of a feudal estate, or by trickery.[37]

Zipes argued that the literary versions of fairy-tales, from the adaptations of the seventeenth-century Charles Perrault, to those of Walt Disney, divested the stories of their earlier affinity with oppositional culture, particularly when the tales became primarily told to children. They have lost the intimate connection between story-teller and audience and have been diluted by a process of literary pasteurisation for commercial purposes. In this respect they came to resemble the conservatism of the fossilised genre of romantic fiction.

There are methodological problems about Zipes' reconstruction of lost oral forms but the major weakness is its narrow restriction to the class antagonisms of feudalism. For example, he interpreted the frequent witch figures in these stories as images of usurers in local peasant communities, the petty representatives of mercantile capitalism on whom many of the peasantry were dependent by a form of debt slavery. The multitude of wicked stepmothers were also decoded as village hoarders of money and exploiters of the poor.[38] This approach neglected the importance of kinship in peasant communities and the possibility that the stories represented a coded form of resistance to patriarchal authority. *Rapunzel*, *Cinderella*, and *Bluebeard*, I suggest, depicted aspects of the oppression of women, in tales which articulated a cry of pain at their intense powerlessness rather than the polite repression of unconscious needs. Analysis of these early forms of popular culture should show how the harsh economic realities of class are both transmitted through and mediated by the mechanisms of compulsory kin ties.

Another ancestor of modern romantic fiction was the peasant or plebeian romance, such as the written novellas emerging in the Occitan province (modern Languedoc) from 1570 to 1790, which provided a 'metaphor of Western marriage', through 'a coded, marvellously disguised "adaptation" of a folk-tale'.[39] Were there English versions? It is impossible to know, but the French novella was an important transitional element. Ladurie's research revealed that written literature in the Occitan region dramatised a key problem in peasant society, namely, how to preserve property and maximise desire.[40] The hero must find the 'treasure', that is real or fiducary capital, by which to marry the girl.[41] The sixty novels appearing between 1570 and 1790 in the local dialect occupied the 'groundfloor of the written language';[42] they distilled in witty, inventive displays of narrative ingenuity a rich flowering of popular culture, in which the mechanisms of plebeian patriarchal marriage were laid bare.

These stories were written by male authors, concerning quests to solve the financial problems of young peasant boys:

> These gentlemen do not pose the other question, which certainly preoccupied Occitan women: namely, the problem of the girls' search, symmetrical with the previous one, for a dowry that will influence the family of the man she loves. In this sense Occitan literature in the classical age is rather a

reflection of the financial obsession of men than an accurate description of social reality.[43]

Such romances were not a realistic reflection of real economic or kin relations, rather, they represented the reshaping of these in fantasy.[44] In the stories, the young males manage to solve by trickery or force the problems that in a hierarchical society are insoluble. Thus the literature was the written equivalent of the older supernatural folklore, which occupied the cultural basement, in Ladurie's building metaphor. In the older folk- or fairy-tales, these problems could be solved only in miraculous fashion by the intervention of sinister forces of magic on the hero's side. But the most brilliant of these novelists of plebeian romance – a rootless, Rabelaisian eighteenth-century parish priest who was savagely critical of the traditional intelligentsia – translated his stories from the older oral genre by 'transforming the all too intemporal beauties of the fairy-tale' into 'the outrageous ugliness of the contemporary village'.[45] Ladurie employed here a Durkheimian structuralism in which he attributed to these fairy-tale conceptions of the sacred a strong causal role in shaping not just the later peasant novellas but also the actual pattern of social rules: life as it ought to be lived.[46] If the class relations of feudal society, including the vital productive and reproductive role of kin, shaped both the older oral and the written narratives, the integrative images of feudal culture also moulded popular aspirations.

By 1850, such stories had lost their artistic quality. Novels now introduced the collisions between individual heroes' desires and the existence of inequality in a direct and critical manner:

> the tricks, the feeble little tricks (such as the discovery of a treasure, a present arriving from a rich benefactor) that our authors readily intended to enable the poor hero to marry the rich girl, these techniques suddenly seem ridiculous. The world had lost its magic. Such dramatic inventions were no longer to be taken seriously. They were now seen as little more than the fantastic justification for an earlier social rigidity that had come to an end.[47]

Yet, in Britain, current popular literature still retains updated versions of these older romances with the quest centring on the woman.[48] The disenchantment of the world is incomplete. The magical mechanisms employed in women's magazine stories, and in

Mills and Boon romances, still engineer analogous fantasy solutions in which social demands and individual happiness can coincide. Societal contradictions are thus transcended. The ideals of such literature are petty-bourgeois representations of a mythical golden age, but they still exert some charm for those whose experience is closest to these imaginative structures – especially for those women whose educational qualifications exclude them from total economic independence.

The transformations of the lower class romance: the puritan bourgeoisie

The archetypal elements of the modern domestic romance can first be seen in Richardson's *Pamela*, which acquired a cult status among both middle-class and servant women at its first publication in 1740. *Pamela* has been regarded convincingly as the first novel. It adds to the fairy-tale resolution of love and wealth, two new dimensions: psychological realism and intense ethical commitment.[49]

Pamela, Terry Eagleton claimed, is the cartoon version of *Clarissa*.[50] Maybe so, but it has also had more influence, for Pamela became the model for popular heroines, prototypically shaping their aspirations. This novel retains the magical social ascent of fairy-tales and perhaps for this reason became an immensely popular text. Nevertheless, it expresses an idealised image of a disciplined gentry class rather than a rebellious lower class, and this displays a new feature of the popular romance.

Pamela is the narrative of a poor servant-girl who, having successfully withstood temptations to yield her virginity to her landowning master, Mr B, is rewarded with the emotional and material fulfilment of marriage to him. Despite the effects of realism, the resolution is indeed a miraculous transformation, an idyllic holiday from the social reality of the patrician class which had been the immediate beneficiary of the Glorious Revolution of 1688. The key to *Pamela*, then, is to see it less as realism than as an ideological charter: a vision of a rehabilitated gentry class which rules through a just patriarchy.

Richardson is usually interpreted as the spokesman of the *urban* middle class:[51] 'The movement for moral reform . . . tended to be mainly supported by the middle class, who fortified their outlook as a group with the assumption that their social superiors were their moral inferiors.'[52] The text does indeed rest on a call to moral reform, but it is the expression of an *agrarian* bourgeoisie,[53] remodelled in the subaltern dreams of a printer, whose class cannot yet stand on its own.[54] Of course, its ethos represents an instance of the Puritan desire to regulate a class grown too rich to care about salvation, but it is also inflected with the tones of the Glorious Revolution, constitutionalism and contract.[55]

The new model patriarchy underpinning *Pamela* retains the vocabulary of the well-ordered family for its depiction of the state.[56] The text specifies a minutely regulated contract for family life which creates a miniature utopian microcosm. In this, a written constitution for the marital division of labour is enunciated, a model for child-rearing is proposed and sexual deviance on the part of either spouse is condemned. Moreover, the domination of the master in the household connotes the resumption of organic relations of lord and tenant on the estate. Pamela's aid permits her master to become a domesticated or reformed gentleman. By refusing him the free play of his senses, she becomes the instrument of a restabilised ruling class.

Within this scheme female subordination is explicitly announced, dependent now on neither force nor command, but on the free acceptance of the woman. Thus Mr B is even able to demand that Pamela will never depress him with an unhappy appearance, but remains free himself from similar obligations. Her activities are limited to the private sphere: his extend to the estate, the hunt and national politics, that is, to the public realm.

It is frequently observed that Pamela's label of 'sauce-box' is not arbitrary: it is less often found remarkable that such a spirited and unyielding woman should melt into submission to her husband. After her 'Exaltation', she becomes indeed a docile wife, whose control is engineered by love: 'Sir . . . I should be unworthy if I could not say that I can have no will but yours . . . I will not scruple to obey you.'[57] The language of power can now be *hidden*: Mr B promises 'that the words COMMAND and OBEY shall be blotted out of his vocabulary'. Despite this, Pamela fears that some inadvertent peccadillo on her part might be 'Laesae Majestatis' (*sic*) or *'Treason to her Lord and Master'*, her husband.

Such female vassalage creates the solid base on which a reformed gentry class can emerge. Sober, sitting up with sick tenants, the reborn Mr B repairs the 'organic' tie between lower order and ruling class. Richardson sees the distinguishing mark of this superior gentry to be its English liberty. In the new images of nationalism denoted in his game of cards, Mr B is stated to be above class or party, ruled only by the Law.[58] The 'plain ace', for him, is the 'law' and is superior to the court cards. Thus Richardson fleshed out a heroic gentry who represented the fusion of bourgeois and aristocrat, which was characteristic of the 1688 settlement. The text advocates spiritual equality and disciplined moderation. These were the terms under which the agrarian gentry proposed a mandate for its indefinite rule: terms which meshed with the fantasies of lower-class writers – such as Richardson – about a just ruling class. Women's popular fiction, even today, still has recourse to such hegemonic gentry figures.

The domestic romance of the 1840s and 1850s: the birth of mass fiction

Many domestic romances of the 1840s were recycled versions of *Pamela*.[59] More often, the romance was located in the world of urban capitalist class relations. Yet however severe its critique of elitism, however much it softened the practices of a market economy with an appeal to charity or 'caring capitalism', opposition to the desire for social reconstruction championed by the new working class was its secret centre.[60] One effect of popular romance is precisely to make the institutions of capitalism – urban or agrarian – seem inevitable, so that the aspirations growing out of the early Utopians' social theory seem to be profoundly incompatible with common sense. In this respect, such popular literature became a vehicle for the intense 'domestic religion' of the counter-revolution of the 1840s and 1850s, in which anti-feminism, anti-socialism and anti-infidelism acquired considerable success after the decline of Owenism and Chartism.[61] Within this prevalent ethos of possessive individualism, the romance offered its own regressive utopia, tying women to dependence within the family with what Anna Wheeler called 'the silken fetters of desire'.[62]

In order to understand that moment at which the domestic romance first appeared in its modern form and with a mass following, it is necessary to locate it within this domestic ideology. Such a religion had its origin in the Puritan revolutionary demand for liberty of men's consciences and in the spiritualisation of the household to which it was yoked.[63] The right of the individual, priest-rejecting conscience was a *male* prerogative, requiring the subordination of wife and children to the spiritually more mature head of household. Yet the Puritan father, ambivalently, required the companionship of the wife if she were going to be successful in her designated sphere of the moral education of the children.[64] As capitalist social relations came to dominate everyday provision of wants, the family acquired a new structural significance as an island of ethical values. Familism was the privatised culture celebrating this unit as the sole arena for altruism: women were its 'moral vanguard'.[65]

The Puritan 'spiritualisation of the household' was originally an ideology rooted in the middle class of small merchants and masters. In the late eighteenth and the nineteenth centuries this doctrine was the active implement for the colonisation of the working class with middle-class values. This was the 'moral disinfectant' that was to halt the diffusion or 'proletarianisation of the Enlightenment' and to discipline the conviviality of the newly urbanised masses.[66] Yet, curiously, such cultural disinfectants arose in very different social settings in the 1840s and 1850s.[67] Two sources can be found. First, a mass fiction was provided for the working class as a charitable or educational gift, either in the form of religious tracts or secular utilitarian magazines (*The Saturday Magazine* or *Penny Magazine*, for instance). Like other forms of leisure which aimed too overtly at the conciliation of classes, this edifying literature was treated with suspicion by its recipients. Secondly, there was a vigorous popular fiction from plebeian writers and publishers – such as those in Salisbury Square, off London's Fleet Street – who were subjected to a continued moral panic. This was the beginning of the luxuriant growth of a working-class culture of pleasure catering for the entertainment of the least literate. The new mass consumption of the romance resembled in many ways the luxury items of the cottage family industry and urban artisan trades of the eighteenth century.[68] Like fashionable clothes, coffee and gin, the romance acquired the reputation of antisocial sociability. From the point of view of middle-class asceticism, such little indulgences displayed a profligate use of money: for the consumers such purchases activated networks providing mutual aid in adversity.

The domestic romance was found in both types of fiction, but was especially important in the second. Its passive heroines and family-centred values nevertheless contained an ideological am- biguity. Like dime novels, although the romances reinstated hierarchy, they had certain democratic inflections: if the heroine ultimately became an heiress, in her 'cryptoproletarian' earlier life she was nurtured by the working class and recognized its claims for justice. Ultimately, however, the populist aspects of the domestic romance did not so much enhance realism as provide the exotic colour of romanticised forms. Louis James, its historian, has aptly called it an illusory realism.

It is not sufficient, however, merely to identify the hidden political agenda behind the apparently innocent narratives of cheap popular literature. These stories sold better than their cultural competitors.[69] It is necessary to explain why women in the 1840s and 1850s should have turned to this form of cultural consumption. It was not an imposed taste, since alternatives also existed in the shape of Chartist novels and feminist magazines. But these were increasingly rejected during this time, in favour of the penny issue romances. Thus magazines which were saturated with the ethos of dependent femininity and familism, *Family Herald* (300,000 circulation), *London Journal* (450,000) and *Eliza Cook's Journal* were immensely popular, while the feminist and radical *London Pioneer* ceased publication after only three years and the radical *Cooper's* and *Howitt's Journals* (25,000) were similarly short-lived.[70] The following chapters seek to understand this paradox and attempt to explain the attachment of its readers to the romance.

To summarise, the decisive material conditions for the romance are: first, agrarian capitalism; and second, the patriarchal mode of domestic production. The romance's promise of happiness originated in feudal female vassalage to husbands. This was adapted to the struggle against the aristocracy with the new injection of Puritan middle-class domestic ideology. Its literary precondition is the fusion of the classic realist narrative form with the older fairy-tale. As working-class women came to share some experiences of their bourgeois sisters through the withdrawal from paid work, they swelled the romance-reading public. Thus the cultural revolution of the agrarian bourgeoisie acquired a broad popular base.

2 Cultural Theory and the Popular Romance

EXCHANGE-VALUE, FICTION AND CURRENT CULTURAL IMPLICATIONS

The capitalist organisation of the fiction industry has two consequences: first, revolutionary expansion of production, a progressive trend, and second, periodic threats to the publication of 'serious literature', which fetters human development. Thus, despite the pessimism of cultural critics from the Romantics to the Frankfurt School, it has to be acknowledged that the technical innovations of both the nineteenth century (steam press and cheap paper) and the twentieth century (glues and new printing technology) have enormously cheapened publication costs and increased consumption. Moreover, the decline in patronage had the effect of freeing writers from political and religious censorship.

Of course, the transition to capitalist modernity took divergent national forms. Existing secondary sources allow me to sketch briefly the main developments of literature for the mass market. The absence of more sociologically attuned studies restricts this to a highly schematic overview of the trajectories in different countries. Nevertheless, this section is introduced to support my main historical point, which is to stress the variability of popular literature, both in terms of the politics and the aesthetic quality of the texts. This survey also suggests the increased contemporary pressures, under the instrumentally rational forces of the market, to fossilise mass literary production within the parameters of known and safe formulaic production.

In France, literature was a crucial arena for the organic intellectuals of the 1789 Revolution, and especially for their popularisers in primary schools, where instruction in the new national language through classroom readers served to displace both patois and King's French. Further, didactic novelettes were disseminated from Paris to the peasantry, bearing both new agricultural ideas and an ethic of democracy. Moreover, even when harnessed to the austere disciplinary rituals of grammatical instruction, such popular literature also expressed wider needs and desires. Through its pages a new humanism contested the older peasant fatalism.[1]

In Britain the arrival of universal literacy was retarded by the tenacity of the eighteenth-century gentry's demands for mass ignorance as the preservative of the 'great law of subordination'.[2] The democratisation of culture met with fewer impediments in America, where the combined impact of the struggle for national independence and the French Revolution created a 'literary revolution' which was envisaged as an integral element of general enlightenment.[3] The first stage of popularisation in America was the growth of the reading public to include workers in offices, houses and factories. It was accompanied by a very early internationalisation of trade through the pirating of best-selling foreign writers for home consumption.[4] From the eighteenth century onwards, the market carried both scholarly works and genre products with a more immediate popular acclaim. Ironically, E.D.E.N. Southworth's romance *The Hidden Hand* was probably better known in nineteenth-century America than Adam Smith's celebrated metaphor of the market.[5]

The commodification of literature everywhere remunerated best those authors who achieved the widest sales. Greater rewards often went to the literary hacks who supervised the recycling of books issuing from the fragmented division of literary labour, rather than to those writers who competed for literary honour on the older artisan or new bohemian models. Hence the force of Balzac's critique of the 'stock exchange of the spirit' or of George Gissing's cynical fantasy of a 'true automaton or Literary Machine' which would cut out the author, allowing the publisher to 'throw in a given number of old books, and have them reduced, blended and modified into a single one for today's consumption'.[6] Yet, as Antonio Gramsci argued, many works now canonised as great literature were once *popular books*, produced and sold by capitalist techniques, a fact ignored by many critics of mass culture.[7] The case of the American market is significant in this respect. For, along with the genre culture – domestic romances, 'cabbage patch' kailyard novels and Horatio Alger's 'rags to riches' odysseys – the American mass public read their contemporaries: Pope, Voltaire, Rousseau, Richardson, Eliot, Beecher Stowe, Twain, Trollope and Hardy. They also *spurned* Melville's *Moby Dick*, Hawthorne's *The Scarlet Letter* and Conrad, perhaps because these texts required higher levels of literacy. This mass readership had always possessed a large number of women: indeed, in the 1830s to 1850s they constituted four-fifths of the American readership.[8] Of their precise class profile little is known, save for the prevalence of the middle class amongst readers of the sentimental novel and the existence of a lower-class readership for Beadle's dime novels from the 1860s, for utopian novels of the 1880s and for John Steinbeck's epic of the contemporary dispossessed.[9]

The canonisation of writers with a popular base suggests that myths about the 'depraved enjoyment' and crude taste of uneducated readers are founded on inadequate psychological generalisation, which take no account of the historical shifts between different 'structures of feeling' on the part of mass consumers. Secondly, as the list of popular writers indicates, best sellers are not necessarily contained within the ideological parameters of the dominant class but may have their roots in oppositional thought. That this was the case in the 1930s with Dashiell Hammett novels and Steinbeck's *The Grapes of Wrath*, is well known, but it also occurred at earlier periods. Thus in the 1880s, *Anna Karenina* (in a 60 cent edition), Edward Bellamy's utopian novel *Looking Backwards* and Sarah Grand's feminist work *The Heavenly Twins*, were all successful with a popular readership.[10]

Undoubtedly there have been stable affinities between particular social groups and types of novel. Yet there have also been the literary equivalent of floating voters, who have alternated between subversive and conservative, 'moral' and erotic, artistically powerful and formulaic texts. As yet our understanding of the conditions determining literary appeal are primitive, although James Hart's pioneering sociology of American popular literature allows a preliminary mapping of the major shifts in discourse within popular novels. His systematic historical analysis confirms that in the 1850s and 1860s best sellers included progressive texts attacking both the slave mode of production and the gender order in which the position of women was perceived as analogous to slavery. Thus Harriet Beecher Stowe, for example, believed that God guided her hand to write her critique of slavery, *Uncle Tom's Cabin*, with its coded feminist analogies.[11] Another cult novel, *Maum Guinea*, by Metta Victoria Victor, was so influential on the abolitionists' side in the American Civil War that some critics consider it to have had a crucial impact in the crystallisation of British public opinion into non-intervention.[12] Social criticism and emancipatory themes were to emerge again in the terrain of best-selling literature in the 1880s and the 1930s. In the intervening years, popular novels lost their radical thrust and peddled the American Dream or aristocratic ideals to the masses.

After the victory of the North in the Civil War, novelists writing for a mass readership contributed to a bourgeois cultural revolution, diffusing not only new hopes for upward mobility but also the legitimacy of unregulated capitalism. Of these, Alger's ubiquitous 'rags to riches' fiction was the most typical popular formula, clearly resembling the mid nineteenth-century epics inspired by Samuel Smiles in Britain.[13] However, by the 1880s, the reduction in wages and heightened industrial unrest was linked to a decline in the production of fairy-tales of self-help. Instead, popular fiction took two paths. The first was an increased fascination with history, including the mythical European feudalism of Charles Major's *When Knighthood was in Flower* and the patriarchal Southern society of novels such as Helen Hunt Jackson's *Ramona*. Hart comments: 'The present of economic turmoil, of entrenched monopolies, predatory trusts and octupus railways faded with the reading of these pretty tales about the American past.'[14]

Secondly, there was a fiction of social transformation, for along with Bellamy's prophetic novel *Looking Backward* there was also Ignatius Donnelly's *Caesar's Column* and later, Upton Sinclair's *The Jungle*.[15] Such a split in popular culture was to be replicated in the depression years of the 1930s. *The Grapes of Wrath* may have been labelled, ironically, the 'first so-called proletarian novel to be so widely read that the working class were aware of it',[16] but it vied with *conservative* historical fiction. *Gone With The Wind*, for example, which was unprecedented in the volume and speed of its sales[17] was part of the paternalist popular tradition. Despite its strong, autonomous heroine, it extolled the virtues of Southern slave-owners and possessed a racist subtext inconceivable in the heroic bourgeois period.[18]

In Britain, popular fiction included radical works too, such as E.F. Marriott's melodrama, *Black-Ey'd Susan*,[19] or the Chartist sequel to the works of Eugene Sue, G.W.M. Reynolds's *The Mysteries of London* – celebrated because it 'lashed the aristocracy'.[20] Yet quite different structures of feeling underlay the Gothic tale of terror, such as M.G. Lewis's *The Monk*, with its sinister Papist conspiracy,[21] or the gentry romance, of which Thomas Prest's *Ela the Outcast* was a highly successful example.[22] Penny-issue literature was particularly varied. It included Defoe, Langhorne, Smollett, Goldsmith, Shelley and Byron as well as numerous popular writers now sunk without trace.[23] Thus, in England as well as America, many canonised writers were once attractive to the mass of their contemporaries: Richard Altick cites Thackeray, Shelley and Walpole as well as Dickens and Trollope, all of whom were cheaply serialised.[24] However, for the lower classes, new fiction not issued in penny parts was too expensive. Until the twentieth century, it was debarred materially to all but the best-paid labour aristocracy.[25]

Moreover, the world-view of plebeian readers in any European society might well have more in common with writers in another period and place than with the current preoccupations of their own traditional intelligentsia. For this reason, Italian popular newspapers of the early twentieth century serialised French nineteenth-century writers such as Balzac who were closer to the concerns of the Italian subordinate classes. Nevertheless, the writers who commanded such a mass Italian following were very diverse. For they not only varied greatly in terms of cultural value, but they also steered their readers alternately in both hegemonic *and* counter-hegemonic directions.[26]

In conclusion, then, studies of America, Britain and Italy have revealed that at certain historic moments a mass public has appeared for important critical realist and utopian texts. Studies of mass cultural consumption also show that the reception of a book may differ dramatically within different strata. Intellectuals may underestimate the powerful political effects of popular novels that they themselves consider marred by diluted social criticism.[27]

Recent developments in the publishing industry

I have delineated so far the ideological and artistic diversity of commercial culture. Despite this, it is the contention of recent writers on the contemporary book market, such as Michael Lane, that at present similarly varied developments are being increasingly jeopardised by the nature of the publishing industry. In particular, these writers claim that in the 1960s and 1970s there was an increase in the number of formulaic best sellers, reduced room for manoeuvre on the part of small-scale publishers and limited potential for the compromises of the past in which a small number of commercially successful genre writers subsidised serious but uncanonised novelists.

Why should these changes provoke a sense of crisis amongst

cultural producers now? After all, such threatening trends have not prevented the publication of new feminist novels in the 1970s. Furthermore, theorists of post-modernism have already predicted a massive shift in the glacial high/low culture divisions of the twentieth century, which will restructure the whole political economy of culture. However, one important development is the rationalisation of the publishing industry in the 1970s and 1980s.

Within the culture industry, the rhythm of expansion, merger and takeover can be detected at various periods. As early as the turn of the century in America, financiers had become influential in the industry, through their control of holding companies containing publishing firms.[28] Yet the rationalisation of production in the 1970s and 1980s also has features distinctive to *late* capitalism. The vertical integration of publishers with financial interests is now a key feature of the industry in Britain and America. It is expected to lead to the imminent reduction of the American industry to control by perhaps as few as seven major companies,[29] while diversification has precipitated shot-gun takeovers in which ill-assorted bedfellows are joined together, as in the control of Bantam Books gained by Fiat in 1974.[30] The vertical integration of different media has been a notable emergent feature in Britain, with firms such as Granada owning Panther, Paladin and Mayflower. By the end of the 1960s, five imprints alone accounted for 70 per cent of all paperbacks sold. Unfortunately, recent examinations of the publishing industry in Britain from an orthodox economic perspective have failed to indicate the Byzantine complexity of new patterns of control and their implications for cultural production. Thus an otherwise thorough investigation into the industry by Peter Curwen, in which it is stated that British publishing consists of both very large corporations and very small companies, offers no assessment of the independence or interdependence of these firms. Moreover, such attempts as these to dispel doubts about the crisis in British publishing provide little reassurance, because their perspective is too narrow to conceptualise any criteria of achievement other than the financial.[31]

Recent rationalisation has had repercussions on the production of women's fiction. From a business viewpoint, the romance is the 'formula of formulas', an invitingly stable product with low risk elements. It was no doubt for this reason that Mills and Boon, established in 1910, was initially approached for advice by Harlequin of Canada, latecomers in the romantic fiction market. Mills and Boon has now been gobbled up by its former pupil.[32] Harlequin itself subsequently swallowed one further rival, Silhouette.[33] Its only other serious competitor, Dell, has now been merged with Doubleday. Thus Harlequin stands at the unconquered heights of the industry, selling in 1979 a mere 168 million copies globally. In 1977, it made $11 million profit on the 75 million copies sold.[34] Indeed, now that Harlequin has shown that books can be sold like instant coffee, the search for world markets has destabilised other more localised fiction industries to an unprecedented degree. George Paizis's research has revealed how France, which had possessed traditional, small-scale publishers in the romantic fiction area, such as Delly and Max du Veuzit, experienced recently an extraordinary increase in formulaic fiction readership. By 1985, annual sales of romantic fiction had risen to 20 million, largely as a result of the heavily advertised cultural contact of Anglo-Saxon authors translated into French.[35]

Monopolisation has revolutionised techniques of production and sales, but at the cost of new, unpublished writers who do not quite fit the 'flavour of the month'. Publishing offices have increasingly been subjected to scientific management, demand has been managed by advertising those books that are standard products and by changing distribution to new outlets in supermarkets and newsagents. Increased use of market research and removal of slow sellers, have resulted in the average American paperback romance having a shelf life of only fifteen days to six weeks.[36]

Further, market forces have progressively undermined many of the safe havens for literary production, based on canonical or 'heresiarch' – dissident – evaluations. The rise of the blockbuster and best seller threaten not only new writers, they threaten also established writers.

The most detailed detective work, undertaken by Per Gedin, shows that in Sweden, for example, reduced mark-up on 'serious' writers leads to their being squeezed out by best-selling novelists. A romance writer such as Victoria Holt makes very high profits on high sales, while a Swedish writer, with respectable sales of around 4,000, makes a loss.[37] Consequently, by 1963, 8,000 copies, and by 1974, 10,000 copies, had to be sold in order to make the same 'decent profit' that derived from 2,000 sales at the turn of the century. The resulting decline in new authors not only means the domination of the Swedish market by Anglo-Saxon writers, but the destruction of the 'seedcorn', as publishers increasingly live off 'safe', already canonised writers. Hence the gulf widens between popular literature, which at present is linked to many regressive ideas, and 'the secret inner monologue', which is the work of the living, critical writer. In Britain, these trends are intensified by the decline in public subsidies, creating a dramatic erosion of book expenditure in public libraries and the abolition of the Arts Council Literature Panel.[38]

This conclusion has been contested from two quarters. Disagreement is implicit in the work of Pierre Bourdieu, who has referred to the rich economic rewards accruing to the publishers and dealers of high culture as they participate in the magic alchemy of making and hallowing reputations.[39] Yet Bourdieu has nothing to say about the economic problems of breaking in to the fiction industry for those not yet canonised. A more explicit defence of the industry has been made by the 'cultural optimists', including here the economic analysis by Curwen, already cited. His review of the publishing industry aims to refute the charge that there is a crisis in fiction. However, he misses the point by showing that fiction *as a whole* is doing well, a point that nobody disputes! He comments: '[I]t is somewhat ironic in the light of the much-heralded death of fiction that it should be responsible for so much of the prosperity of the home market.'[40] Yet the crisis applies to 'serious' and especially new writers, not the best-selling literature responsible for the rise in sales he has noted.[41] Paradoxically, Curwen's statistics *sustain* the crisis argument, since he shows the increased capital per head of publishing employees (1963, 137; 1977, 192) and the 'nerves' in the industry when low output resulted in collapses in investment in 1975 and 1981. This increases the plausibility of the explanation that buoyant sales in fiction are likely to be due to greater resort to safe, genre products supported by more aggressive and innovative marketing techniques. Curwen has failed to demonstrate the health of the non-formulaic fiction industry.

Finally, the cultural optimists note that from the initiation of the new literary mode of production, with the birth of the capitalist book trade, alarms have sounded about the fate of the book. Historical evidence is mustered to show the periodic booms and collapse of parts of the publishing industry, as in the crises in American paperback production in 1840 and 1900.[42] Yet, despite contemporaries' doom-laden prophecies of over-production or of the exhaustion of suitable novelists, good writing was not subsequently undermined. The corollary is that the present stage is similarly a period of restructuring rather than decline.

The pessimists have not yet adequately addressed the complexity of the market in the book industry, nor its history of revival. However, substantial reasons exist for doubting the happy coincidence of cultural needs and market interests, the pivot on which their case rests. It is these which have led Michael Lane to conclude:

'British publishing is gravely ill.'[43] For when cultural production emerges full-blown in its value or market form, it becomes the vehicle of instrumental economic transactions which distort communication between producers and consumers. Paradoxically, this development may have been facilitated by those publishers most concerned to rescue the public from dictation by a Reithian cultural elite, by championing an aesthetic pluralism or democratic anti-authoritarianism.[44]

Thus a new group of male and female 'Young Turks' are bearding the dens of the traditional public-school, Oxbridge-educated editors who now lament the passage of their golden age of gentlemanly professional activity.[45] But a deeper process is evident, like the tip of an iceberg, in this recomposition of elites.

The key shift is the rigorous rationalisation of literary production in terms of its profitability. In large concentrated firms, accountants become the managing directors or chairpersons and insist on calculability: precise budgets, timetabling, even five-year plans. Thus the subsidising of uncommercial books such as poetry or new fiction by the sales of best-selling general or genre books – as practised by Collins, Gollancz or Allen Lane – become hard to sustain: 'It will be difficult, if not impossible, to carry out such cross-subsidisation when the investors demand the maximum rate of return on their money.'[46] With the bureaucratisation of the oligopolistic company, Lewis Coser et al. have pointed to the parallel pattern of declining creativity.[47] Editors see authors less; only safe bets are made. The room for editors to move laterally into smaller houses is eroded.[48] Finally, outside specialist bookshops, the greatly reduced life of a book denies available 'shelf time' in which contemporary equivalents of writers such as Henry James or William Faulkner can emerge and develop reputations.[49] The short lifespan of a paperback requires special ordering from publishers for books as young as six-months-old.[50] Such changes in production and distribution are likely to fossilise genres and will have a particularly adverse effect on the choice available for uneducated working-class and lower middle-class readers. Against the optimism of the dual market approach or Bourdieu's differentiated markets, it is worth recalling the constantly increased number of copies needed to break even. Small- or medium-size publishing houses cannot remain untouched by this massive wave of change, so that as tightly specifiable demands on budget sheets are introduced, they will normally suffer. Such enterprises are likely to be either brief concerns, being elbowed out of the distribution networks by the big companies, or they are gobbled up.

This is relevant to the question of popular literature under the broad umbrella of romantic fiction, for it is mainly conservative popular writers who have provided the most profitable novels. My research indicates that most lower-class readers of popular books are unaware of the availability of alternatives to the contemporary best-selling genres.[51] Meanwhile, more 'pre-cooked' books from novel factories and more hack writers have 'solved' the demands for productivity at the popular end.[52]

Thus, without subscribing to the traditionalists' commitment to a spiritual aristocracy, it *is* still worth noting the valid element in their subjective perceptions of decline. On this Lane has commented: 'I believe they are the expression of a fundamental crisis in the world of books that springs, in turn, from a fundamental and revolutionary crisis in contemporary culture.'[53]

Given the history of cheap popular literature, it seems that contemporary publishers have grasped the forces leading women to seek compensatory relief through fiction but they have underrated the untapped demand for popular novels which are realist and critical, thus bearing witness to the unilluminated lives of the majority. My research shows that a significant proportion of uneducated readers found pleasure in one such book, Agnes Smedley's *Daughter of Earth*. This suggests that, with different distribution, there is a wider potential readership for such writers.[54]

How are we to understand the meaning and evolution of the best-selling genres of women's fiction? So far, I have discussed the impact of the formulaic romance as a commodity on the publishing of fiction. I now want to turn to the wider sociological analysis of the romance's popularity.

THE USE-VALUE OF THE POPULAR ROMANCE: THEORETICAL PERSPECTIVES

Mass culture has a chequered history: sternly rejected at its birth by the gatekeepers of Literature, it reappears under several disguises. It is the territory of modernism's nostalgia for the popular; yet it also yields writers for rediscovery, and is belatedly credited with developing in new directions the potential of each genre. Lastly, the degraded forms of mass culture become the subject of sociological exploration, for the most ephemeral novels can have haunting hegemonic effects. Walt Disney adventure comics, Barbara Cartland romances and Mickey Spillane thrillers ironically acquire a reflated currency as the hidden sources of class, gender and ethnic domination.

The theoretical work of monitoring these secret caches of obedience has been aided by Gramsci's writings on popular literature in the *Prison Notebooks*.[55] These ideas supplement his better-known studies of ideology, which have already advanced Marxist and feminist studies. Within this context, he explores the sources of pleasure in popular reading.[56] He suggests, first, that these novels attain their popularity by connecting with 'the philosophy of the epoch', that is, they offer collective representations of the sentiments and world-view flourishing among the 'silent multitude'. Drawing his examples from the work of Alexandre Dumas, whose novels were still much read when he was writing in the 1920s, Gramsci suggested that the source of their success was that they permitted their readers to construct an idealised self in the character of the hero:

> The serial novel takes the place of (and at the same time favours) the fantasizing of the common people; it is a real way of day-dreaming. . . . One can refer to what Freud and the psychoanalysts had to say about day-dreaming. In this case one could say that the daydreams of the people are dependent on a social inferiority complex! This is why they day-dream at length about revenge and about punishing those responsible for the evils they have endured.[57]

Thus, in the case of Dumas, the readers are 'intoxicated' by the main characters' decisive intervention to restore belief in a justice which people suspected no longer existed. Since everyone has some experience of injustice, petty or great, this creates a fertile soil for such a novel's success. Gramsci also suggested that the structures of novels such as those by Dumas could have engendered the concept of superman in the writings of philosophers like Nietzsche – for intellectuals still read popular novels in the mid nineteenth century.[58] Gramsci was also the first to extend to mass culture the Marxist analysis of religion as an opiate, later to be followed by Brecht, who referred cynically to the culture industry as 'a branch of the capitalist narcotics industry'.[59]

Gramsci also had a theory of the utopian appeals of popular books. Dumas tempts the petty-bourgeoisie and minor intellectuals with an 'artificial paradise', which contrasts with 'the narrowness and pinched circumstances of their real and immediate life'.[60] Unlike more mature forms of utopian thought, such paradises are contradictory: Dumas's novels are democratic yet depend on their readers' fascination with power; nationalism is insinuated into the deepest narrative structure, yet Dumas drew back from the racism which characterised the thought of contemporaries such as Gobineau.[61] For Gramsci, then, an adequate approach to popular novels required classification with both political criteria (conservative-reactionary, democratic, racist, nationalist) and an analysis of the genre (sentimental, adventure, Gothic, historical and detective novels).[62] Gramsci regarded cultural value as independent of such questions of genre and public accessibility. Thus, unlike Dumas, Balzac was indeed a great writer, yet he, too, was popular, his public success deriving partly from his construction of 'supermen' figures, such as Vautrin.

In general, then, Gramsci suggested that in societies in which the lower classes are systematically denied control over their own lives and in which their surplus-value is constantly pumped out by capital, popular literature offers compensatory satisfactions – images of action and excitement to contrast with lives of drudgery and tedium. The plenitude of the happy ending nourishes wilting hopes. Gramsci, then, did not adopt an essentialist definition of the popular, in which it is equated with progressive literature. Certainly, Brecht defined the popular in this way, including only that writing which took the standpoint of the people, expressing and enriching their forms of expression and transmitting the views of the most advanced section. By contrast, Gramsci's study was of everything that was diffused amongst the broad masses, even if it represented interests hostile to their development. Popular culture was for him an arena of struggle over the ideas made available to the uneducated, and in this respect I shall follow his method.

In terms similar to those used by Gramsci, Ernst Bloch's *The Principle of Hope* also fused Marxist and Freudian theory, illuminating a wide range of cultural phenomena from music to detective stories.[63] Bloch has clarified more lucidly than any other writer the nature of 'escapist' literature. Moreover, he was also amongst the first Marxists to insist that kitsch as well as more authentic popular culture was worth studying in that it revealed 'the dream of the world'. Bloch argued that the most ideological magazine story must nevertheless be viewed as possessing a utopian core which constituted in part the pleasure of the text. Indeed, in the absence of a more analytical understanding of such human needs and of the role of the imagination, Marxism was doomed to be economistic.[64] Popular genres would be increasingly colonised by the irrationalist fantasies of the Right, to which the historically marginal strata, such as the contemporary peasantry and bourgeoisie, were especially susceptible.

Bloch also situated literature within the wider context of the pursuit of individual or social hopes, some traces of these searches suggesting magical transfigurations of experience – as in the mythical geography of Eldorado or India envisaged in feudal Europe,[65] some indicating more mature and concrete utopia – like those visions in which capitalism creates the objective conditions for the possible future, the 'not yet'. Moreover, if the carnival or festival was celebrated partly for its secular or anticipatory promise, Bloch also thought it revealed the aspiration to be released from material and political oppression. Modern rationalised production created in the worker a desire to turn to crafts in their free time and to retreat to the countryside; the general growth of imposed work fed a mass search for non-alienated leisure, of which escapist reading was merely one alternative.

Bloch's erudition enables us to grasp the historical conditioning of such magical escapes and the class differences in their content; he argues persuasively that all literature has an escapist allure, since both images of individual desires and of the resolution of social contradictions derive from a utopian substance which fulfils 'escapist' needs. From the Renaissance onwards, great literature has developed a wishful image of world-improvement, which is not restricted to the utopian tradition of Sir Thomas More, Campanella, Fourier and William Morris. Such images are of two basic types: literature can appeal to the 'Not Yet Become', when realism in the broadest sense is allied to a belief in the potential for social change; alternatively, fictions of harmony and peace can be introduced within an *ideological vision* as in the pastoral nostalgia for an idealised aristocracy.[66]

Thus the utopian function in great writing consists in a vision of the new and objectively possible social reality which goes beyond the contemplative depiction of what exists. Bloch refers to this in the language of dreams. The night-dream is a regressive form of consciousness in which the wishes are symptomatically clothed in the language of desire and its inner tensions; it recapitulates the early stage of life when individuals long for fulfilment through love or by making their fortune. The anticipatory consciousness of the day-dream, however, is the vision of a possible world-order, a more serious fantasy than the nocturnal images:

> And the great – that is realistic works of art do not become

less realistic through the notation of latency [the latent future] . . . but more realistic; since everything real mingles with the Not Yet within that space . . . there are enough differences between these two kinds of dream . . . the mode as well as the content of wish-fulfilment diverge in them insuppressibly . . . the night-dream lives in regression; it is indiscriminately drawn to its images [good patriarchal authority, rural harmony] . . . [But] the daydream projects the image into the future . . . the content of the nightdream is concealed and disguised, the content of the daydream is open, fabulously inventive, anticipating, and its latency lies ahead.[67]

In the day-dream, Bloch adds, there is a necessity of renunciation as well as a recognition of human needs.

This begins to unravel the tangled skein of popular thought about escapism. In these terms, contemporary romantic fiction includes night- and day-dream elements. Like the serious day-dream, it revolves around moral obligations, but like the inconsequential creations of the night-dream, it conveys one or more regressive images: good father-figures, land-owning heroes as guarantors of social order, dependent heroines. For this reason, the classical romance paradigm depends on optimistic wish fulfilment at the cost of illusion. Thus in the case of the most formulaic writing, the function for the personality is similar to that of a nature-reserve in an industrial city, providing the refreshing reassurance of the known.[68]

Within such a regressive consciousness are all the pre-rational stereotypes of good and evil, the 'atavistic archetypes' which have conflicted with Enlightenment ideals since the period of the progressive bourgeoisie: Jews, negroes, homosexuals, gypsies and women.[69] Bloch's point still holds for the 1980s: even recent best sellers deploy homosexuals as villains. In 1970s magazine stories, the whore was used to similar effect.

Bloch identifies the escapism of American magazine fiction, especially, with such regressive images: 'The magazine story thus remains . . . the most [moving] in its feudal images, the most miracle-believing in its capitalist images.'[70] He contrasts this with the less 'passive' popular literature of the thriller, the adventure story and, earlier, the fairy-tale, with the heroes' active rebellion in taking the goods of the rich from them. Popular criticism and images of liberation circulated within these stories, which on occasion provided the politics of great works, as in the case of Beethoven's Fidelio.[71]

Bloch's antithesis between active and passive stories has to be reconsidered in the light of new versions of the romance or magazine story. He also fails to analyse whether the fantasies and prefigurative emblems of an enlightened world are *gendered*, despite his recourse to male sexual imagery in describing the most simple and universal idylls of happiness. Women's day-dreams, as Frigga Haug points out, may also express images of internalised gender oppression and its transformation.[72] Finally, Bloch fails to explore the arena in which reading occurs. There is evidence from my discussions with Scottish readers that most women do not view the formulaic genre as realist, but as something different, a parable which provides entertainment. Such readers initiate a tacit contract to enter these mythic worlds in return for the pleasures of temporary oblivion. I shall elaborate on this knowing pursuit of illusion in Chapter 6. Despite these imperfections, Bloch's theory, with its sensitivity to the historical specificity of fantasies of escape, is the basis from which I shall explore the genre most characteristic of women's fiction, namely the domestic romance.

Feminist theory in popular cultural studies has tended to restrict its scope to a narrow psychoanalytic focus and has failed to assess the wider ideological effects of these novels.[73] While it is perceptive about gender, it has ignored other aspects of the writers' social consciousness, particularly the images of class, ethnicity and power embodied in the formulaic romance. I maintain that it is essential to adopt a wider approach to assess whether this genre serves to reify or demystify social reality, and the broader political implications of its fantasies. And in this respect I intend to provide for the romance the study that has already been undertaken for the dime novel,[74] the thriller,[75] the spy story[76] and science fiction.[77] I now turn to other cultural theorists who may help in mapping out this territory, and who can be compared with Gramsci and Bloch.

Q.D. Leavis: *cultural segmentation and its discontents*

For Queenie Leavis the popular romance represented lower-class nostalgia for 'the world we have lost'.[78] She was part of the second generation of theorists of modernity, whose reactions were dominated by despair. Her book on contemporary cultural divisions was a central intellectual resource for the critical revolution spearheaded by the magazine *Scrutiny* and a significant English component of the general re-orientation of social thought after the collapse of utilitarianism. Yet, as Francis Mulhern has commented: 'Uniquely among its European siblings, the name and self-proclaimed nature of this English discourse on community was "literary criticism".'[79] Queenie Leavis's concern was to crystallise the social issues raised by the modern theory of culture and society. She adopted a dual methodology: a psychoanalytically attuned sociology was applied to mass culture and its audience, while a literary criticism, antipathetic to any systematic analysis of the conditions of literary production, was deployed for 'great literature'.[80]

Her pioneering analysis of the segmented literary market has been misleadingly interpreted as an élitist nostalgia for a leisured cultivated minority. In fact she sharply attacked ritualistic displays of Higher Learning which served only the maintenance of class closure and the pursuit of genteel academic 'profit-making'.[81] Her 'minority' was, rather, a humanist vanguard, besieged by an enterprise culture but committed to the democratised 'march of the intellect'. Thus she praised the nourishment of a tradition of autodidactic workers with the works of Tom Paine, William Godwin and G.W.M. Reynolds, contrasting with this the ineffective nature of later compulsory education: 'It is a tragic fact that State education . . . could only damp this enthusiasm for "enlightenment" or else side-track it.'[82]

Of course, the weakness of *Fiction and the Reading Public* was its facile assumption that because of the *uneducated* character of their publics, all modern forms of *commodified mass culture* were *inferior*. Queenie Leavis denigrated without comprehension contemporary popular arts such as radio, film and jazz, this last being dismissed for its 'lascivious syncopated rhythms' inhibiting 'normal development'![83] While recognising that forms such as the novel had initially possessed a popular readership, she sweepingly rejected any potential for artistic quality in current commercially successful forms of writing. Further, by means of contrast, she perpetuated a false conception of *pre-capitalist society* as integrated around a single culture. This illusory feudalism led her mistakenly to seek the origins of the later divided culture in 'industrial civilisation' alone. Finally, while she abhorred the simplified popular newspaper journalism catering for a working-class public and linked it to the fragmentation and fatigue of factory labour, she was only vaguely aware of the fetishised social forms on which this rested.

Queenie Leavis stratified literature into, first, 'great art', that is, complex, analytical, morally sensitive works, grounded in wide

experience of life, second, 'middlebrow' and third, 'low brow'
fiction. Her deep antipathy to class inequality is illuminated by her
hostility to the narrowness of Bloomsbury as well as to middlebrow
novelists who hawked their 'herd-prejudices' of 'snobbery', status,
power and racism.

The low brow category included a genre analysis of the 'domestic
romance'. Leavis approached the best-selling novels of Marie Corelli
and Florence Barclay as responses to the moral confusion and need
for wish fulfilment of their readers. Essentially, she viewed these
writers as providing a cultural equivalent to the declining churches,
providing the reassurance once offered by salvation. If modernist
texts such as Virginia Woolf's were unattractive to a mass
readership, she contended, other novelists gave those with the
'fiction habit' the strong narratives and attractive characters with
whom they could identify. Such best-selling 'low brow' books use

> an emotional vocabulary which provokes the vague warm
> surges of feeling associated with religion and religious
> substitutes, for example, Life [sic], death. love, good, evil,
> sin, home, noble, gallantry, purity, honour . . . There is this
> terrific vitality set to turn the wheel of morality.[84]

Her questionnaires to writers revealed that these novelists have no
pretensions to literature: rather they see themselves as craftworkers
catering for the needs of 'the heart' as opposed to the 'head', for
'uplift', and for emotional 'masturbation' – aims which Leavis
spurned as anti-intellectualist panaceas. At her best, then, her
account clarified the 'lived' pre-rational roots of ideology in a way in
which Marxist explanations of the tenacity of reactionary ideals have
rarely succeeded in doing. Thus, for Leavis, the fleeting, fragmen-
tary and arbitrary character of the social relations of modernity
paradoxically sustained the most regressive medieval values.

The importance of women in this ill-educated romance readership
was acknowledged. In the inter-war years, such women readers
were recruited from all classes. Yet Leavis failed to explain the
specific needs *provoked by their subordination*, to which such novelists
responded. Instead, her remarks hinted at the emancipated woman's
disdain for popular readers' 'emotional self-indulgence' or 'day-
dreaming', bearing a striking similarity to Freud's obtuse judgements of the repressed culture of adult women in his 'On
femininity'.[85] Raymond Williams later formulated a more fruitful
view of the dialectical interaction of the social and the individual by

exposing the forbidden discourse within the day-dreaming, the rebellious qualities of desire beneath the constraining structures.[86] However, it was Richard Hoggart who initially developed Queenie Leavis's sociological analysis further when he explored the character of working-class culture.

Hoggart and popular aesthetics

Hoggart aspired to an exploration of working-class 'common sense' in proto-Gramscian terms, showing how their stock of knowledge is not harmonised into an intellectual *system*, but is still *practically rational*.[87] He had two purposes: to delineate the social reality which produced this culture, and to demonstrate the role of the popular arts in sustaining such distinctive perspectives. Both middle-class Marxists and Leavisites were attacked for misrecognising the purpose of such art. In particular, such approaches were condemned for constructing the working class either as noble savages within an urban pastoral or as heirs to a caricatured impoverished taste. Nevertheless, Hoggart himself differentiated a healthy from a degraded popular culture, contrasting the inter-war artisan arts with the new mass culture, which, as a mere 'candy-floss' or intellectual junk-food, spread attitudes of 'indifferentism', 'contemporary disillusionment and doubt. . . . great emptiness . . . disenchantment'.[88] Thus earlier popular *art*, represented by pub songs and cheap magazines – *Peg's Paper*, *The Oracle*, *Secrets* – were part of an urban folk culture or an outworker capitalist tradition in which working-class storytellers still supplied from their homes the bulk of the fiction. With its demise, the consumer is persuaded to buy goods that have negligible use-value.

For Hoggart, the middle-class critic, however, is mistaken when he/she expects the aesthetic value of this genuinely popular culture to lie in its *extension* of experience or knowledge. The clichéd character of the magazine stories has to be understood in another way, not as 'serious literature' but as the emotional or religious centre of the culture – 'uplift' rather than instruction. Thus working-class society is to be seen anthropologically, as possessing a different culture or, in celebratory tones, in terms of its humanist victory over economic adversity and an atomising individualism:

the writers use cliché, and . . . the audience seems to want

cliché, . . . they are not exploring experience, realising
experience through language. . . . If we regard them as
faithful but dramatised presentations of a life whose form and
values are known we might find it more useful to ask what
are the values they embody.[89]

Now Hoggart's sharp distinction between 'experience' and 'values'
has to be questioned. For he seemed to argue that literature was
incorporated into the oral culture in a particular way, so as to
enhance *values* through pleasurable reading but not to undermine an
older transmission of *experience* through word of mouth. But this
raises the difficulty of those periods when the working class (or at
least a significant minority of it) consumed different genres to the
domestic story. Amongst these were revolutionary romanticism,
Chartist poetry and the industrial novels of working-class writers.
Working-class readers then formed part of the wider public for
critical realism and for a vision of the new at these times. The
development of the distinctive women's popular fiction and
aesthetic that Hoggart described was not automatic but the result of
the complex growth of nineteenth-century pragmatic accommodation to the late bourgeois world, which shaped even the 'contract'
between readers and writers. Indeed, despite the deep-rooted need
for wish fulfilment and the similarity of developments in other
European societies, it cannot be assumed that such readers will
remain permanently cut off from a literature which is realist in the
broadest sense.

In brief, Hoggart failed to see working-class culture as the arena
of momentous historical battles over its content and form, for
example over its adoption of middle-class family values or
conceptions of childhood. For the culture which he portrayed as
unified is in reality a braided plait of ill-matched strands – that of
Catholic Irish former peasants, Protestant skilled workers, patri-
archs, radicals and socialists.

The central core is disseminated through women, whose role he
celebrated without elucidation. Indeed, his thematic focus on home
and marriage is ultimately misleading because it led him to veil the
contradictory realities within the patriarchal family and workplace
which surface in these stories in inconsistent forms of thought.
Hoggart perceived the domestic story as enshrining the religious
heart of the culture. But the aura of the urban kailyard community –
which he further romanticised – has to be desecrated in order to
grasp the culture's inner mechanisms. Only then will the precise
language of class be understood and the status of such ritualistic

fiction compared with other accessible forms for lower-class women. On these issues, Hoggart's much-used text was silent.

Raymond Williams and cultural materialism

In his 'fraught, dissentient affair with Marxism',[90] Williams provided a crucial dimension for thinking about popular literature which was missing in the *Scrutiny* – Hoggart approach. He distinguished both the periodical fiction and the best sellers of the 1840s from the great realist tradition of the novel, especially by the former's incapacity for radical questioning and its preference for fairy-tale escapes: an 'illusory realism'. Such best-selling fiction usually depends on ascendant ideals of social character and in this period it was organised around heroes who were either self-made men – the dominant structure of feeling – or representatives of the gentry – the residual structure of feeling. Both heroic types have remained a feature of popular literature to the present day and are actively preferred by readers of romantic novels. Yet unlike the earlier Leavisites, Williams emphasised the 'moral regulation' or *hegemonic mission* of such fiction:

> a large part of the impetus to cheap periodical publishing was the desire to control the development of working-class opinion and in this the observed shift from popular educational journals to family magazines (the latter the immediate ancestors of the women's magazine of our own time) is significant. Respectable schemes of moral and domestic improvement became deeply entangled with the teaching and implication of particular social values, in the interests of the existing class society.[91]

However, the precise relation between the 'ruling ideas' of the bourgeoisie and the conceptions of best-selling writers was, for Williams, a complex issue. Since hegemony was not imposed but 'lived', such writers could only take on *selective* elements of dominant thought. In the context of the stories of the 1840s, Williams delineated how a wedge was inserted between the constituent elements of the Protestant bourgeois ethic. The industrial interests of the Protestant middle class had led them in the seventeenth century to abandon the traditional feudal moral economy which was based on customary wages and prices together with charity for the poor.[92] Yet the 1840s best-selling story-tellers still retained elements of such a pre-capitalist moral economy, for although narrative devices certainly linked success to the work ethic, economic failure did not lead to a parallel attribution of poverty to indolence. The popular novelists' direct experience resulted in the rejection of this simple individualist equation. With such an example, Williams's perceptive readings decoded precisely how the demotic literature of the 1840s embodied representations not just of 'a whole way of life' but also of 'a whole way of struggle'.[93]

Major and popular writers possessed some common elements, but Williams emphasised that Elizabeth Gaskell (especially in the first volume of *Mary Barton*), Dickens and the Brontës had all questioned 'with maximum intensity' the conventional assumptions of the Protestant ethic and market-based achievement obligations, transcending the form within which the stock endings were couched. Hence the ambiguity of the more realist texts; embodying an emergent structure of feeling, they registered alienation and yet still bore the traces of a world-building, progressive middle class.

Later structuralist interpretations of literature implicitly *challenged* Williams's framework. They questioned the privileging of certain texts as channels for a 'pure' critical realist or humanist tradition, undiluted by the bourgeois or élitist currents swirling in the muddy sub-literature beneath. For example, by offering a different interpretation of Charlotte Brontë's *Shirley*, Rachel Harrison viewed the popular romantic novel as *a genre with a single discourse* which is found in *canonical* and *uncanonical* texts alike and which offers imaginary resolutions to the social cleavages of class and gender.[94]

However ingenious and historically sensitive this version of structuralism, Harrison's reading placed all the emphasis on the moment of resolution in *Shirley*, neglecting the text's unmasking of power beforehand. The main difficulty is Harrison's conception of Brontë as the prisoner of ideology, although one who dreamt of freedom. For her, the text is a more effective ideological machine precisely because it temporarily exposes contradictions, as in its images of the mill-workers' sabotage and the protracted suffering of the dowryless women. It is these class and power inequalities that Harrison believed were 'naturalised' by the novel's conclusion.

However, this view severely understated both the consistent questioning of political economy throughout *Shirley*, and the urgent 'return of the repressed' in the portrait of Caroline Helstone, which together created dramatic effects of the 'maximum intensity', in Williams's phrase.[95] Harrison's approach to the ending also ignored the different modes of reconciliation in the novel. Williams distinguished between novels in which conflict was merely set up to be solved, as in best sellers (or some semi-canonised works like *North and South*) and those novels which, despite their wish-fulfilling endings, became part of the 'culture of protest'. Novels of this sort possessed a closeness to the subordinate culture, as in *Mary Barton*.[96]

If, unlike the Chartist novels, *Shirley* has no clear perspective of an alternative social order, Brontë none the less both lays bare the forces producing day-dreams and also cruelly tears the illusions apart. Unlike the stereotyped devices of infraction and lack which are the narrative motors of the Mills and Boon novel, Brontë motivates Caroline's quest with powerful images of social fragmentation (the bare tables of the unemployed; the sumptuous meal of the fat clergymen; the abandonment of Caroline by her mother as the sole means of escape from her unhappy marriage).

Thus Harrison's analysis precluded sufficient recognition of the subversive thrust of this novel, which retains its impact despite its vision of a heroic bourgeois paradise at the end. However, if *Shirley* *can* be distinguished from the unproblematic reflection of dominant ideas, as indeed Williams's approach had suggested, this is not the case with its pastiche versions in the 1980s. This argument is advanced in Chapter 5.

Developments in the structuralist theories of literature

Some of the recent disputes over 'the canon' or the archeology of Literature were fought over the terrain of the romance.[97] The return to formalism by Lévi-Strauss marked the erosion of the space between 'high culture' and popular culture. Thus the novel could be explored in similar terms to the romance as an autonomous artistic product, extraordinarily like the pre-capitalist fairy-tale in its appeal to mythic structures, its imaginary unity and narrative development. As a consequence, the earlier critics who had established the distinctive literary works of the bourgeois pantheon by stressing their *formal realism*, became unacceptable. The currency of 'bourgeois classic realism' was devalued and that of modernism dramatically raised due to its deconstructive devices. 'Literature' simply became those texts that had been inserted into the bourgeois literary formation. In practice this meant that these texts were categorised as largely 'reactionary', to use Alan Sinfield's term.[98] Thus the boundary between Literature and non-Literature needed remapping: in principle, radical cultural studies would have to rethink the whole question of the classification in terms of a *political* aesthetic.

In effect, this move meant that the canon became increasingly identified with 'ideology'. Thus Eagleton, in his later work, stressed that, with the papal imprimatur of an inner professorial elite, the canon acquired the repressive force reminiscent of the Inquisition: no dissent was permissable since 'it is at this point that the canon is trundled out to blast offenders out of the literary arena'.[99] In this view the consecrated books themselves became weapons of an *ideological discipline*: 'If the masses are not thrown a few novels, they may react by throwing up a few barricades.'[100] Implicitly, Literature was viewed through a functional lens which linked it to earlier *mystificatory* concerns, such as the theological justifications of the dominant class on the part of the Established churches. Unlike them, it operated through the construction of a seemingly benign liberal sensitivity rather than any dogma.

The shift to structuralism can also be situated in the debate over popular literature between Tony Bennett and Roger Bromley.[101] Bromley addressed the puzzle of the mysteriously anachronistic popularity of the romance. He traced the origins of the modern best-selling form to the 1840s and 1850s, denoting its specific ideological structure as *petty-bourgeois*, particularly in its contradictory combination of independence with loyalty, enterprise with obedience. However, the petty-bourgeois aspect was viewed as *disguised* in the romance as a woman, whose opposition to the bourgeois world-view occurred only at the level of private resistance. Moreover, her dissatisfaction took the form of an isolated disquiet, not incompatible with the celebration of possessive individualism, imperialism and the domesticated role of her gender. The romance, therefore, accomplished a pleasurable transformation in which issues provoking conflict, such as the relations between capital and labour, could be symbolically annihilated, largely through the device of textual omission. Thus the plot, the exact class delineation of characters, and the geographical setting, are the 'noisy sphere' of the romance, the equivalent of the market place in modern economics. What Marx called the 'hidden abode' of capitalist class relations, that of the extraction of workers' surplus-value by capital in the sphere of production, can be similarly equated with the concealed arena of the romance, that is its generation of surplus-meaning, reinforcing bourgeois domination.

Bromley's view of the romance at this time failed to do justice to the fusion of gentry and bourgeois forms found within it, an omission he subsequently rectified. Moreover, it underestimated the discontinuities in popular writers' representations of *women*. A fuller account would highlight the appearance of some discontents about modern patriarchal civilisation: in writers of the 1890s like Charlotte Yonge, as well as in recent best sellers. However, a more fundamental criticism was levelled by Bennett, who argued that it was problematic for a Marxist to employ bourgeois critics' conceptions of literature.[102] The Marxist realism/ideology dichotomy could not be identified with these critics' literature/popular culture distinction and indeed could cut across it.

However, the problem with recent 'canon' theory like that of MacCabe or Bennett is that it led to an over-expansive identification of the 'bourgeois' ideological sphere, which became coexistent with (post-Renaissance, pre-modernist) literature. It thus ignored the critical or counter-hegemonic thrust of many writers at the time of publication and meant that literature was perceived to aid the hegemonic supremacy of the dominant class in an unproblematic way. It was in this context that the intervention by Kiernan Ryan was important, for he argued powerfully against such a closed, determinist view of the impact of the dominant class on all thought, seeing canonical post-Renaissance literature as having a 'dormant progressive' content.[103] By contrast, for Eagleton and other post-Althusserian critics, the nineteenth century might have witnessed the death of God, but the twentieth century was witnessing the death of Literature, its disguise of aesthetic autonomy being stripped off to reveal the defence of power beneath.

Yet the recent concern with Literature as an academic canon has reified the role of university English curricula in establishing cultural assessments of aesthetic value. Paradoxically, literature in the wider sense has always included the unconsecrated canons of fellow-writers, radicals and, in some periods, women, which have overlapped, extended and contextualised the university canon. Thus rather than reject the present consecrated canon for being chiefly bourgeois, male and white, it is more appropriate to ask what social processes led to the academic canonisation of a writer.[104] More crucially, structuralist approaches attributing to the universities a monopoly over the definition of 'Literature' are analogous to the historian identifying 'Religion' only with the Anglican Church and neglecting the Primitive Methodists. In this context the academic preference for using form or beauty alone as the test of canonical Literature was always an embattled position, countered by others who saw the distinctive literary roles of writers as bearing witness to the truth or as the 'education of desire'.[105]

Bloch's Marxist account of ideology and utopia

The view that literature is identical with other ideological discourses was attacked by Bloch as long ago as 1947. He argued persuasively in *The Principle of Hope* that literature has a 'cultural surplus', beyond ideology, which explains its enduring interest outside the period in which it was produced. Such literature, for Bloch, might occasionally be extended to include some best sellers, although not to genre writing in general. The 'cultural surplus' emerges from literature's anticipatory utopia and is not limited to the high moral seriousness of some bourgeois literary forms.[106] So, following Bloch, it might be better to view art and literature as human achievements, like higher mathematics, of potential benefit to all: including those outside the privileged styles of life from which cultural producers have so frequently emerged. Literary production cannot be simplistically reduced to the writers' class of origin, not least because it is mediated through other group 'sieves', such as schools and brotherhoods.[107] Artists, for Bloch, are neither the mouthpieces of class myths nor the officials of sacred mysteries.

Bloch also argued that literature (with or without a cultural surplus) could only acquire an *ideological* significance by offering its own *utopian* appeals. In the context of a mass cultural form like the romance, this draws our attention not just to the petty-bourgeois patriarchal character of much popular literature but also to its images of hope, especially the ideas of plenitude which even this literature keeps alive. I have developed this approach by pointing out the heroine's leisurely choice of the best interior decorations or the detailed representations of the heroic couple's rich food. A recent study by Paizis of the boom in romantic fiction in France has drawn comparable conclusions, showing that the essence of escapism is the vision of a holiday-like freedom from all alienating experiences:

> The romantic novel acts as a testing-ground, not only of fantasies but of aspirations, and this takes place in the isolation of the home. In the private fantasy, however, there is also the collective experience of women. Escapism implies not only social criticism, but it also implies hope . . . the very idea of escapism gives an idea of what is being escaped from, that gives rise to its need.[108]

This also explains why the heroes of romances are independent gentlemen or free professionals; well-off, but never exclusive in their use of privilege. It also explains why the heart of the romance is the negation or suspension of everyday categories, permitting the heroine to be neither ruler nor dependent.[109]

Aspects of Paizis's readings of these gardens of earthly delights might be questioned. My research has suggested that the compliance of the heroine to the hero in the traditional romance still locates these texts within the ideas of male mastery found in the tradition from *Pamela* to the 1930s magazine stories. Even where images of mastery are absent, the wider patriarchal order is still embedded in the narrative through recurrent devices such as the homosexual villain, the separation of spheres and the veneration of the family. Despite these qualifications, Paizis's general approach is fruitful.

The utopian theory has recently been developed by Fredric Jameson to apply to best-selling novels and films. He shows how the characters perceived as social types illuminate the underlying contradictions of modern America. For example, the Mafia of *The Godfather* attracts precisely because the *gemeinschaft* founded on ethnic loyalties speaks to a readership caught in rationalised but empty routines. If the ideological thrust of the narrative derives from deflecting hostility from capitalism onto organised crime, this is possible only because of the allure of the utopian longing it also fulfils:

> To reawaken in the midst of a privatised psychologizing society, obsessed with commodities and bombarded with the slogans of big business some sense of the ineradicable drive towards collectivity . . . in the most degraded works of mass culture as . . . in the classics of modernism – is surely an indispensible precondition for any meaningful Marxist intervention in contemporary culture.[110]

Such an approach points the way ahead for the cultural analysis of popular literature.

Janice Radway has elaborated Jameson's utopian theory with an added feminist perspective in her recent study of the romance. 'We read books so that we won't cry,' comments one of her respondents, or again: '[The society of the romance is] the world as I'd like it to be, not as it is.'[111]

This subtle account uses sociological techniques in order to focus on the active romance public, spatially isolated but linked by their mutual enjoyment of the published texts. She derives her conclusions about this wider mass public from interviews with a network of readers in the American Midwest: women who not only read romances avidly but who received romance reviews written by her main ethnograpic informant, a bookshop assistant. For Radway, each formulaic reading is a 'community' performance and a compensatory act. Central to this ritual is the fantasy, but Radway suggests this pleasure has to be disguised as learning. In contrast, my research has suggested a differentiation of popular readerships according to the salience of fantasy or learning in each. Thus for Radway, the hidden rationale of the romances is the vicarious nurturance they offer, which temporarily reverses women readers' general denial of their own needs in caring for others. The acceptable formulaic story engenders in the readers a regressive sensation of child-like well-being which they defend as less harmful than alcohol.

This phenomenology of reading has many valuable insights but also some limitations. Radway does not explain the wider social world-views encoded in the romance. She also fails to address the question of why some women are attracted to the formula and not others: she implies that these books possess a universal use-value for women, a view which I will challenge. Finally, she has a laudable concern to understand romance-reading not as false consciousness, nor as feminist opposition, but as a meaningful act. Yet as such, she consistently over-emphasises the elements of resistance to patriarchy held to be buried within her readers' favourite formulaic plots. She concludes with a disclaimer:

> Certainly, my study does not challenge absolutely the notion that mass-produced art forms are ideologically conservative in the sense that they restore at least temporarily the claims of presently existing institutions and practices to the loyalty of those who participate vicariously in these forms.[112]

Nevertheless, two divergent claims are made earlier: first, that romances 'counter-valuate' a patriarchal and commercial ethos.[113] For this she provides virtually no evidence save the character of the stories' conclusion, despite her own admission that the hero is always a powerful, materially well-endowed figure. Second, she proposes that the romance is critical of patriarchy: 'the methodology highlights the complex and contradictory ways in which the romance recognises and thereby protests the weaknesses of patriarchy.'[114] The method at stake requires linking, dialectically, morphological studies of the texts with the ethnographically exposed nature of the reading act. However, Radway misleadingly attributes a quality of resistance to the harmonious romance form precisely because of its readers' temporary suspension of repressive controls. It is one thing to read these formulaic romantic texts as utopian and quite another to claim that their mythic universes disclose a critical realism.

In the context of these problems, the study of Scottish readers' 'magical escapes', in Chapter 6, offers an alternative formulation. It illuminates the sociological underpinnings of the Bloch tradition on utopia and ideology in order to explore further the social reality within which the reception of literature occurs.

Part II
TWENTIETH-CENTURY ROMANCE TEXTS

3 *Melodrama and Magazines: Cheap Fiction in the 1930s*

FAMILY MAGAZINES

In the 1930s a number of cheap magazines circulated amongst a readership largely composed of working-class women. I have chosen a representative sample of weekly family or women's magazines, selecting those of the most economical design, with the lowest prices, and studying one or two stories every month. Where possible, the period analysed was July 1929 to July 1930 or failing that, the first year of the magazine's publication in the 1930s. Not only was this a time of industrial restructuring and financial collapse, but it was also the last era before the birth of the modern, glossy, mass-circulation women's magazine in 1932. Stories had a much more central place in the older type of magazine and were often the sole diet of fiction for their readers. The affectionate niche they acquired in the lives of their reading-public was attested by many of my respondents with working-class roots, who recalled their mothers snatching brief interludes from heavy domestic labour to enjoy the little luxury of *Silver Star* or the *People's Friend*.

Although these titles contained a genuinely popular fiction, it was nevertheless divorced from the radical themes and narrative structures of the Chartist story or proletarian realism. Yet it is this fiction which is still recognisable within the 'withered ideological branches' of 1980s formulaic romances, distinguished from canonised literature not just by its patriarchal paradigm, but by its unquestioning depiction of an enduring world of traditional duties. Despite its remoteness from the long-term rational interests of its readers, it can be plumbed to see how the middle-class romance form was adapted to take account of the deprivations and the wish-fulfilment hopes of an oppressed lower-class readership.

By the 1930s, organised religion was declining but other sites for ideological transmission, such as these family magazines, assumed a greater importance. Two-penny publications like D.C. Thompson's 'feminine five' (*Family Star, Red Letter et al.*) were perceived as part of the realm of pleasure. This created a fertile terrain for the influence of their readers, particularly through a sensitivity to their dreams and needs. The form in which such political and ethical ideas were couched was still, in the inter-war years, that of melodrama. To use Raymond Williams' terms modernism might be the *emergent* 'structure of feeling', and classic realism the *dominant* structure, but the *residual* structure was still saturated in melodrama.[1] Thus, in striking contrast to modernism, myths were employed throughout the magazine narratives to form a stable, unambiguous and comprehensible universe. Through these devices, alien eruptions of the monstrous 'other' were ultimately excluded, desire was harmonised with order and reality was apprehended without angst.

Of course, the melodramatic story acquired its credibility by the selective use of bourgeois realism, chosen to throw into relief both the hidden terrors and the moment of reconciliation at the end.[2] Nevertheless, the melodrama rigorously screened out the shocks of modernity by creating in its positive heroes and heroines totally unified selves. It eliminated, especially, the sense of the coexistence of terror and routine, excess and order: such multiple realities might erupt in the dialogic, disturbed universe of the modernist novel but were unknown in contemporary romances and magazines stories.[3] As both radical doubt and illicit desires broke free of their repressive anchorages, a pre-rationalist common sense and an optimistic belief in social justice still prevailed at the pole of mass culture.[4]

Clearly, readings of these texts might diverge. It is only under certain conditions that such fiction delivers its potential ideological effects. In particular, sufficient realism is required for readers to suspend their disbelief, that is, some correspondence must exist between their experiences and those represented in the story world. Only then will the 'plausibility structure' emerge in which ideological themes can acquire consistency and force. A second essential requirement is the systematic absence of ambiguity, evident in the dramatic simplifications of moral and political thought in the magazine stories. Thirdly, such cultural commodities must be popular, in that their representations cannot undermine the most cherished interests of their lower-class readers. Indeed, the mode of melodramatic fantasy requires the critical depiction, however fleeting, of the anger and resentment of working-class women, whilst superseding these in imaginary moral revenge or desire. In these circumstances, I would suggest the ideological potential of the fiction is considerable, especially in the absence of rival world-views derived from trade-union experience or radical politics.

Initial impressions of the 1930s stories suggest a mythical world in which simple Christian or fairy-tale symbols are deployed to create predictable narrative developments. Much of the fiction thus amplifies the codes of patriarchal morality, by such devices as the representation of an unmarried mother – or other patriarchally ambiguous characters – in the role of villain. However, where everyday material experience moulds popular thought in an oppositional form, the writers cannot simply negate this. To be accepted by their readers, they have to take account of long-standing currents of working-class criticism.

For example, despite the bourgeois ethos of the magazines, none of the 1929/30s stories contain positive images of the workhouse. No narrative device could divest this of its connotation of Poor Law Bastille and render it a legitimate instrument of discipline.[5] Indeed, of the 144 stories studied, there is only one with any reference to the workhouse, and this bears traces of deep-rooted popular anger.[6] Its title, 'Whom God hath joined' encodes an ironic allusion to the arrogance of a ruling class prepared to 'put asunder' men and women bound together in marriage. Its drama derives from the magical escape of one such old couple from the austerity of the workhouse regime.[7] This example shows that there are limits on the views of the dominant class which can be made palatable for a working-class readership.

More regressively, where chauvinist and racist constructions had acquired a practical adequacy as explanations of working-class deprivation, a rich soil existed for the melodramatic portrayal of the racial 'other'. Villains in this fiction are stereotypes from nineteenth-century 'scientific' racism; monstrous 'dagoes' (Italians), 'half-crazed Africans' and 'wily Indian women' still stalk the pages. (Orientalist and racist discourses had already permeated numerous forms of popular entertainment by the turn of the century; Bennett, for example, reveals that the first day-trippers aimed at African models in the shooting galleries of the Blackpool promenade.[8]) These magazine stories orchestrated the same xenophobic fears.

Such popular culture has a dual aspect which can be stated baldly at the outset, but which requires more research.[9] On the one hand it eludes all but the deepest currents of history, with its recycled plots and stereotyped individualist or common-sense ideas. Yet, on the other hand, it possesses a dynamic character, both in its changing models of heroism and in wider respects, such as its shifting connotations of commodity consumption. Thus 1929/30s stories depend on images of a 'bad girl' or 'whore' who is condemned as much for luxury consumption as for her anarchic sexuality.[10] Traces of such attacks on illegitimate consumption still remain in the 1970s, but by the 1980s the wayward figure of instant consuming passions has disappeared. Even if the readers' finances do not permit the actual practice of these strategies of consumption, images of abundant commodities now feature as backgrounds to the fantasy content of the stories, especially in the highly formulaic literature. Indeed, in one magazine (*Woman's Weekly*) and in the cheapest romances, the fiction often revolves around intricate details of interiors, complete with names of contemporary designers and shops. Through the 1980s an intertwining of discourses has occurred, in which the advertising text increasingly conceals its game behind an appeal to the acceptable values of 'art' or the subversive pleasure of the joke, while the fiction contains elements of the commercial advertisement. A passage in *Antigua Kiss* by Anne Wheale is typical: '"A firm I can recommend for beautiful fabrics in the English taste is Colefax and Fowler in Brook Street. All their chintzes are based on old designs. But of course, being English, you'll know them",' or later, 'they ate at the flat, . . . eating the delicious cold delicacies from Harrods' or Selfridges' food halls – smoked salmon from Scotland, imported French pâtés seasoned with truffles, stuffed with prunes from Agen.'[11] The commodity provides images of bliss, and becomes a substitute for the rural nostalgia of earlier women's popular culture.

The romance formula

All the magazine stories of 1929/30 operate within the reformed patriarchal assumptions described as the 'formula'. This confirms life-long, monogamous marriage, chosen by the partners themselves, as the setting for desire; it offers a Madonna image of women as a glorified wife–mother role and it represents the private sphere as the only context for unalienated existence.[12] As part of popular culture, this formula dates from early capitalism. It is linked both to the enhanced time discipline and competitiveness of the market and to the simultaneous contraction of the leisured plebeian life which had once flourished in cafés and pubs.[13]

By the 1850s the working-class family had been virtually besieged by competing authorities seeking to shape its structure. In Britain, first housing visitors, and subsequently teachers, social workers and psychiatrists, operated with an image of the ideal family, an image which has been heavily moulded by bourgeois assumptions. A 'spectacular intervention' to remodel the cells of social life took place along similar lines to those reported for France by Donzelot.[14] In both societies, the working-class family was progressively stripped of its distinctive sexuality, especially its licensed petting ('bundling') and the acceptance of pregnancy followed by marriage. Lodgers and other non-family members were excluded from residence; surveillance of children was increased.[15] The enhanced personal choice of the modern family coincided with active attempts to manage it, as a major shift occurred from 'the government of families to the government through families'.[16] From the 1850s onwards, the family magazines were among the chief instruments for the popular diffusion of middle-class family regulation.

These little parables of family life all offer women the promise of happiness through marriage and children. Nevertheless, in the 1930s, this desire operates in a world of material scarcity. Thus contemporary magazine stories often question the nature of the class system and the source of poverty. The social integration signalled at the stories' endings is frequently premissed on the recovery of riches or the sudden elevation of the hero and heroine. The prevalence of such fantasies of transformation are much more marked then than in the magazine fiction of the 1970s and 1980s, while the redemptive or utopian strain of the conclusion is a more openly *material* dimension in the 1930s lower-class magazines, despite the stigma attached to egotistic consumption. Thus the pleasure of the 1930s story is comparable to the imaginary paradise of religion: it envisages a land of milk and honey, of secure self-sufficiency. In contrast, in the 1980s magazines, material goods are a less important element of the resolution.[17] With the exception of some widowed heroines in *Woman's Weekly*, money and food are no longer the crucial symbols of material plenty. Further, if economic troubles appear at all, it is at a more abstract level, in the form of a fear of inflation or of competitive failure. More usually, class relations of production are neglected altogether. Questions relating to gender roles – and particularly to women's work and sexuality – have become more important issues within the narratives.

Yet, whether in relation to gender or class, magazine stories have rarely functioned as critical realism. Apart from the implicit reversal preserved in the wish-fulfilment ending, any oppositional consciousness evoked in the 1930s genre is ultimately defused. In particular, any appeals to active trade union organisation or to other forms of workers' dissent are countered within the stories and such practices exposed as dangerous.

Central to the 1929/30s magazines is the dependence of women and the regulation of a privatised family life. Paradoxically, despite the ethos of universal brotherly love, all the signifiers of altruism and personal care are corralled into family life, most notably in the form of women's service to husbands and children. Precisely how has the ideal of familism been transmitted in popular cultural forms? First, the inter-war stories' titles clearly signal that this is the ethical mode in which they are to be read: 'They said she was a bad lot', 'Hard ruler of her home', 'Led off his feet by a vamp', 'Roger Brand, love cheat', 'Her sister's sin', 'The shadow on her name'. These convey a preferred reading of the narrative in which a religious morality orders the aesthetic pleasures of the text.

Second, the endings invoke the paradise of Christian mythology in which the couple are 'one flesh', the family unit is paramount and any emergent class loyalties are transcended as ephemeral. This final haven of rest is anticipated by the narrative opposition between two women, the ethical heroine, who possesses the inner piety and dedication of the Madonna and the evil woman, who creates obstacles to romantic love or family unity.

A paradigmatic story of such a typical 'Madonna of the mills' is a serial from *Weekly Welcome*, 'Her traitor friend',[18] in which the heroine, Nancy, a clerkess, is separated from the mill's manager, whom she loves, by the Machiavellian skills of a fellow worker, a textile warper called Muriel. Muriel marries the hero after he has been blinded in an industrial accident. Yet it is through Nancy's intervention that a successful operation is financed for the recovery of his eyesight and it is also through her intervention that he later recovers his 'moral vision' – the discovery that Muriel has committed bigamy serving to dispel his earlier illusions. However, only in this respect does Nancy act autonomously: otherwise she shares the passive fidelity of the Victorian Angel in the House. In contrast, her rival has a dangerous mastery of the world, revealed not only in her youthful marriage and calculative remarriage, but also in her instrumental religiosity, skill at blackmail and manipulative virtuosity.

This Madonna/whore dyad will appear time and time again in these stories. Although familiar, the 1930s social type of popular Madonna should be briefly itemised in terms of her knowledge, personality and appearance. First, she has a consuming commitment to duty. This duty is recognised (in Kantian terms) as performance of actions which do not give pleasure, thus as separated from interests. Love is occasionally explicitly defined, as in 'Three years of stolen love', as doing what is good for the other person even if this means denying oneself: a verbalisation of what is implicit throughout the 1930s genre.[19] Secondly, the heroine invariably displays her *work ethic* within the family, as an extension of this devotion to the other: 'She would work from morning till night just to make him happier. And if she could do that, it would be ample payment.'[20]

Hence there is a mutual sacrifice: the man's work ethic must be shown in the labour market, the woman's is exhibited within the family. The secularised form of the Protestant work gospel requires the woman's unstinting activity within the house: indeed one homeless heroine works 'like a slave'.[21] Domestic labour has replaced the charitable work of the middle-class Victorian heroine. However, the 'industrious little wife', with her love of 'cleanliness and comfort in the home'[22] is constructed around one ambition: to offer personal service to the husband. Hence the young girl shows through her 'sweetness and gentleness' her fitness to be a 'perfect wife', preparing herself for an arcadian dream with a man who will 'take possession of her life'.[23]

Marriage is thus intrinsically gratifying. This is recognised by the orphaned servant of 'Three years of stolen love', who comments, on becoming the wife of her employer, that it 'seemed to her as though she was stepping into paradise'[24] – ironically, after marriage, her social life is depicted solely with her husband's kin. In the 1990s, defamiliarised through time, the 'paradise' of the ending would perhaps be read rather as a form of confinement, against the grain of the text.

This literature, then, operates with a splitting device in which the idealised heroine must display a devotion to domestic labour while the predatory 'whore' is the reverse, an independent, confident, unenclosed woman.[25] Denoted mainly by her sensuality, she lacks the vulnerability which the sweetness and quiet docility of the heroine indicates. Thus the pursuit of fun or sexual experience is the quintessential mode in which the breakout from social control is shown: patriarchal deviance initiates all other forms of deviance in women, even murder. The 'other woman' is 'A danger to every wife', as one title puts it.[26] Thus in the 1930s stories, as in Samuel Richardson's novels, the paramount moral virtue in woman is her exemplary practice of pre-marital and extramarital chastity. Consequently, a perennial problem for the heroine is to distinguish between the legitimate pleasures of love and the delusions of passion. The stories can be read like earlier Puritan etiquette books, as guide books to the ideal husband, elevating those with an 'ethic of responsibility' and denigrating others whose sexual freedom transgresses marital property rights.

Although these stories celebrate neither male machismo nor a double standard, an apparatus of narrative techniques addresses women as the guardians of sexual regulation. They recount, sympathetically, lower-class girls' experiences of naïve sexual seduction by their masters, continuing an older popular literary tradition which had recorded the stigmatisation of the woman and her child, and her descent into a region of economic semi-slavery.[27] However, these magazines possess a more individualist rhetoric than the older plebeian or radical romance, for the upper-class family is now portrayed as injured by the man's delinquency.[28] In contrast, radical forms like the Chartist stories of the 1850s had depicted the gentry as displaying a singular disregard for the moral purity of any of their male members.

Secondly, the 1930s stories *amplify* the stigma of illegitimacy: and thus intensify women's oppression. Far from solely emphasising the propertylessness of the bastard and the mother's difficulties in nurturing the fatherless child, they underline the moral horror in which these acts are held by multiplying the heroine's suffering. In this way, the popular romance as a genre picks up the baton where the church courts had given up the task of social regulation.[29] Until the mid eighteenth century the fear of bastardy had been structured in a legal apparatus of ecclesiastical accusation and punishment, in which barefooted, white-shrouded men and women declared their culpability at the church door.[30] This was succeeded in the nineteenth century by the institutionalisation of many unmarried mothers in Poor Law workhouses or mental hospitals.[31] From this date, moral regulation is also included within the popular narrative structure itself, constructing the enhanced status of legal marriage as a consequence. The ideology of the romance thus separated chastity from its origins in property transmission and increased the 'policing' of the working-class family.

The key narrative is the bigamy plot in which a girl innocently marries a man who wilfully conceals the secret of his first marriage, or in which the man is a blameless tool of the profligate Jezebel figure. The various obstacles and complications which the heroine suffers in the course of these narratives of bigamy can be stripped away: she is rendered homeless, she cannot get a job, she is abandoned by friends and family. These are contingent elements of the story's logic, elaborating her odyssey of suffering. The essential requirement emerges from the fact that the discovery of bigamy always results in the separation of hero and heroine even if they are in love and are economically self-sufficient. Hence it is the *namelessness* of their children that constitutes their shame.

Numerous stories refer to this ritual infraction of patriarchy as the reason for the heroine's sense of contamination and her subsequent highly moral desertion of the one person whom she can most trust. And since the transmission of family names occurs through the inscription of patriarchy in the law of the state, it could be said that through the melodrama of multiple marriage the working-class reader was encouraged herself to venerate the Law, 'the political Father'. Such a plot emerges in a *Lucky Star* story in which the hero discovers that the wife he thought had died in a fire had in fact survived. He has inadvertently committed bigamy. Despite the material abundance of the lovers, their passion and her pregnancy, the heroine gives up her husband to the legal wife. She is now structurally equivalent to a fallen women: 'she shuddered at the searing knowledge that her child would come into the world – nameless.'[32] Hence the clash of right and right, love and duty, requires the catastrophe of the heroine. The whole plot structure turns on the jeopardy of the living reality of family life for the sake of the Law.

How are we to understand this motif? It seems unlikely that the stories reflect the actual incidence of bigamy.[33] The explanation probably lies in the combined attraction to the writer of various merits possessed by the bigamy plot. First, in the absence of practical opportunities for divorce, the bigamy device allows the writer to show a girl suffering through a bad marriage and then being emancipated from it by the discovery of bigamy, to regain a better existence with a proper husband. Second, it permits the elaboration of a legal definition of marriage as an equal contract in which each spouse becomes the property of the other, thus masking continuities in patriarchal regulation. Third, it invites the introduction of a Jezebel or whore type whose destruction of the legal norms of monogamy reinforces the community of the 'good' citizen versus the outsider.

Heroines and their work

These stories do not exist in an identical mental universe to those of the Victorian middle-class novelists, for whom even an unmarried working woman was represented as problematic.[34] Women's magazines of the 1930s feature plots in which women are shown to be as capable of achieving production targets and intellectual attainments as men. However, in every case the working woman is reintegrated into the domestic world after marriage. An example is *Family Herald's* 'Caroline Anstruther'.[35] As a brilliant don, Caroline had initially infuriated the hero when, as a student he had to share a university maths honour with her – a woman. Years later, a headmaster, he falls in love with Caroline as she awards prizes at a neighbouring school. This precipitates a conflict between his ideals and her work. Ill-health intervenes, forcing her to resign from her university work and to assume a traditional dependence. The fateful obstacles to her marriage to the hero are thus miraculously removed. Like the weak nineteenth-century hysteric, then, her body denies her independence.[36] Some *contradictory* elements remain in the text: the heroine depicts the man's need for supremacy as philistine, but the social order is nevertheless restored via the 'natural' destiny of womanhood, which is 'To be their own charming selves, to make a man's home happy. To sew and cook, and dance and sing. To nurse little children, and keep the whole world sweet.'[37]

This destiny is established unequivocally for heroines who choose to continue a career after children. The resolution invariably returns the heroine to the private sphere, the agent of her transformation often being an older and more perceptive lower-class woman who has privileged insight into children's real needs: 'Nanny's wise old heart ached for the wife who risked losing love for a thing so silly as a career.'[38]

More characteristically, it is not the heroine's initial defiance of the patriarchal law (as above) which sets the plot in motion but economic necessity which forces her to take a job. These stories thus display dramatically the nature of women's experience as a *reserve* army of labour. For heroines of this type are caught in a double bind, between right and right; in order to save their families, they must risk destroying them. Hence these plots portray married women's wage-labour as a precarious enterprise fraught by risks in which women's sexual vulnerability constantly exposes their marriages to unacceptable dangers. The closure of the narrative always results in the restoration of the husbands' breadwinning capacity and the withdrawal from paid work of the wives.

'She took off her wedding ring' conforms to this model, in which the danger besetting the married heroine without a ring is emblematic of the general disruption of the social order in the

Depression.[39] Yet the story also affords the heroine an opportunity to express her pleasure in work, her sense of fulfilment and purpose in being part of the process of cooperative manufacture. It thus represents a bizarre but not uncharacteristic synthesis of women's productive experience, authentic desire and working-class male interests.

Nancy King's false depiction of herself as unmarried to counter the marriage bar in the local glassmaking works leads her into difficulties in resisting the advances of the works' manager. She seeks her husband's protection. He courageously fights the man and is doubly rewarded: first, with the lucky offer of a job by a bystander, and second, by Nancy's discovery that she is pregnant.

This story represents the inter-war recession rather as Engels saw the downturn of trade in 1844: as an extreme form of social disorder with confused gender roles. There is a deviant belief, to which the manager subscribes, that the woman who is not kept by her husband is simultaneously not expected to be faithful to him, since '"[you've] a right to please yourself and live your own life"'[40] – a view which is energetically repudiated by Nancy. Hence the characterisation of the manager as a villain simultaneously rules out any wider question of women's sexual autonomy and reaffirms the link between romantic love and monogamy. Yet while this story finally reinstates traditional gender divisions, the representation of women's productive labour is by no means wholly negative: the heroine conveys the ambiguity of her experience, her dislike of being a 'cog in a busy machine' and her awareness that only men get skilled jobs while women are restricted to the unskilled. The narrative also acknowledges her pride in participation in the production of unshatterable glass in a way which suggests a knowledge of factory production: 'yet there was a fascination in seeing how the thing was done, how the glass was made which would not smash in a dangerous way, but remained intact even when cracked through some tremendous contact with a hard object.'[41]

Nevertheless, in sharp contrast to literary realism, the narrative resorts to mystification to explain the hero's misfortune. Lacking any context of crisis or rationalisation in industry, the subjective sense of exposure to bad luck is left as the only explanation of the hero's redundancy: '"It's as though Fate has got a downer on me and George just now"'[42] and '"it's only until our luck turns"',' remarks the heroine, deciding to take the factory job.[43] Ultimately the extraordinary transformation of an ordinary man in the street into an employer creates the magical donor figure familiar from folk-stories who grants George the reward of a job and simultaneously permits the heroine's fairy-tale re-entry into the feminine private sphere at the end.

This story displays most clearly all the basic features of the paradigm: the attribution to women of rationality but not a being-for-herself, the image of the married woman as a (paid) worker, but only as a supplement to professional motherhood. The treatment of male redundancy is also instructive. Other stories reiterate traditional hostilities towards 'masterless men' or the unemployed, playing on the fears that the workless are scroungers, gamblers and idle womanisers. Indeed, no *hero* remains unemployed at the end of these tales. Thus in one typical narrative, 'Scandal ruined her life', a married women worker is represented as exploited directly by her lazy husband, whose unemployment is seen as a form of willing parasitism on his wife comparable to that of the pimp on the prostitute.[44] In such extreme circumstances, the heroine is compelled to work, but she must still demonstrate absolute loyalty to her lord and master. Despite the stereotyped hostility with which the unemployed man is delineated, the heroine is consigned by her femininity to unrebellious suffering. The fantasy solution lies in the sudden freedom which allows her to replace a bad master with a good one.

The female Other or 'whore'

If the Madonna is submissive to the law of the father the magazines' Jezebel or 'whore' is the female Other who is uncontrolled by guilt or shame. Where the heroine may infringe petty rules but essentially holds family values sacred, the Other denotes sexual and economic excess. For her, love is degraded into mere passion or lust, a form of disease undermining female property rights in their spouses. It is she alone who is at home within the anonymous modernity of the metropolis or the suburban uniformity of ribbon development. Her hedonism is boundless, expressed in a love of clothes, dancing and card-playing, the coded modes of revolt against Puritan sexual asceticism. This sumptuary ethos has its roots in the underside of bourgeois society, revealed in the texts in 'vice rings' and homicidal 'crime rackets' which are grafted via the female Other onto the innocent proprieties of families. Moreover, this *femme fatale* is an *unnatural mother*: children in her care grow sick and fade away.

Hostile to the work ethic, she must search for progressively refined modes of parasitism. She is the 'gold-digger', the blackmailer, the bigamist.

The invariant connotation of the 'other woman', then, could be called 'smeddum', spirit or unruliness (following Lewis Grassic Gibbon and Christina Larner), a quality of dangerous self-determination which was, *inter alia*, the commanding trait of the heterogeneous Scottish witches.[45] After the end of the witch-hunts, smeddum reappeared in altered form in ambivalent descriptions of the nineteenth-century 'madwoman in the attic'.[46]

Although the last witch was burnt in Inverness in 1706, popular literature as late as the 1930s still sometimes named the female Other as a witch.[47] Thus in 'Branded by Satan',the literal truth of a religious cosmology is attributed when the dangerous woman possesses, like witches earlier, the Devil's mark on her neck.[48] In this and other stories it can be seen that the shift from a religious to a secular world-view occurred relatively late in magazines circulating among the poorest and most uneducated women.[49]

More typically, the 'whore' or witch has lost any earlier religious connotation. Nevertheless, such untamed, undomesticated women are still the most characteristic *villains* within these stories, their fallen nature requiring their death for the rebuilding of social integration. We can delineate several major types, including, first, the spoilt, maladjusted girl, whose unmanageable sexuality is caused by insufficient repression in childhood; second, the widowed stepmother whose property interests conflict with those of legitimate offspring; finally and most important, the rich daughter who seduces the lower-class hero. This social type is fundamental to popular literature. The clearest example is *The Oracle's* 'Two women loved Jim', superficially a classic bourgeois story of rags to riches but one to which clings fragments of more radical plebeian thought.[50] It depicts an iron worker, Jim Pettifer, dedicated with almost Stakhanovite ardour to the process of experimental innovation while continuing his routine job as an underpaid furnace man. His disciplined limitation of leisure to two hours on Sundays includes his time with Millie, whom he has encountered at her work in the iron stores. The role of the *femme fatale*, Violet Melton, the ironmaster's granddaughter, is to disturb this delicate economy of the emotions, that is, to offer a radical intrusion into Jim's competitive and rationalised world through the charms of eroticism, gambling at cards and dancing. Since it is her influence over his employer which permits him the liberty to experiment after hours, Jim's resistance to her seduction is gradually weakened. He

ultimately regains from Millie, the heroine, the strength to give
Violet up. His happiness with Millie is ensured by his scientific
success and by his appointment to a managerial position at a rival
firm.

What is at stake in this story is, first, a craft consciousness which
gives the story a democratic tone despite its ending. This implicitly
criticises those inter-war developments – such as Taylorism and the
Bedaux scheme – which were regulating the labour of productive
workers like this hero, by separating scientific work from
production.[51] Secondly, by making his major obstacle to self-
realisation the female Other, the romance can carry elements of the
more critical fairy-tale. For the role of the *femme fatale* within the
narrative structure can be further clarified. She represents the
luxury, leisure and élitism characteristic of the post-heroic bourgeoisie. In this story – and elsewhere – she exhibits in condensed
form the stereotypes of the evil capitalist. Hence the narrative
displacement of readers' frustrations onto figures such as these can
permit a redemptive image of a democratic company, in which
good workers are recognised and rewarded. This is a vision in
which the negative elements of class conflict can be sealed off.

The class images of 1930s stories

The popular magazine story has been indelibly marked by bourgeois
ideas. Yet this conclusion is surprising, given the argument of recent
writers who have contended that the middle-class culture that
produced Andrew Ure and Samuel Smiles was an 'aborted
rebellion'.[52] Thus, according to Martin Wiener, after 1850 the
businessman's moment passed 'the purpose grew dim and the
audience turned away. Business was pushed to the periphery of
British social and cultural concerns to be criticised and disdained.'[53]
Such an assessment of British industrialists fails to address fully the
sharp critique of Perry Anderson and Tom Nairn's similar thesis,
which had also lamented the 'supine English bourgeoisie', in E.P.
Thompson's memorable 'Peculiarities of the English'.[54] Like them,
Wiener can be criticised for failing to see the inner transformation of
the feudal aristocracy into an agrarian capitalist class and for
confusing a gentrified domestic life with the absence of middle-class
economic power. Moreover, Wiener has not only totally ignored
the nineteenth-century bourgeois public sphere of mechanics'

institutes, lyceums, literary and philosophical societies but also neglected the cultural agencies which spread middle-class individualism to the masses.[55] One forgotten source of such legitimation is the popular story.

If we look at the same sample of 1929/30, this does indeed yield evidence of the widespread diffusion of a bourgeois ethos. Thus heroes are usually represented as economically successful, while the work ethic is an imperative for all. Such fiction appeals to the reader by reiterating critiques of the aristocracy, for both careers open to talent and marriages based on romantic love are adopted from the world-view of the progressive bourgeoisie. Similarly, numerous stories reproduce versions of the business morality diagnosed in Max Weber's *The Protestant Ethic and The Spirit of Capitalism*. A discipline of self-denial is still celebrated as the necessary condition for the acquisition of wealth.[56]

Relentless labour, often linked with saving, is the single most frequent connotation of heroic status. It is attributed to heroes from the dominant and dominated classes, to the land-owner, farmer and doctor as often as to the artisan or factory-worker.[57] The heroine, as I have shown, also appears under the sign of hard work, in opposition to the sloth of the 'other woman'. But although many writers link ascetic work to material comforts or success, the inherent value of labour discipline is the principal theme of these stories, as in the Protestant tradition. Hence such romances contribute to an internalised oppression, in which workers are taught to abandon their impulses towards shunning estranged work.

For an aristocracy, labour demeans. Yet in this fiction, it is productive work which creates a mature adult. Consequently, a new democratic conception of 'gentleman' emerges, a structure of feeling evident in one story's concluding confession: ' "I wanted my son to be a gentleman. I – I didn't want him to dirty his hands – just as if a man is any the less a gentleman because he has dirty hands!" '[58] In another of this type, 'True to him always', a young working girl is revealed by an unexpected bequest to be a member of the ruling class. The discovery threatens her youthful love for her companion from the slums, who reflects that he 'had been born and bred in the underworld . . . [while] Peggy was a lady'.[59] Yet after exiling himself to Australia, her former protector regains the right to marry her. His virtuoso devotion to work elevates him above other men, most notably a socially superior fellow-migrant: 'a lazy good-for-nothing . . . the younger son of a family [sic] [who had] failed at the jobs he had had in England'.[60]

Finally, in a further story centred on work, 'Blind to her Folly', the labour ethic negates even the anticipated romantic ending in the didactic interest of a prudent marriage.[61] A young girl, initially rejecting her parents' unremitting poverty for the allure of a young man with a 'bad reputation', comes to acknowledge ultimately the wisdom of her father's stern perspective. For it is he rather than the youth who is vindicated in the conclusion, which illuminates the truth of his maxim – 'young people with energy to gallivant don't know the meaning of work'. The end privileges her father's socially unrewarded actions: 'he worked hard', 'he did his best'.[62]

Within this individualistic logic, debt and fecklessness is as grave a deficiency as in Smiles's *Thrift*. Villains, for example, appear as the long-term unemployed or as tramps. Such figures represent obstacles to dominant class interests: they are ideological relics traceable back to late medieval fears of the unsettled 'masterless men', for whom the Vagrancy Acts had so long prescribed the violence of branding, flogging and execution. Thus these tiny bourgeois melodramas link tramps with moral evil just as recent stories link social security claimants to scrounging. In marked contrast, other strands of popular fiction, such as Chartist novels, have presented the penniless wayfarer as the victim of property relations and thus heightened awareness of illusory freedoms.[63]

Work commitments can be the source of 'sin' as in 'A danger to every wife' when a hedonistic shop assistant imposes herself on the hero's hospitality, tempting him to forego his vows of fidelity while away from home as undermanager of his firm's new branch.[64] Work may create ill-founded rumours of infidelity for travelling salesmen and other vulnerable groups (as in *Lucky Star's* 'They told her a pack of lies').[65] Yet if work commitments are always imperative for men, they are always dispensable for married women, for whom such an achievement ethos is inappropriate.

Further indirect evidence of the importance of individualism is also provided by the characterisation of domestic servants as villains, for servants are excluded from the freedom of wage-labour to pursue their market advantage wherever it is offered. The structural dependence of the servants' position, creating conflicts with expectations of male independence, explains their frequent choice for criminal or morally dangerous tasks.[66] These disapproved characters are also often denoted as artists and musicians, perhaps because such groups were carriers of an enduring resistance to money as the sole measure of productive value.[67]

The ephemeral and escapist literature of mass culture then turns out to be favourable to a market society in ways which Wiener has not considered. Of course, such magazine stories are not chosen by editors solely for their didactic aspect nor are they as a genre ideological consistent. For example, there is also evidence in the cheap family papers of the continued appeal of *the gentry class* with a superior, non-materialistic way of life, rooted in the pastoral refuge of the countryside. Strangely, too, the conception of urban life contains scattered elements of the Marxist critique of capitalist society, while the vision of rural life embraces utopian aspirations for a social order without conflict or wage-labour. Paradoxically, twentieth-century women's romances, like advertising, continue to be structured around the urban–rural opposition, despite the fact that the pastoral ideal has long receded from canonised literary texts. Its role is to serve as an 'ideological elastoplast' to solve the problems raised by the discontents of work and an unplanned market system.

The nostalgic association of the gentry with a more healthy organic society has to be negotiated, however, through the bitter folk memories of the realities of patrician rule. Thus a moral criticism of gentry élitism and their dehumanising treatment of the lower orders are themes that consistently appear. Disapproved gentry fail to recognise the suitability of a lower-class girl for marriage although she may be good enough for sex; members of the subordinate class are falsely suspected of crimes. In these imaginary documents of social injustice there does surface a cry of pain against the 'injuries of class'. This is delineated graphically in a story such as 'Sunshine Sal – the girl who loved a swell', when the East End heroine, falsely accused of a theft, expresses her innocence in tones which hint at the existence of a working-class culture of protest.[68] Yet the class chasm displayed in the narrative of injustice in 'Sunshine Sal' is ultimately resolved by redeeming figures from the upper class who act with true public spirit. Their disinterested concern is expressed particularly through the class-blind dedication of the young hero, a doctor in an East London charity hospital. The fate of the heroine herself is magically altered when she learns she is a foundling, by birth an aristocrat. Thus both she and her family experience a mythical transformation of their lives.

The *foundling* device found in this and other cheap magazine stories allows the nobility to be disguised as working men and women, as 'cryptoproletarians'. This was a favourite motif of middle-class writers of the 1890s' *'in darkest England'* school.[69] As Michael Denning has suggested, in a rich analysis of American dime novels, an elaborate metaphor is implied: a worker (the model is often a miner, who is descended from gentry), is more powerfully cast as nature's gentleman in his role as foundling.[70] The radical element of such popular literature is the fusion of two elements – 'essential gentleman' and miner. This is an important insight. However, both the women's stories and the dime novels must also be seen as one way of achieving the fantastic ending which answered the cravings of their readers, the removal of material anxieties from the working-class family.

Like the modern fairy-story and the American dime novel, the pleasures of these tales lies in their capacity to satisfy such material fantasies while subscribing in many ways to hegemonic ideologies. Differences between the popular genres also emerge. In the 1870s and 1880s, dime novels featured lower-class images of revenge. For example, gypsies, their images condensing the strongest connotations of an uncowed and non-proletarianised poor, bring to book a corrupt and powerful millionaire capitalist in order to reinstate the legitimate, just senators of a true republic. In the dime novels, too, strikes are always won.

In contrast, women's romantic family stories lack even this limited gesture towards oppositional culture. Not only do they frequently depict accommodation to poverty, but they conjure up images of an inevitable passage to proletarian existence for those seeking independence by criminal or other deviant means. Yet, like the dime novels, they also offer 'magical narratives', figures of utopia, in which the problems of both bourgeoisie and workers in a market society are dramatically erased. These wish–fulfilment mechanisms have the same appeal that Marx and Freud noted for religion, an appeal to hope. This is sometimes addressed in the fiction itself. For, as one heroine reflects on the fantasies of the films she watches: ' "An' it would be unbearable here . . . if I didn't think there was something better somewhere . . . it's better to live in a fool's paradise than no paradise at all." ' [71]

Such narratives of escape are marked in numerous ways by the contemporary social relations of production. In the 1930s, one story, 'Wish a wish', illustrates a typical suspension of reality when a little shopkeeper is saved from the danger of an impending supermarket and hence from the forces of big business. [72] I have already indicated that many of the stories end with offers of a *job* to solve problems of unemployment. [73] Finally, *money* alone is a transformative force of endless fascination to the writers. Story after story depends on imaginary gifts, legacies, rewards and treasure. Through these means their protagonists make the leap from the realm of necessity to the realm of freedom.

In Chapters 4 and 5, I turn to current romantic solutions. I note particularly in the 1980s the new, benign appearance of capital under the heroines' autonomous direction. Thus in our own period the unity of the traditional romantic formula begins to fragment.

METHODS OF STUDYING POPULAR GENRES: CONTENT ANALYSIS AND THE MYTH OF PURE OBJECTIVITY

Representative texts must clearly be studied in more detail, which poses the problem of method. The 'Great Divide' between mass culture and modernism created an intellectual division of labour between sociology and literature. Content analysis became established as a tool for the authorititative reading of popular culture, and close criticism for literature. I want to argue against this methodological apartheid.

It has been traditional among sociologists to study large volumes of popular literature by content analysis in order to report on issues such as the ethnic or class characteristics of heroes. Such quantitative summaries are held to permit the description of contrasts between cultural images and social reality with a high degree of objectivity, precision and rigour.

However, this research instrument is neither as objective nor as detached from the observer as might appear, since the procedures used all imply an *insiders'* cultural knowledge. It is impossible to study fiction without understanding how it is moulded by literary forms and conventions. Thus to assess, say, how representations of sexuality have changed over a period, it is insufficient to record simply the frequency of episodes, and essential to interpret the portrayal in terms of the genre (melodrama, realism, etc.) and the protagonist to whom such actions are attributed. For example, it is the opposition between the actions of the heroine and those of 'the other woman' (a 'gold-digger' or 'wanton witch') which creates the crucial ideological effect. To assess content I have to understand the rules which the writer deploys and this implies a minimum of cultural competence. In the short story, such rules extend to *literary traditions*, such as the pastoral, to *stylistic devices*, like irony or allegory and to *images*. The connotations of these can be fully revealed only with some cultural capital. In other words, interpretation depends on a knowledge of the discourses which the writer brings into play. Such cultural competence is used in the production and the reception of even the simplest popular literature.

For this reason there is no mechanical or direct method of imputing values to content: both narrative structures and character conventions have to be understood in order to assess whether one item of content is equivalent to another. In this process, content analysts first study 'natural' language to understand the authors' discourse, noting phrases such as 'A's [the hero's] face was haggard from overwork'. Even at this level, some discretion is required to identify denotations of 'hard work'. They then gloss this with sociological interpretations of folk categories, such as 'the text affirms a work ethic', which can never be directly imputed from the fictional content.[74] Philosophically, the content analyst is dancing through minefields.

Despite this unavoidable element of subjectivity, my analysis of magazines in the 1930s does assess the frequency of themes or images. Hence it depends on crude counting (of the numbers of characters unemployed, or socially mobile, for example). Some otherwise excellent studies of mass media, such as Judith Williamson's *Decoding Advertisements* suffer from the absence of any quantitative assessment. For example, she does not reveal the proportions of advertisements using the different rhetorics she has meticulously described, such as the images of traditional as against modern women, or the frequency of the preference for nature as against culture.[75]

However, I have also employed a more qualitative approach than content analysis, using concepts from literary theory and demonstrating my interpretation of a text by quotations. A full ideological analysis should reveal that the cultural sphere is an arena of struggles over clashing signs where, even within a single text, both subordinate and dominant class and gender contend for legitimacy.[76]

If the use of literary concepts is necessary, it is wise also to be aware that critics often reveal their own originality and cultural capital by the sensitivity, breadth and daring of the decoding. Thus the subjectivity of the critic may be *maximised* rather than being merely an ineradicable interpretative element.

Finally, popular literary genres cannot be reduced to the representation of underlying conflicts between capital and labour, despite the importance of the latter. I argue throughout this book that such novels and stories are concerned centrally with how women should live and the character of the relationships between public and private, existence and potential. In brief, there are certain indispensable theoretical components for the analysis of the romance genre. These are, first, a class analysis; second, concepts of gender

MELODRAMA AND MAGAZINES   71

and sexuality, which display the character and regulation of the private sphere; third, the Freudian–Marxist tradition developed by Bloch, Pierre Macherey[77] and Fredric Jameson (especially through the exploration of the 'political unconscious', significant silences and internal contradictions of the text); finally, fourth, the terms Raymond Williams employs: 'experience', 'structure of feeling' and 'the knowable community'. By these means, it can be shown how the contest for hegemony operates as the realm of ideology is mapped out in the form of the story.

4 Catherine Cookson:
Realism and Utopia

Catherine Cookson, OBE is the leading exponent of what can be called the 'social democratic' subgenre. Her success has not been ephemeral, for the novels written in 1950 and 1954 still command an immense readership. The breadth of her appeal can be gauged from Public Lending Right statistics: the first two-and-a-half years' monitoring, show that Cookson represented 1 per cent of all adult fiction library loans and that at no point has she had less than 23 titles in the 100 most loaned titles. In 1986 29 Cooksons were in the top 100, and 27 in 1987.[1] Such evidence of popularity was supported by the spontaneous recommendation of the Scottish lower-class women I interviewed and is the reason for studying the author in some depth.

Catherine Cookson is arguably as much the architect of the post-war class compromise as was Harold Macmillan or Ernest Bevin.[2] Unlike most writers of popular fiction, she has rejected a cultural politics of the survival of the fittest and individualism. Nor do her books fit the category of proletarian realism, organised around a transformative vision of a new world, to be achieved by collective, rational action. Cookson's fiction resolves disruptions mainly through the utopia of the individual couple. To elaborate, they are fundamentally structured by a romantic love ethic, combining companionate marriage with sensual desire. This is dovetailed into a reformist vision of material prosperity, which is embedded in a conception of a humane, class-reconciled capitalism.[3]

Like many popular writers, Cookson's narratives revolve around intensely dramatic action. Her stories hover on a precarious border territory between melodramatic genre writing and realism, in which congenital deformity, murder, incest and witchcraft accusations threaten to push her novels beyond serious (sur)realism into mere fiction. At her best, Cookson uses melodrama for realist objectives;

her writing reveals 'how things really are', displacing the masks of authority to expose the economic and sexual interests underneath. It is perhaps in these sociological and historical concerns that there lies the key to Cookson's genuine popularity with working-class women, for, despite their nostalgia for a Golden Age, they do contain moments of illumination. Moreover, they are written vigorously, alternating the Standard English of the narrator with the pithy, regional dialogue of the lower class. This linguistic compromise undoubtedly aided her success, for it allowed her to break with the local understandings of the regional lower class to reach a wider popular audience. The working-class characters have a dignity and emotional range which derives from her own upbringing as part of a subordinated class and gender.

It will be argued that Cookson's novels cannot be seen simply as the creative product of an *individual*, and their uneven mystification assessed simply in terms of the author's difference: her exotic kin ties or inner loneliness. Of course, it would be difficult to explain the significance of bastardy in her novels without knowing that Cookson was herself illegitimate, as she explains in her autobiography. Yet this account can also be read differently, to show how her novels are shaped by a wider collective history of class and gender relations. For Cookson represents the 'respectable' working-class cultures of the occupations dominant in the North-East, particularly the shipbuilders, seamen, miners and dockers. Moreover, the wish fulfilment of industrial regeneration and cross-class unity have decisively moulded the regional consciousness of the Cookson novel. It should be stated at the outset, however, that this approach differs from the only other academic account of her writing, which argues that 'Cookson's work is to a large extent a reworking of themes from her own life-story.'[4] In my view, this is an inadequate explanation of both her novels and the reason for their popularity.

Cookson was doubly situated within the working-class culture by illegitimacy, not just her own, but through her work in a workhouse, where her surveillance of unmarried mothers led her to ascend the staff hierarchy. This gave her privileged insight into the repression of sexuality and the double standard, permitting her to interrogate the nature of asceticism, in tune with the wider hopes for self-expression in the 1960s and 1970s.

Material for melodrama was supplied directly from her own childhood in Tyne Dock, Jarrow. She was born in 1906 into the family of an Irish Catholic docker, a family in which were concentrated the tensions common to unskilled workers. Her early desires were to avoid physical danger in fights, to be called 'Mrs' when she was adult, because her mother, 'Our Kate', was not, and to escape from her class without being labelled an upstart.[5] Initially she was cast in the role of sister 'Katie', to her mother 'Our Kate', and the autobiography has as its centre the fraught relationship between mother and daughter. Her father was unknown to her, but according to her mother was a gentleman. Fed on her mother's descriptions, this figure became the first subject of her daughter's day-dreams, just as later the fantasy of a love binding together the servant and gentry spheres became a structural element of her many novels.

Cookson's grandfather earned 3s 6d a day as a docker. In periods of recession he resorted to the workhouse, retaining a profound fear of ending his days there. Her mother's childhood had been so impoverished that she walked barefoot and begged bread: 'I used to envy my mother these things because I longed for such poverty that there would be no money for drink.'[6]

'Our Kate' had been branded a fallen woman for her brief infraction of the marital rules. Her daughter was to develop a heightened sense of her absent father's power, magnifying both his culpability for her mother's drinking and his responsibility for her own career as a writer. In the gentry blood flowing through her veins, she located her own 'sensitivity' and her consequent literary production.

Her illegitimacy created a prolonged fear of authority. Also, for the stigmatised girl there was a rupture in the solidarity of the neighbourhood: 'It was in this small community [of East Jarrow] that I lived until I was twenty-two, in it but not of it, accepted yet rejected.'[7] The suffering provoked by illegitimacy lasted until her nervous breakdown in 1945.

Her mother became the financial mainstay of the family, earning money by washing, repairing boots and replacing windowsashes. Despite her grandfather's patriarchal aura – his policing of the family with horsewhip and belt – his economic insecurity induced a dependency on his relatives. He was a staunch Irish Catholic, rambling, when drunk, of English tyrants. Katie was taken from a Protestant school to a Catholic one, a school she hated for inculcating a form of religious terrorism in which all Protestants were consigned to hell. Here were the germs of her later rejection of institutionalised religion, which now acquired the character of a fearful system of supernatural sanctions rather than the repository of truth or consolation. Her subsequent moment of dissent from popular Catholicism was to lay the foundations of her novels.

Throughout her writing there emerged a cynicism about the social functions of religion deriving both from her awareness of the Churches' support for power and her perception of the discrepancy between the beliefs and actions of the devout.

Out of this household so poor that her Christmas stocking was only parcelled vegetables, Katie started her first job in a workhouse laundry. The workhouse was a paradoxical combination of individual opportunity and oppression. Her autobiography retailed the experience of unsupported single mothers confined in the Institution for fourteen years until their offspring, segregated from them in the children's home, were ready to start work. In her interviews, she commented bitterly on the superiority of staff diets to those of inmates and recounted how attendance at the unhappy meetings of the separated spouses made her vomit.

This understanding of the direct connection of women to the State through the Poor Law may have heightened in Cookson the sense of the family house as an arena of private individual control, a refuge from which the less eligible poor were excluded. This structure of feeling was to resonate through the novels, alongside the simultaneous perception of the home as a terrain of coercion, discipline and disorder.

Efficiency at work led to promotion as workhouse laundress in Hastings, where she was regarded initially as a 'nigger-driver'.[8] She left to start a home for invalids, becoming burdened with the difficult presence of her alcoholic mother. She married a 'gentleman', a grammar-school mathematics teacher of whom a Jarrow friend remarked, '"By, you've done well for yourself".'

Miscarriages and years of overwork led her to become mentally ill. After electric shock treatment, she discharged herself. She now acknowledged that in her childhood she had 'developed the faculty of seeing two sides of everything',[9] an early response to the sectarian bigotries of Jarrow which was useful for the novelist. Writing became her only amulet against the fear that swamped her in her breakdown. It solved her need to come to terms with her childhood and yet to neutralise the corrosive effects of pity. Apart from this, and the fact that she was not motivated by commercial interests but learnt her craft in a writers' group, we know very little about her aims or her intended audience. She has stressed that she regarded herself as a realist novelist rather than a romantic fiction writer. However, her interviews suggest she saw her writing not as the voice of a class or group but rather as the harvest of her own personal experience and early struggles. When asked publicly about her youth: 'Your childhood must have left deep scars?', Cookson replied, 'Scars, yes, but I extracted sixty-eight novels from it too!'[10]

Her novels can be read within a wider feminist-materialist perspective. I shall start with the early contemporary realism, which, in her choice of working-class subjects, bears a marked resemblance to the writing of the 'Northern renaissance', especially the work of John Braine, Stan Barstow, Alan Sillitoe, and David Storey. Yet the closer portrayal of women, coupled with the optimism of Cookson's endings, contrasts with the bleak anomie of these writers.

MAGGIE ROWAN (1954)

Despite its date, *Maggie Rowan* also has some affinity with the proletarian realist novels of the 1930s,[11] and like this form, Cookson's text breaks with the individual hero, alternating instead between the voices of two mining families. These protagonists stand as typical representatives of Durham pit communities, from inter-war recession to the post-war period, immediately prior to nationalisation. Raymond Williams has written of the extension in the proletarian novels from family loyalties to the ties of local community, work-place and class, a perception which he links to developments in capitalist productive forces and relations. Cookson does not write from an explicit egalitarian or anti-capitalist framework, but her narrative does depict heightening social contradictions. In *Maggie Rowan* the announcement of redundancies and a pit accident are presented as galvanising miners' attitudes into a refusal to accept earlier social relations within the industry; the austerity of the conditions under which pitmen work justifies good wages, freedom from the fear of unemployment and from unacceptable supervision.

Characteristic of women's writing, Cookson's texts shift the domestic and sexual spheres to the centre of the stage and away from their more marginal role in the proletarian novel. A relative optimism emerges in relation to the economic aspirations of the face-workers. But the more problematic area for Cookson is the sphere of women's work, fertility and marriage. The fantasy ending offers an imaginary reconstitution of the working class on affluent foundations. Rejecting individualism and the market, natural wants such as childlessness are solved by gift – in this case the spontaneous present of an illegitimate baby – while the overcoming of both anti-social sexuality and repressive asceticism is promised. The utopian ending reasserts women's traditional caring role for men. It also symbolically recharges the Methodist lay preacher tradition in the pits. Cookson thus privileges a stratum of organic leaders who are embodied in the second hero: 'Christian' and 'flexible' men prevail over 'dogmatic', 'hardbitten' malcontents. I suggest that the reformist adaptation of working-class radicalism to capitalism represented in the tradition of Methodist unionism is the hidden centre of all Cookson's naturalist novels.[12] In order to understand *Maggie Rowan*, then, the character of Methodist trade-unionism must be grasped, together with its hegemony in the North-Eastern coalfield until the 1880s.

Maggie Rowan *and Methodism in the North-East: the tradition of class compromise.*

Recent research has shown that after bitter struggles between the 'coal barons' and miners in the first two-thirds of the nineteenth century, a stabilisation of class relations took place. Favourable changes in the market for coal in the area were conducive to the development of a group of literate and self-disciplined miners who turned to the Liberals. These men and women were Wesleyan and Primitive Methodists who forged a culture of class conciliation, founded on the sliding-scale system of 1875–90. Wages were adjusted to the market, hence to the profitability of the firm. From the 1860s until 1914, and especially from 1870 to 1896, Methodist ideas of 'moral force' undermined the radicals' or socialists' diagnosis of class conflict and retarded their union's affiliation to the national structure.

Surprisingly, then, mineworkers were latecomers to the Labour Party relative to other unions. Moreover, the Durham and Northumberland Coalfield was the last region to join the Mine-workers of Great Britain (MWGB) in 1893, and the region supported the Liberals, and then the Lib-Lab alliance until the First World War.[13] The Durham Miners' Association, formed in 1869, emphasised accommodation and negotiation as paramount goals and was regarded tolerantly by coal-owners:

> The leaders advocated moral force rather than strikes to promote the miners' cause. . . . The Durham, Northumberland and South Wales mines carried this to another stage by instituting the sliding-scale whereby miners' wages were tied

to the selling-price of coal . . . [thus] propagating an assumption about the harmony of interests of capital and labour.[14]

This perception of harmony was fiercely contested in the 1890s.[15] Nevertheless, the earlier 'moderate' tradition was buttressed by the regional buoyancy of the market, an effective challenge to feudal elements such as the Yearly Bond, the appointment of independent checkweighmen and the coal-owners' paternal control. Robert Moore argues convincingly that the Methodists' religious leadership aided the call to harmony, particularly since some coal-owners went to chapel along with the miners.[16] These chapel communities, made up of miners 'set apart' from their fellow-workers by their sobriety and sense of salvation, operated as the idealised base for the appeal to collaboration.

By the end of the 1880s, this Methodist culture was beginning to be attacked by socialist and secularist contestants for the leadership. With a dramatic drop in profits, a hostility emerged from the rank-and-file miners to the Methodists' 'soft settlements', along with a critique of their narrow canons of respectability.[17]

Methodist working men and women are the collective heroes of many Cookson novels. Though rarely named as such, Methodist culture, shorn of its religious idealism, still possesses contemporary significance for Cookson, as an ethical and conciliatory mission. Among her villains are the socialist critics of this tradition, along with those standing for the dark side of Methodism, the domestic tyrants, elitists and hypocrites, whom her novels symbolically annihilate.

Thus, in the course of the narrative of *Maggie Rowan*, a contrast is drawn between mining before and after the Second World War. The first pit accident and redundancies trigger intense class conflict: 'Bloody bloodsucker,' the manager's agent is jeered, 'Why don't he get hisself doon?' 'How would he like to keep seven bairns on forty bob a week, eh? You can't keep a bloody great mansion on that, can you? And who keeps him and his like in fancy houses? We do!'[18]

Political leadership, then, vacillates between those who bitterly voice grievances, and those, like the hero, Tom, whose class-conciliatory tones can only be convincing when he shares both the working conditions of the pitmen and rigorous observance of the group's ethical rules. Tom, the Methodist lay preacher, is portrayed as having as his primary concern the fate of the men in this world rather than the next:

His talking to the men and the fact they listened, men like the
hardbitten Blackett and Findlay, had not pointed out to
him that his path lay in saving souls, it merely strengthened
his primary idea that more could be got over if you worked
alongside of them, breathing the same air, your sweat
washing off the same dust, and in your brain as in others
ever the secret fear that one day . . . the pit would get
you.[19]

Despite the sharp divisions over tactics, the text serves to explain
and justify the demands of the organised miners, subverting the
initial view of the heroine, Maggie, that they are bigoted, ignorant
and lazy. Her successful, but individualistic escape from the mining
valley is delineated as class desertion. In her husband's words, she
is merely 'aping the swells'. Maggie's cult of efficiency, displayed in
her rationalisation of his bicycle shop, is contrasted with his former
pleasure in self-directed tasks. Moreover, *Maggie Rowan* contains a
systematic opposition between riches and well-being. 'It wasn't in
Maggie's plans that there was to be much cooking yet [at his
mother's] though the house might not be any too spruce, there
was always home-made bread . . . .'[20]

Thus the image of bloated capitalist is tied together with that of
the career woman, Maggie. She is portrayed as a woman obsessed
with domination, who overturns the social order by imposing
female power and who despises the work of women. The story
validates these traditional skills, underwriting a work ethic of
domestic labour. Maggie's pursuit of wealth is revealed to be
mistaken, the electric fire she had bought is replaced at the end by
a coal fire, and cups of tea and food now flow where previously
only eating out had been favoured. Maggie's earlier initiation of
action is replaced by personal service of a menial kind, proof of
good will towards her husband, such as scraping his boots. The
same coding applies to the second problematic heroine, Beattie: her
essential worth is portrayed washing or wearing an apron. It is not
that wage-labour for women is contrasted with domestic labour,
since both Maggie and Beattie continue to work, but rather that
female domestic work is valued, against both the pursuit of capital
and the egoistic pursuit of pleasure.

The ending of the novel is utopian in a double sense. First, it
offers a vision of a middle way, between the sexual repression of
the Methodist characters and the happy-go-lucky spontaneity of
the Catholics. The older generation's dichotomy between austere

self-control and the tabooed sexuality of the prostitute is transcended in a figure such as Beattie, another problematic heroine, who becomes ethical as well as sensual and thus cannot disrupt family ties.

Despite its simplistic perception of women's subordination in gender roles, the novel is realist in its exposure of the antagonisms within the mining industry and the community. Secondly, its conclusion retains a profound economic optimism, typified in the reflections of the second mining hero, who interprets the post-war material progress of the miners as an unassailable and permanent consequence of a shared moral understanding.

The centrality of the Methodist union leadership is the thematic structure on which the entire narrative rests. However, Methodism is not mentioned at all in her autobiography. This aspect of the novel is inexplicable in terms of the writer's own direct experience. Where, then, does this double utopianism come from? Two complementary sources can be found: first, the intense commitment to class reconciliation in the 1840s' 'Condition of England' novels,[21] and second, the peculiar combination of Smilesian self-help and collective improvement found in the local Methodist union leadership's calling. These ethical views are still compatible with an appeal to both a broad North-East readership and a wider international public. For Cookson's novels in general, and *Maggie Rowan* in particular, identify certain ineradicable features of Northern industrial society which the subordinate class find intolerable, such as unemployment, low pay and overbearing authority. The narrative explores the new communal tensions for which affluence is both the salve and the irritant (as in Maggie's business success), and creates a powerful image of the older accommodative Methodist stance regaining the central moral ground. Taking a working-class perspective, the novel symbolically reconstitutes the 'alien' elements within the class, both those such as Maggie seduced by individual wealth, and those like the militants, who wish to push further and faster the transformation of capitalism. Hence a deceptively simple domestic fiction has been produced collectively, especially by the anonymous miners with their early Liberal leadership, who shaped the nineteenth-century cultural traditions of the North-East. The inventive handling of these themes by Cookson serves to secure the old messages in the new dilemmas of post-war trade unionism.

At this early stage of her writing, Cookson displays a

distrust of social mobility as a solution to injustice. 'Don't do it!' is the underlying message of *Maggie* and *Rooney* (1957). By the time of *The Round Tower*, in 1968, she has a more ambivalent response, with a simultaneous fear of the arrogant authoritarianism of the new rich and an idealisation of the ambitious vision of the young hero. Nevertheless, if his material self-improvement is validated, it is also partially stripped of its fairy-tale qualities, as the hero's success as a lorry contractor requires not just bank loans from a wealthy benefactor, but bribes to win contracts. In this, and her later novels, the cross-class marriage becomes the central sign of hope for the social order. However, in a reversal of Lawrence's dichotomy between the sensuality of male workers and the impotence of the upper-class man, sexual vitality is attributed by Cookson to lower-class women.[22]

COLOUR BLIND (1953)

This text focuses on ethnic divisions within the working class, elaborating the extensive totality of Tyneside and thus predating Enoch Powell's infamous prophecy of the 'rivers of blood' flowing from continued immigration. *Colour Blind* covers the period 1912–30 in Jarrow, when Arab settlement took place in the Holborn district adjacent to the Fifteen Streets area of the native workers. A central figure is an African seaman, James Paterson, who breaches ethnic barriers by marriage; a lesser role is played by an Arab, Hassan, who emerges from the shadowy 'Other' of Holborn – the exotic place enclosing Arabs with 'sweet smells', a space both alluring and taboo in the novel, from which white women are utterly debarred.

Cookson's opposition of Holborn to the Fifteen Streets structures a narrative which draws its force from the early colonial labour migrations to Tyneside and which, even at this early date, Cookson fruitfully sees as prefiguring many aspects of post-war ethnic relations.[23]

The ideological burden of the story is contained in the Preface, which denies the truth of racist claims but views such antagonisms as ineradicable. 'God is colour-blind,' asserts the less bigoted of the two Catholic priests introduced in the story. However, the narrative revolves around the social undercurrents which undermine this divine liberalism, bringing in the wake of breached racial barriers a chain of devastation: acts of violence, abandoned wives, distorted family forms. The novel bears a tragic vision, showing the romantic moment of the cross-racial marriage at the end to be merely a temporary ebbing of the tide of racial hatred, not a foretaste of its imminent retreat. A subtext suggests a more hopeful and rationalist trajectory for working-class consciousness, in which the self-educated come to reject rival nationalisms and sceptically question received truths. Yet within the Cookson text, the fundamental response of the native workers is a defensive exclusiveness towards migrant workers: a strategy to delay, contain and suspend the pressure of the 'reserve army' of labour that they represent.

The chief protagonists are the McQueen family, living in poverty in the Fifteen Streets with only their talent for illicit acts of survival and their humour to keep them from the workhouse. Bridget becomes pregnant by James Paterson. Despite her marriage, her mother tries to arrange a 'still-birth' from the local abortionist. The baby survives. She appears white although her father is African.

Bridget is caught between the incestuous hopes of her brother, Matt, and loyalty to her husband. A fight between them leaves Matt scarred and requires James's flight. Rose-Angela, the daughter, is submitted in childhood to the jibes of teachers and children, in adulthood to the loss of employment. A job with a painter saves her from destitution. When she discovers that one of his models is her father, she puts at risk the growing love between herself and the artist in order to nurse her father secretly, thus concealing him from the law and her uncle's retribution. James's dignified death frees her to marry the artist, whose work extends his awareness beyond the narrow identities of the local community.

The novel opens then, in Jarrow, with endemic poverty for the McQueens and their neighbours, a situation in which they see only powerlessness, compelled as they are by the workhouse and insecurity to live out their lives on poverty wages:

> Here they had a roof over their heads. And it wasn't a workhouse roof, although he knew that the latter contingency had only [just] been avoided . . . But God was good and had shown his special providence . . . when all around weeping women and grim-faced men had watched their last sticks of furniture being carried out by the bums before

> wending their way to . . . the grim gates [through] which,
> once entered, a family was no longer a family but merely
> segregated individuals, with numbers on each of their
> garments. When this happened, the McQueens had stood
> close together, defying Life's blows with their laughter. . . .[24]

The 'special providence' is iconoclastically criticised by means of the
subversive laughter which Cookson charts episodically throughout.[25] The laughter crystallises as cynicism, as when an adolescent
starts work for £1 a week and is told to keep quiet, '"for when the
Government gets wind you're having three meals a day, they'll find
some bloody way to bring them down to one, or owt."'[26]

In *Colour Blind* migrant workers appear responsible for reducing
native workers' living conditions in housing while adding competition to local restaurants and brothels. Cookson explores here the
interweaving of popular racism with the lived reality of class
relations. Colour divisions assume the character of an Indian
juggernaut, beyond the comprehension and mastery of anti-racist
intervention. The defensive structures of working class racism are,
however, fortresses that can be breached, both by the growing
migrants' quarters and by sexuality itself. Bridget's beauty creates
bridges across the hitherto impermeable worlds of Colour and
White. She is drawn to James by his membership of a labour
aristocracy (his savings of £35, literacy and religious beliefs), but
also by his greater sensitivity to her needs than was usual in Jarrow
men – 'he treated her like a Queen'. However, the cross-racial tie
breaks up traditional family solidarity, while the community erupts
in jealous and vindictive rage, which exposes the half-caste child to
abuse. The Catholic Church is complicit with stigmatisation, while
the African's mission-school Protestantism inadvertently stokes up
sectarian antagonisms.

Thus, at the end, Rose-Angela's dying father reflects on his
fractured family:

> James had always felt that life was full of contradictions . . . .
> A man wanted something and he got it and he thought it
> made him happy . . . . He was happy for a time but it was
> not good. For sixteen years he had paid for that bit happiness
> [*sic*]. And others paid too. Everything in life must be paid for
> but some things were charged too high a price. In a moment
> of illuminating truth he knew that his daughter must pay and
> go on paying, for . . . inside Rose-Angela was black and the
> tragedy of his race lay buried in her blackness.[27]

This exploration of racial divisions produces the only Cookson novel in which the writer dispels the fairy-tale optimism of the romantic ending and suggests that the social order cannot be reintegrated. Yet at the level of deep structure, the story is not totally consistent, for it also operates with a progressive conception that working class ignorance is being replaced by rationality. This is indicated by the nuanced view of the world of women in the initial stages of the novel. The introduction of the 'fixer', an abortionist, is used to reveal the underground resourcefulness of women in actively handling their fertility, but also the unacceptable nature of traditional conceptions of racial purity, seen in the abortionist's willingness to destroy a healthy infant. Opposed to her are the more optimistic emblems of the local doctor, science and art.

If the abortionist represents the pole of tradition, literacy dissolves bigotry on the opposite pole, also within the working-class. Cavan McQueen, Bridget's father, is the protagonist who stands closest to the culture of sceptical, secular working people. He is the bearer of a more enlightened and democratic vision: 'if he had not spent his last threepence on buying a hundred books he didn't want he would never have known this new world.'[28] Cathy, his wife, burns his books, only to be aghast at the utter grief their loss provokes. From this she emerges changed, too, for she loses laughter but gains thought – leaving the traditional world of unquestioned parochial solidarity behind her.

Cavan represents the working man who questions cherished beliefs about nationality and religion ('Christ was a Jew'; 'St. Patrick was an Englishman'). It is his voice that Cookson silences with the bitter pessimism of the ending.

Cookson's novel bears some resemblance to the historical development of Tyneside communities and their migrant workers. The shipping industry in Britain was the first to bring in black and Arab labour to solve its manpower problems.[29] Native seamen shunned the arduous work of stoking the fires in merchant shipping, while tramp steamers disrupted family life with indeterminate and long voyages. Colonial seamen were a willing reserve when native labour was scarce. Thus ships' crews became further stratified, with the Empire moulding new patterns: 'the market could be likened to a pyramid at the pinnacle of which stood British and European seamen with the various nationalities and races of the Empire occupying the middle and base layers.'[30]

This stratification was frequently interlarded with wage differentials between coloured and white British subjects, which the Seamen's Union failed to contest. The shipowners' increasing preference for cheap colonial labour became inflammatory in 1911, 1919 and 1948 when attacks on ethnic minorities occurred in Cardiff, Newport and Liverpool. White workers in the overstocked casual market sought to restrict migrant labour. The Chinese laundries of Cardiff and the Arab boarding houses of Holborn in Jarrow became the arenas for the 'bargaining by riot' of white crowds, led by a Seamen's Union resolved to preserve exclusive access to all non-menial jobs for their native members.

In Tyneside, the same dynamic fuelled the 1919 riots against the community of Arab seamen. Wages were equal, but Arab and African seamen were alleged to perform unpaid overtime and to receive favours in recruitment. The Arab boarding-house keepers became the special objects of local workers' venom for they were held to combine the odious qualities of pimp and crimp, procuring white prostitutes, shanghaiing men in good times, and bribing the bosses in bad.[31]

In 1930, at the Mill Dam, in the Jarrow area of Holborn, a confrontation occurred which differed from the earlier Holborn riot in crucial respects. This time the disaffected seamen's minority movement defended fellow Arab workers unsuccessfully against the new imposition of a rota, intended to limit migrant seamen's work in a recession. In 1931, destitute Arabs, cut off from employment by this rota, applied *en masse* to the workhouse, incidentally the same Harton Institution in which Cookson herself worked in the inter-war years. Three months later, fifty-eight Arabs were deported.[32]

There are thus two recorded occasions on which colonial labour prior to the Second World War became an important issue in the locality. In the light of this, what is the status of Cookson's novel? Does *Colour Blind* negotiate popular ideas in order to better defend dominant (racist) ideology or does it represent the welling up of critical anti-racist responses? It should now be clear that the novel dredges up and refracts communal 'structures of feeling' rather than revealing the essential social relations of industrial disputes. A Tyneside 'Grapes of Wrath', set around such 1930s conflicts over colonial seamen would have structured the novel entirely differently, teasing out divergent contemporary parallels and highlighting the worlds of capital and labour rather than the passionate responses invoked by moral and sexual taboos. Thus, although all the protagonists of a competing proletarian realist perspective are interwoven into the story, she opts for a tolerant but pessimistic middle ground: the Negro as Romantic noble savage, native workers' racism as unbreachable. Her tragic vision ultimately stems from the defensive reaction of native workers and it is their lived experience which underpins the author's conception of common sense.

POPULAR MEMORY AND HISTORICAL DREAMS

Georg Lukács states that the historical novel centres on 'middling heroes' rather than world-historical figures or leaders, and that it displays how historical forces were made and experienced by individuals.[33] Walter Scott's novels are chosen as the model, since they reveal how economic restructuring occurred after the Highland Clearances by focusing on 'typical' individuals. This fidelity to the changing reality of social relations he distinguishes sharply from the 'costume history' characteristic of pseudo-historical novels.

Does Cookson offer us historical novels or costume drama? The answer is, both. Certainly, union-organised labour has for her a peripheral and crisis-generated place in historical struggles rather than a decisive or formative role. *Maggie Rowan* apart, allusions to strikes and to unions are perfunctory. It could be said, though, that running through her historical novels is a concern with the North-East as a region, which is peculiar in that there were preserved here many pre-capitalist relationships such as the Yearly Bond, which first retarded then disguised the development of capitalism itself. Cookson stories are grounded in certain structural features of the region: especially the widespread nature of domestic service for women, the hostility of the agrarian ruling class to popular education, the coercive structures behind *noblesse oblige* and the array of repressive punishments meted out to the working class.

Katie Mulholland (1967), one of the most widely known of her novels, represents these aspects of social reality in the form of historical melodrama.[34] It contains the archetypal narrative organisation of her historical novels, tracing a miner's young daughter from extreme poverty and sexual exploitation to comfortable marriage with a wealthy, yet sensitive, Norwegian sea captain. Her rape is the motive for a family vendetta between the landowning Rosiers – from whom came her assailant and employer – and the Mulhollands. Pursued through two successive generations, the rape provokes murder, her father's unjust hanging and Katie's imprisonment. On her release, Andree, the captain, provides her with property and ensures her education as a 'lady'. However, Katie's tranquillity is destroyed by two subsequent events, her illegitimate daughter's innocent perpetration of incest and her brother's unhappy family life as a Palmer's shipyard worker. The feud is only healed by the death of Katie's Rosier tormentor, figured in the narrative as a monstrous figure of demonic energy and exploitative force. Its residual hostility is only annulled by the marriage of her great-niece, Bridget, to Daniel Rosier III, a visiting American businessman and the son of her emigrant daughter's unlawful union.

Cookson adopts a narrative sequence which has its origin in the Greek Oedipus myth, so that its structural rhythm of dehumanised sexuality, bastardy, adoption and unknowing incest, could be reduced to a simple psychoanalytic level. These plot functions, however, are typically tied to a gentry ideology of paternalism, at stake also in *The Mallen Trilogy, Tillie Trotter, Feathers in the Fire* and – with a transformed ingredient – *The Girl*. In these, the device of the gentry protagonist who rapes or possesses untrammelled sexual power is linked to his use of *economic* power, as landowner, to extract unwarranted surplus labour. Underlying such action is an elitist disdain for his peasantry, miners or servants, represented as a deviation both from the aristocratic ethos of protection and from the bourgeois conception of the stewardship of riches on behalf of the whole community.

Katie Mulholland, then, celebrates two key events in the miners' history: the abolition of coercive feudal controls over the miners and the accountability of the checkweighman to both masters and men.[35] The novel surveys the passage from bondsmen and women to (male) proletariat, the first pages dealing with the belated struggle by the miners to shake off serfdom. To what extent is this melodramatic exaggeration, as reviewers have suggested? Katie's family is depicted living in caves after being turned from their tied cottage. Yet this was indeed the experience of evicted miners and their families in the 1831 strike, which lasted four months and during which men were sentenced to death for assaulting blacklegs or to long prison sentences for picketing.[36] The strike was led by a Primitive Methodist, Tom Hepburn, to whom one character, Katie's father, has a resemblance. The novels's stress on the severity of a legal system which hung and transported trade union activists has a resonance in local events, too, for in 1832 seven Jarrow men were sentenced to death for union membership.[37] The choice of 'keeker' (checkweighman) as a villainous figure derives from the well-documented employment of the 'keekers' by the coal-barons to cut labour costs by alleging short weights, for which miners were heavily fined.[38] This novel (and *Tillie Trotter*) also reveals the gender division of labour in which village women undertook domestic labour in gentry households at wages beneath those acceptable to male lower-class members, a pattern strengthened by the abolition of female underground labour, described in *Tillie Trotter*. It also encompasses, through the figure of Katie's brother, Joe, the flight away from accidents and ill-health in the local mine with the search for better employment at Palmer's shipyard.

The first stage of *Katie Mulholland* deals with the disintegration of the village moral economy. The narrative sequence of rape, bastardy and innocent incest, by which Katie is tied to the villainous gentleman, Bernard Rosier, is emblematic of this more general injustice. At the heart of these conflicts was the coal-owner's unacceptable refusal of permission to build a chapel: hence also his estrangement from the jurisdiction of the local nonconformist community:

> The men had to fight to be allowed to erect it and use it. It was awful, they had to fight for everything. Yet they didn't want to fight, they wanted to discuss and negotiate, but the masters weren't for that. They wanted to . . . blame the union for agitating them . . . .[39]

In the book's second stage, the scene moves to the urban capitalist structure of Jarrow. Palmer's expansion, together with some individual mobility and material security in the late nineteenth century, suggests a solution to the problems posed by the Rosier *ancien regime*. But just as Bernard Rosier episodically re-emerges to shatter Katie's peace, so Palmer's Works are episodically torn by industrial disputes. Charles Mark Palmer fails to honour obligations: he locks out his workers and imports Irish labour.

In the final stage (1920–40), the arbitrary closure of industrial plants such as Palmer's accentuates the wasteful cyclical rhythm underlying the advances: 'poverty was so stark, so raw, it was like looking on a body from which the skin had been ripped.'[40] Two possible scenarios are sketched. The first is presented through Bridget, Katie's great-niece, who marries a Communist, Peter, an unemployed Palmer's clerk. This path is rejected, for such class disaffection is seen as alien, and is connoted in the novel by the 'duty' uppermost for Bridget in the marriage as well as its childlessness. Instead, she embraces the third-generation son of the Rosier family, ultimately marrying him. He is horrified by the poverty of the slumped city and yet his relaxing, hedonistic demeanour embodies the author's hopes for continued prosperity via American capital exported to the British periphery. Thus, possessing the hereditary mystique of the English gentry from which he is descended, Rosier III permits the implant of American investment which will preserve a fertile and enduring union of classes. Hence, *Katie Mulholland*'s popular success may lie in its stripping away of ideology via its images of raped country and a skinned town, together with an appealing vision of an affluent future in which purified elements of the old are combined with the new.

In *The Black Velvet Gown* (1983) Cookson elaborates the historical themes of her earlier novels to pinpoint the character of patrician rule in the 1830s. The social relations of aristocratic landowners are seen through domestic servants' eyes: a disillusioned sansculotte's vision of feudal social order emerges. *The Black Velvet Gown* is thus a portrait of 'Old Corruption' in William Cobbett's terms, a portrait painted with unusual venom and vigour for a best-selling writer.

The novel highlights the control of marriage and sexuality for the transmission of property. Two dislocations of this mode of control are exhibited: the dower house is occupied by a member of a landowning family, Percival, who has been disgraced for either homosexuality or paedophilia and lost his tutoring job in an Oxford college. This unacceptable sexuality has unanticipated consequences, in that it becomes the means by which the children of the Millicans extend their education. They are themselves doubly displaced, first by the death of their miner father, and then by his unusually high aspirations for them. Literacy thus has key significance as a disputed terrain fought over by self-taught workers against a solid phalanx of the gentry seeking permanently to monopolise their knowledge. Seth Millican and his daughter, Biddy, both acquire some learning. Such a cultural understanding, across class lines, is a fraught attainment and one which forges new relationships. Hence the second dislocation of the novel, in which Lawrence Gullmington, the sensitive second son of the gentry family, marries Biddy, who despite her literacy is still despised as the 'laundry slut', the lowest species of domestic servant. Such a breach of etiquette earns him disinheritance, an ineffective sanction, since the outcast Percival has left the dower house to the couple. From this security, they envisage starting a school, which Biddy pointedly insists will take both girls and boys.

Thus while demystification of the nature of gentry rule is an important thematic concern of this novel, the redemptive figure of the good gentleman is retained. Elaine Showalter has drawn attention to the frequency with which Victorian novels used a 'blinding, maiming or blighting motif'.[41] Through such experience, the arrogant hero lost his complacency and the alien hubris of class pride, his humiliation producing the fertile ground on which social *integration* could be imagined at the closure. A similar structure operates in the Cookson novels, in which the good man is flawed and loses his full gentry membership: in this case, by paedophilia; in *Tillie Trotter* by the loss of his legs in a pit accident while finding out how his miners worked.

It is the progressive extension of natural rights which animates the heroine, Biddy and which leads her to insist on her liberty as a servant, her rights to free time and to teach other degraded women servants while learning herself. Her education is itself revealing, for it includes the ethical humanism of Lord Chesterfield's *Letter to his Son* as well as the radicalism of Shelley: it is primarily a culture of non-politicised class compromise, uninfluenced by the development of Jacobin democracy, Owenism or Chartism. Nevertheless, in refusing to knuckle under to unreasonable gentry demands, Cookson's heroine is the 'last of a long line of protesting peasants',[42] and as such is the clearest celebration of this spirit of resistance. However, it must be added that the writer depicts most fellow-members of the Millicans' class as irretrievably sunk in rural idiocy. Nor does the appearance of industrial workers in later historical novels engender a basis for social and industrial democracy. Rather, urban workers are seen as irrevocably split by regressive sectional concerns, fomented by businessmen who cynically undermine native workers' organised power by 'calling in the Irish'.[43] The lower class is thus seen as fragmented between, first, those who resist proletarianisation, as in the case of Ned, the respected, fierily independent horse-dealer of *The Girl*; second, its progressive but often isolated members, like the Millicans; finally, those whose exclusion from the public sphere results in a collective envy or 'ressentiment' , denying to others what they lack themselves.

The mapping of the past, which Cookson undertakes in her regional historical novels can be further elaborated. Marc Bloch once commented on the French folk memory preserved in the feudal epic: 'the embroideries of the tale are all worked upon the fabric of historical truth'[44] – similarly with Cookson. I have already said that her stories vividly display obstacles to popular education in the nineteenth century. Whereas current academic interest has focused on the competition between State, commercial publishers and the radical press in the battle for popular literacy, Cookson's novels give us a sense of the 'microcosmic' social relations at stake as villagers break out of their place, and an array of sanctions is used to keep them there.

The political interest in the use of physical punishment by those in power is a constant theme of her writing. It is difficult to know whether these sanctions are fictional intensifications of social reality or whether the writer is acting as chronicler, recalling customs such as flaying which have since slipped from public memory. Given the historical corroboration for some melodramatic passages, which at first sight appear purely imaginary – as in *Katie Mulholland* – it is more likely that they spring from the oral transmission of local historical knowledge.

Images of violent retribution occur frequently. Refusing to 'bow her head', Biddy is strung up on a laundry pulley by members of the nobility. Katie's father, in *Katie Mulholland*, is wrongly hanged on the gibbet. The dark side of the 'patrician theatre' with villagers given a party at the lord's coming-of-age, is represented in the man-trap laid in the local woods: 'You know, . . . ther's two kinds of folk I hate', says the horse-dealer, 'them as lay man-traps, and women what take whips to flay bairns.'[45]

The landowner in *Feathers in the Fire* maintains seigneurial control by the custom of flaying any unmarried pregnant girl, in a ceremony of public degradation. The tradition here is doubly interrogated both for its barbarism and its common inconsistency, for in this case the father of the unborn child is the agent of the girl's punishment.[46] In *Tillie Trotter*, miners learning to read are submitted to the village stocks for transgressing their proper place, while the belting, whipping and battering of women and children by figures of authority is a frequent motif. Cookson thus breaks with idealist illusions of an organic pre-capitalist community by her insistence on *extra-economic* coercion, by which the aristocracy at once maintained their hold on the land and fêted the majesty of the law. Such quasi-feudal sanctions are depicted as enduring at least until the 1850s, being succeeded by the fear of hunger or the 'deep secret fear that [they] would end up in the work-house'.[47] The novels typify the shift from the location of power at the site of the body to the internalised control of consciousness.[48]

PATRIARCHAL CONTROL OF WOMEN'S SEXUALITY

It is not easy to classify Cookson's novels as simply or consistently subversive of patriarchal ideas. They fall more clearly into

Showalter's category of 'feminine' rather than 'feminist'.[49] Nevertheless, she has explored women's experience, and celebrated women's work and family commitments, while showing the detailed connections between the preservation of classes and the control of sexuality and marriage.

Cookson sees the channelling of sexual drives into marriage as a precarious attainment. The aristocracy, in particular, are viewed as the perpetrators of unregulated and violent sexuality: their victims are lower-class women. In this respect, Cookson continues a tradition of popular story-telling found in Chartist novels and earlier melodrama, which depict the upper-class seduction of the innocent.[50] Within the farm-labourers' and miners' community generally, rape invoked the sanctions of kinfolk, due to 'damaged goods' being exchanged at reduced prices, thus making the single girl less marriageable. However, economic dependence on the gentry constrained the predictable revenge for the girl 'taken down' in this way. Hence Katie refuses to identify her assailant when she realises her father's retribution would result in the family's eviction and loss of employment. In *The Mallen Streak*, the gentry of the 1850s are shown raping with impunity. Again, the girl's tenant father is effectively disarmed by his dependence on the landlord.

The Mallen Streak bears within it a characteristic and unresolved inconsistency. On the one hand, the novel explores the relativism of class sexual codes in its contrast of the sexually unregulated aristocrat with later, more disciplined men. Yet the novel is also structured by an opposing and more regressive idea – that action is motivated by inherited genes. On this reading, the novel demonstrates that biological determinants mould the personality, creating tragic clashes with social rules. The oscillation of the writer between these two theories (historical and biological/psychoanalytic) can be explained, perhaps, by the popular novelist's privileging of a 'good read' above clarity.

WOMEN'S SELF-DISCIPLINE AND ITS CONTRADICTIONS

Women's passionate attachments do not automatically coincide for Cookson with marriage, although this is felt to be the aim. Illicit enduring common-law marriages are shown as an alternative pattern, especially between servant and master, lower-class girl and upper-class man. These emerge as the unintended consequence of puritan control of wives' sexuality: one of Cookson's constant themes is the awesome power of asceticism in transforming young innocent 'Madonnas' into repressed, middle-aged matrons. Thus the novels supply numerous images of the frigid, waspish, orderly matron, whose own susceptibility to social control makes her the embodiment of domestic tyranny. Typically, as in *The Girl* or *Feathers in the Fire* such characters use religiosity as a weapon with which to beat others and as a rationalisation for their own powerlessness.

Partly as a consequence of this dislike of puritanism, the removal of the barrier between the legitimate and the illegitimate is crucial in Cookson's sexual politics. This is framed in the language of a more natural, emancipated sexuality rather than as a feminist attack on patriarchy. The main protagonist of *The Girl* articulates this view:

> 'if every man carried blame for what he dropped on the way, ther'd be few in these hills walking head high. Things like that happen, 'tis nature, and whose to deny nature when it comes at you. Not me for one, so I blame no man for fathering a bairn, not me.'[51]

The ideological force of legitimacy is connected in these novels to the incarceration of rejected pregnant daughters in the workhouse, the flow of homeless mothers into the underpaid domestic service of the gentry and the swollen ranks of prostitutes. These consequences of the moral horror about illegitimacy which Cookson's novels delineate spring particularly from primogeniture.[52] Hence Cookson's choice of the historical novel, for bastardy only becomes of social significance when land or family capital are transmitted in this way. It is her achievement to have exposed the 'surplus repression' to which this led.

Coming from her experience of working mothers, the theme of 'redundant women' is largely absent. Rather, her perspective depends on a comparison between the craft work done by men and that done domestically by women, in terms of their equivalent resilience, skill and resourcefulness. Minute detail is included of women's domestic labour, so as to enhance its use-value. Further, the necessity of love for socialisation is a key theme. Many novels (i.e. *The Invisible Cord*, *The Mallen Trilogy*) are worked out round the idea that a deficiency of love in childhood causes subsequent monstrous defects of personality. This is linked to the theme of bastardy induced by rape, for such illegitimate children fail to spin maternal bonds and – affectionless – they provoke catastrophe: 'As his mother, she should have loved him but she couldn't, he had been a separate being from the moment he had left her womb.'[53] Further, Cookson's historical novels often depend on a subversive delineation of women's legally covered status (*femme couverte*): '"You have no rights; you are my wife, what is yours is mine and what is mine is me own."'[54]

REIFICATION AND UTOPIA: THE ENDINGS

Fairy-tale endings appear in many of Cookson's novels, permitting the heroine to marry a man who has land or capital. Alternatively, the heroine's happiness is tied to a gentry benefactor, who creates the conditions for a proper marriage (see *Rooney, The Black Velvet Gown*). There are many levels at which this could be explained. First, the psychoanalytic level, at which the gentleman hero has to be understood as the solution to the trauma of the author's own illegitimacy, the absent but powerful father, and the search for a husband who embodies these qualities. Secondly, on the level of artistic structures, Cookson's 'artistry of escape' lies in the way she handles formulaic elements of the romantic novel, which includes the marriage of a low-born girl with a high-born man.[55] As the most dramatic form of class conciliation, this ending could then be interpreted in terms of the themes of 'two nations' and social unity found in the industrial novels of the 1840s.

There is, thirdly, another level at which I think this gentry figure needs to be interpreted, springing from Cookson's childhood in Jarrow, her awareness of the rhetoric of the paternalist face of capitalism and of workers' sense of dependence on a single huge company. This dependence has been defined as resulting from dominance of the labour market: 'In this situation, people are likely to develop contradictory attitudes: an exaggerated deference on the one hand and a dull resentment on the other.'[56] The imaginary figure of the good gentleman in her novels thus mirrors the ideal paternalist capitalist. In order to substantiate this point it is necessary to trace the signficance of living in Jarrow for Cookson.

Jarrow emerged in the second half of the nineteenth century as virtually a one-industry town, with a population intimately linked to the fortunes of Palmer's shipyard. Charles Mark Palmer was a titanic entrepreneur, the first mayor and the MP until his death in

1907. A subsequent member of the family was to preside over the winning and losing of a great industrial empire.

The novels' endings embody the structure of feeling produced by economic dependence, which coincides with the patriarchal dependence of women on men behind the romance. Essentially, Cookson gentry characters are split into good and evil figures, sustaining identification with the worthy and rejection of the unworthy. Class interests are not imputed to good gentry. The bad gentleman bears the unique responsibility for the structural contradictions of capitalism. Thus in such characters as Bernard Rosier is concentrated lower-class hatred of exploitative coal-owners, the corrupt use of the police by the rich and the lesser vulnerability of the upper class to penal sanctions.

Another such figure appears in *Katie Mulholland* – Sir James Lithgow, the Lower Clyde shipbuilder and steelmaster, who organised the demolition of yards such as Palmer's during the concentration of shipbuilding production in the inter-war years:

> in 1930 when the razor of nationalisation had started at one end of Palmer's throat, and Sir James Lithgow [. . .] the strong man of steel, had chewed at the other with his plan for a rationalised industry, the blood had flowed so quickly that Palmer's had become like an anaemic giant. . . .[57]

Palmer's had employed 10,000 men in 1919: when it closed, 80 per cent of Jarrow became unemployed.[58]

When single companies have such life and death power over townspeople, it is not difficult to see the source of a hierarchical, unitary consciousness amongst working-class people. When Cookson published *Katie Mulholland*, researchers found a diversity of perspectives existed amongst Tyneside shipbuilders, varying from a perception of class conflict to a hierarchical viewpoint. Nearly a third of workers expressed a sense of embattled unity with management in their firm or industry, against other firms, regions or industries – a consciousness which was neither deferential nor static.[59] It is this latter dependence on the company which is expressed symbolically in the idealised figure of Cookson's good gentleman.

Cookson's novels come out of a 'distressed region', from exposure to the wasteful rhythms of industrial shakeout and capitalist restructuring. Her writing represents both working-class critique of a market-dominated society and an older element of paternalist thought, inherited from the contradictory consciousness of paternalism and exploitation which bound together eighteenth-century plebeians with the commercial landowning patricians.[60] Thus in her novels can be found many of the values based on human need which H.F. Moorhouse has shown come from the radical repository of the working class itself and which may well have their origin in pre-capitalist foundations.[61] Such values are associated with the moderate, Methodist-led union organisation which was dominant from the 1870s to 1890 in the region's pits, as well as with a responsive employing class. We have seen how increasingly the formula has had to be reinvigorated by an Anglo-American businessman hero or by the divorce of the good gentleman from economic power. Hence, even in the stories with the 'regressive' solution of the moral capitalist, the fairy-tale ending is partially undermined by the earlier demystification: 'The lock-out had come,' she writes of 1852. 'Their earthly god whose name was Charles Mark Palmer, who had promised them that if they played square with him he would play square with them, had joined up with the other steel-masters.'[62]

It is only by grasping the homology of the structure of Cookson's novels and the structure of a class-conciliatory, paternalist capitalism, that we can fully grasp the significance of her popularity. It was the belief that the employer would be able to solve the problems of the region which motivated many workers (as in the trust that Palmer's management were offered in their last efforts to reorganise production in Jarrow). Cookson's fairy-tale endings represent both an undiminished hope that such class unity can be found as well as an expression of resistance to rationalisation. It is for this reason that the novels can be interpreted as combining realism and utopia, providing records of working-class experience and values, but simultaneously offering refuges for conservative myths. The 'political unconscious' of the Cookson family saga is paternalism, desired not as rhetoric but as reality.[63]

5   Genres of the Popular Romance: 1970s and 1980s

Recent best-selling romances have an ambivalent stance towards the patriarchal and economic orthodoxies from which the genre was constructed. The feminine subculture of virginity and dependence still survives, but such texts have now been gently satirised even in the women's magazine press: in the West of Scotland, a representative author, Barbara Cartland, was angrily derided by my respondents. Furthermore, bourgeois economic and class perceptions have been increasingly interrogated within the romance texts. Despite the persistence of many individualistic assumptions, opposition to 'Victorian values' can be detected within some recent romances, including the presentation of strikes as legitimate defences of workers' interests and the linkage of exploitation to high rates of profit. Moreover, new themes have been broached: the vulnerability of domestic servants and employees to the sexual advances of their employers, the rights of women to education, the historic double standards favouring men under family law. Writers such as Catherine Cookson, Jessica Stirling and Jan Webster are concerned less with the atrophied individual dramas of love, characteristic of formulaic romantic fiction, than with developing realist techniques within the kin-centred form of the family saga.[1] Their implicit question is: How is modern society possible?

Thus the anticipatory delights of this fiction include an image both of a good society and of love. But these novels are not just magical transformations of the real within the desired wish fulfilment, they are also re-enactments of regional history. As such, they provide a *folk history* and a *popular political theory*.[2] They define and re-define what is acceptable now in the light of their discourse about the past.

Before we consider how popular novels diverge in the 1980s, the genre as a whole can be characterised initially. First, in comparison with spy stories, thrillers and Westerns, the romance elevates the sphere of private life *vis-à-vis* exchange relations and paid productive activity. The texts may or may not be patriarchal in tone, but women's housework, childcare and sexuality is celebrated.[3] Such a valorisation of the domestic craftswoman, however, is typically tied to a radically individualistic conception of character which minimises the pervasive effect of social structures in general and naturalises gender divisions in particular.

Secondly, domestic romance has an underlying commitment to 'the middle way'[4] or the exclusion of 'extremes', political and personal. For this reason it is underpinned by a rhetoric of class conciliation.[5] Given that much contemporary literature is pastiche,[6] it is striking how many of these novels are pastiches specifically of the Victorian 'condition of England' novels of the 1840s. They are therefore centrally concerned with the relations of labour and capital. Kathleen Tillotson has shown that, in middle-class literature, this seam was authoritatively considered exhausted by the early 1850s and was avoided from then on.[7] The subject continued to be of lively concern to popular readers, but narratives revolving around central questions of class then shifted to the terrain of subliterature. Indeed, as I have suggested particularly in Chapter 2, fictional portrayals of the unacceptable faces of both the aristocracy and the bourgeoisie have continued to shape readers' everyday political attitudes, providing a cultural armoury for opposition to both elitism and extreme individualism. This highlighting of contradictions increasingly illuminated the 'dark side of capitalism', especially the impersonal logic of rationalisation and regional unemployment.[8] However, in the 1980s a new social type emerged: the female '*idol of production*'. This structure of feeling centres on a celebration of the market and contrasts most markedly with the earlier social democratic subgenre of which Cookson is an example. Thus the genre possesses structural universals which can be deployed with strikingly varied contents. These will be explored in two major forms, the traditional gentry–bourgeois romance and the woman-centred idyll of modernity.

THE GENTRY–BOURGEOIS ROMANCE

Literary modernism in Britain has taken a predominantly regressive form, regretting the passing of the aristocracy and the organic village, and it is not surprising that much popular writing should be indelibly stamped with the same mark. Within the dominant strand of the romance, the gentry emerge as the only class which can assume responsibility for social unity, that is for forms of solidarity which cannot be achieved via the market freedom to pursue self-interest. Mainstream writers, such as Victoria Holt, Catherine Gaskin and Norah Lofts, describe a mystically unbroken English history in which the gentry has the paramount political role of healing social conflict. Thus, woven within these narratives are two themes, the nature of true authority and the source of the money needed for this task.

The family alliance of protagonists from the feudal and bourgeois classes restores the continuity of the paternalist order which is, in turn, invigorated by money derived from industry. The integration of the two classes is achieved through the dramatic *emblem* of *a passionate and fecund marriage*. Thus throughout these texts there is a double signification of sexuality and power. The old order is threatened by the luxury and rapacity of the male members of the landowning or industrialist class, whose opportunistic action both ruthlessly neglects the fragile identities of the women and ruins their families financially. The imperative need to solve such material problems is heightened by aberrant sexuality: the heroines are initially illegitimate, anorexic or profligate in their attachments. Thus the malfunctioning of the private sphere amplifies the distortion of the public sphere or economy. A stable marriage can only emerge when the class problems have been solved. The union of land and gold is the signal for the correction of the patriarchal order.

A typical example of this genre is Holt's *The Pride of the Peacock*, set between 1870 and 1900, in which declining feudal power produces a period of social disorder. This is signified by the sale of the ancestral mansion of a bankrupted aristocratic family to a *nouveau riche* Cockney who has risen from obscurity to own South African mines. The concurrent imposition of a female-dominated regime within the gentry household is defined as an over-repressive 'world turned upside down'. The correct balance between desire and legality is only re-established when the heroine, the illegitimate daughter of the gentry family, returns triumphantly from South Africa, having tamed the philandering heir to the Cockney mine-owner's property. It is her role to act as the intermediary between the aristocracy – from which she comes – and bourgeois money – into which she marries. The mine-owner hero convinces her not only that his sexual attachments are focused on her alone, but also that his rigid labour discipline of the 'childlike' Bantu miners combines profit with morality. The gentry, purged of its excess, is thus symbolically reinstated through the heroine in the feudal mansion. Like her mother, the heroine's first child is conceived with desire, but unlike her, he is also conceived within the prescribed rules of marital alliance.

As pastiche 'condition of England' novels, the modern gentry–bourgeois romances are more regressive than their prototypes. The labour–capital theme in *Peacock* might be compared with the similar issue in Elizabeth Gaskell's *North and South*. Yet the perspective of *Peacock*'s heroine lacks even the limited demands for industrial democracy urged on Mr Thornton, the mill-owner, by Margaret, the female protagonist of Gaskell's novel. Moreover, the separation of spheres in Holt's novel takes place entirely within the conventions of nineteenth-century domestic ideology, so that the narrative is devoid of the realist tensions of gender over women's access to the public sphere generally implicit in the more critical canonical texts. Thus in *Peacock* an exchange occurs in which the heroine acquires a petty cultural monopoly over taste – the right to advise on the quality of opals from the South African mine – yet her former responsibility as a woman for their employees' welfare is transferred to her husband. To the positive hero is now attributed the managerial prerogative of total and unquestioned control over workers.

This agreement becomes the basis of the reunion of status and riches within a new stable order. Externally, the old feudal forms are restored – the heir is born in his rightful place in the gentry house – internally, the feudal order has been gutted and replaced with bourgeois money and the gospel of work. Thus *Peacock* creates a mythical social history in which an ideology of sexual and labour discipline has been enunciated so that society can be saved from rancorous class and gender envies.

This fantastic harmony of gentry and bourgeois interests, conducted within the Victorian language of gender, is the essential model of the traditional romance or family saga. Its ideological structure is constantly repeated. Thus in Catherine Gaskin's historical romance, *Promises*, set in 1880–1939, there is an even clearer repetition of the discourse of the 1840s, in which the romance takes on the Christian redemptive mission noted by Marx.[9] In this version of the modal text the illegitimate heroine is replaced by a foundling heroine, whose absent parents are Leeds factory hands, victims of the distorted human relations which have shaped working-class experiences of early industrial capitalism. In this novel, the exclusiveness of the aristocracy prevents any alternative return to an idyllic agrarian society, while the masses appear as a menacing presence, with their potential role as gravediggers of the industrial order conveyed through fleeting images of their slum housing, their involuntary abandonment of children and their wife-beating. The ending is constructed through an idealised cross-class 'Holy Family', marked by acceptance of the common people on the part of the rich and the death of characters whose commitments were to their sectional interests alone.

Lally, the heroine, who has been endowed with a profound social perceptiveness along with the marginality of the foundling, has become the architect of social unity, binding together servants and masters, the deluded and the sane, the aristocrat and the millocracy. Her role is legitimated by her Christ-like agony at the wealth and privilege of the ruling class, which is symptomatically evident in her infantile silences and her youthful anorexia.[10] Yet there are sharp limits to this humanism. Although the advocated change of heart requires a return to human interdependence, the representation of key social conflicts, such as the General Strike, is invariably *from the vantage point of the dominant class*.

However, the traditional gentry–bourgeois texts should not all be typified as recycled *Pamela* or 'condition of England' novels. Some exponents of this genre also encode female dependency quite differently. The link between marital exploitation and property institutions has been increasingly interrogated within these texts.

The paradox of such anti-patriarchal transformations of the genre is the simultaneous persistence of rural, feudal nostalgia. The organicism of the traditional village community is still retained as the key response to the crises inherent in capitalism, especially the decimation of entire industries by market forces. Thus at the resolution of such modern family sagas as, for example, Susan Howatch's *Penmarric*, only the *male* domination of *women* is seen as oppressive: the deferential tenant–miners' bond to their lord embodies the natural order of things and is reaffirmed.[11]

THE ROMANCE OF THE MODERN WOMAN: BOURGEOIS SOCIETY MINUS PATRIARCHY

There has been a volte-face in images of gender in the 1970s and 1980s. If a typical scene in 1930s stories was that of a woman tearing up her employment contract to dedicate herself to her family's needs, in the romance of the 1980s the heroine achieves – without any tragic costs – spectacular business success and happy children. However, in the hands of Judith Krantz and Barbara Taylor Bradford, the new quasi-feminist romance is built on more than a revised politics of gender. It signals a break with the earlier ethos in which feudal tradition was asserted against the twentieth-century wasteland, with the gentry representing the fiduciary guarantors of a money economy. For modernity has now been eagerly adopted and the new formula reverberates with the necessity of permanent change. If a central experience of modernity is awareness of the importance of the 'transitory, the fleeting and the fortuitous'[12] in social life, in these fictions such forms of interaction are welcomed as progress: late capitalism is lauded as civilisation.

No longer modelled on the Madonna, the heroine in this genre has requisitioned the honorific image of the male entrepreneur as restless Promethean developer. No longer defined by her family identity, she has become the quintessential self-made woman. No longer tied to the sphere of conspicuous consumption as in the jazz rhythms of the flapper or the sensuality of the film star, the new Modern Woman is the active figure, the innovator in production. Within the recent family sagas set in the 1890s, such characters move in the territory of historical fantasy as originators in the sphere of mass market commodities: they are the first citizens of the consumer revolution – the women's magazine editors, fashion house proprietors and chain-store owners within the tradition of Bon Marché and Marks and Spencer.[13] Their power is evident through the new visions of legitimate consumption. Readers are welcomed by them into a world of luxury goods which have ceased to be weapons of exclusion, but continue to serve as objects of the imagination.

Today's entrepreneurial heroine, figured at the turn of the century, lacks the contemplative passivity of the male *flaneur*, the street-observer of the nineteenth-century literature of modernity.[14] Yet, like him, she moves anachronistically at ease in the masculine spaces of West End hotel or editor's office, unconstrained by the regulation of the public sphere which had earlier cleared from the city all but murder victims, prostitutes or widows.[15]

The repressed passivity of the traditional heroine has now been stripped away. It is the new heroine alone who calculates the minutiae of all business decisions and she alone who turns the fortuitous shocks of modern life into opportunities for commercial triumph.[16] No longer naïve, the female entrepreneur expresses the blasé attitude which Georg Simmel and Walter Benjamin denoted as the defence of the over-stimulated personality against metropolitan experience.[17] The fragmented totality of the city galvanises rather than depletes her resources. And in a last neat twist of romance conventions, Judith Krantz even makes her latest heroine the initiator of sexual action, possessing the secret knowledge of arousing desire, formerly the prerogative of the experienced male.

In these novels, the bourgeois rationalisation of industry is accompanied by a panegyric to the future seen in an anti-tragic mode. And rationalisation – technical rationality – is not for the new heroine an iron cage in which she is trapped. On the contrary, economic power at its most concentrated and diversified is linked mythically to sexuality and fecundity. Consequently, publishers refer to the new genre as S 'n F (shopping and fucking). These are indeed the fairy-tales of modernity.

Barbara Taylor Bradford's historical novel, *A Woman Of Substance*, is a representative text, which Bradford believes could only have become popular now. She has flouted the conventions of the formulaic romance by reproducing in Emma a modern Moll Flanders – ambitious, quick-thinking, materialistic. The narrative revolves around her business success.

Emma's epic ascent from the misery of a mill-worker's cottage to the ownership of a department store chain and multinational holding company is accomplished by planning and unremitting toil, that is, through classic asceticism.[18] Yet she also lies, manipulates and exploits her sexual charm to enter the safe passage of the corporate rich – actions which were marks of the stigmatised 'other woman' of the 1930s stories. Emma's revulsion from her first husband's sexual demands, for example, takes the form of mental arithmetic with her business accounts while he rolls around on top of her – an unemotional response much more characteristic of the 1930s' female Other.[19] Indeed, Emma is obsessed with money, with both its multiplication and calculated deployment; her sweetest pleasure is in the business failure of her competitors.

Emma's heroic gifts are matriarchal wisdom and virtuoso entrepreneurial vision. Her precocious leadership and inner restlessness is revealed in her early schemes as a servant for the rationalisation of the mill-owner's housework. Her exemplary financial skills and innate taste are constructed individualistically in terms of business 'genius', a genius underpinned by her stress on disciplined work within a calling. From this point of vision, the social relations of capital and labour virtually disappear from the text – symbolically dissolved in the cult of entrepreneurial personality.

Yet if the 'spirit of capitalism' animates the shop and garment industries Emma first nurses into life, this is a progressive or heroic capitalist ethic, mythically unadulterated by racial or religious discrimination. For the approved characters typify *the modernising energies* of a managerial stratum fighting *against the closed ranks of the Establishment*. Like the Irish builder and the Jewish manufacturers also honoured in the story, Emma survives by talents and wit: 'Nobody outsmarts me!' is her maxim. Nevertheless, at the conclusion, she herself cements her family into the gentry by intermarriage and her bequests to her heirs seem, to the dis-enchanted reader, to recreate caste-like elements within the newly formed money relations. Such inconsistencies are symptomatic of the fantasy ending.

Through such narrative devices, many conventions of the romance persist, despite the re-evaluation of the heroine's role. The mill-owner's porcine elder son is a stereotyped figure of upper-class excess. Other familiar and regressive images are also retained: the self-obsessed homosexual; the socialist who advocates equality only so long as his own property interests are not involved; the insane woman. Such folk-devils have a demonological role chosen from a conservative discourse. Moreover, beneath the ritual genuflections to the 'middle ground' and 'balance', inherent in the narrative structure of the romance, it is the rhetoric of the Right which supplies the more subtle coding of the novel and the Right's world-historical figures – Lord Kitchener, Winston Churchill, Lord Beaverbrook – who stand approvingly in its wings.

This saga is, then, an extended celebration of money-making; at its heart is the morality: 'Accumulate! Accumulate! These are the words of Moses and all his prophets!'[20] The market-place for Bradford is a new Arcadia. For her world-view is formed by a populist delineation of classes as legally closed, impermeable estates into which entry to outsiders is blocked. In *Woman of Substance* such plebeian radical perceptions are directed solely at the gentry or agrarian capitalist class. In contrast, the urban industrial world still retains the fabled pavements of opportunity. Yet motifs such as Emma's preoccupation with market success or her innovations, evident in her early housework 'plan', are susceptible to different readings. The text can be decoded as simply legitimating the modernising forces of capital, or – and this was the reading favoured by my respondents – as expressing the hope that *women* may now gain control over their own destinies. Emma's personality is miraculously immune from the distortions of success. Thus, in providing images of the wonderful life of the rich, Bradford's strong heroine avoids any penetrating gaze which seeks to enquire too closely into the effects of unequally distributed riches and power: the text teaches how things 'of the world' are desirable and it is acceptable for women to wish for them.

Such a turn to hedonism is summarised most clearly in another novel of the same genre, Shirley Conran's *Lace*.[21] One of her heroines remarks:

> The collective mass of American women form the biggest money-spending force in the world. [We] will not only show them how to spend it, we'll also show them how to make it, how to earn it and how to multiply it. It's time we thought more about money and had more of it for ourselves.[22]

The general invitation to consumption as leisure masks the inequalities of economic power concealed beneath the business-woman's 'room at the top'.

Not all of the 1980s genres can be fitted into the two main types above.[23] The *social democratic* novel often combines feminist images of patriarchy with a sympathetic commitment to the labour movement. The critique of the pursuit of a market logic creates not only the hope for small, organic enterprises but also the valorisation of certain local (non-political) trade union organisations, strikes and the wider possession of civil rights. Such an extension of the old gentry–bourgeois model is developed from the perspective of the working class themselves. This subgenre shares with proletarian realism certain powerful and virtually universal narrative devices, such as the pit accident precipitated by managerial greed, which suggest a sensitivity to the propertyless character of the popular readership. Nevertheless, the recognition of a pragmatic trade unionism and of the claims of labour for social justice often still resonate within the language of the gentry tradition.[24]

THE ROMANCE OR FAMILY SAGA AND THE MYTH OF SOCIAL UNITY

I have illustrated the central importance of the gentry in romances and family sagas and have distinguished the particular importance of this class for an attack on unbridled capitalism.[25] What are the roots of this fictional structure? In his illuminating discussion of Daphne du Maurier's *Rebecca*, Roger Bromley has suggested that the unspoken reference of this text is to the inter-war Depression, that is, to contradiction and crisis within the bourgeois order.[26] By remarriage and departure from his country house, Rebecca's gentry husband aspires to a paternal rather than a magnificent role. Through this role he will fulfil the heroic task of refounding the State. His commanding position as a gentry hero derives from his understanding of the deficiencies of the existing society and from his new union with an impecunious, lower-class woman, thus indicating that the couple have acquired their moral authority from the whole society.

The thriller has an entirely different genesis. Its birth depends on the emergence of the hero as an exemplary competitive figure within the possessive individualism of the bourgeois order. His reassuring strength derives from his capacity to quell the conspiracy threatening the social order.[27] In contrast, the classic family saga and romance base their appeal on the redemptive role of a reformed gentry.

Bromley's assessment presupposes the domination of the industrial bourgeoisie, with an appeal to the gentry when crisis threatens the normal ordering of class relationships. However, in the light of recent research, this assumption must be questioned.[28] There is compelling evidence for the view that the gentry or agrarian bourgeoisie had so effectively coupled 'high farming' with agricultural wage-labour that they were superior to industrialists in property and income throughout the nineteenth century. I accept Perry Anderson's conclusion that 'They were capitalists, although rentiers, innovators although patricians. . . . Until the late nineteenth century, they managed to have the best of all worlds: the profit of the entrepreneur and the prestige of the aristocrat . . . .'[29] If this was so, then the protracted political domination of the aristocracy a full century after the Industrial Revolution 'was no mere cultural quirk. . . . It reflected certain real and continuing disparities of material situation.'[30] Paradoxically, then, the industrialists who precociously ushered in capitalism in its classic form in Britain still retained a subaltern relationship to the agrarian and commercial interests. Nineteenth-century images of a pastoral community, within both the 'high' and 'low' literature of industrial Britain, fitted logically into such an agrarian bourgeois perspective, and added to the rhetoric within which social unity was modelled.[31]

Anderson's account fails to elaborate on the much earlier transformation of the agrarian order, in which the seigneurial lords of an unfree peasantry had become partners in the operation of agrarian capital. Moreover, like Wiener, he has also neglected the sources of *urban bourgeois hegemony* in popular culture. Nevertheless, the modern family saga of Howatch, Gaskin and Holt retains these rural traces, which obtained their decisive character from the moral economy of the eighteenth-century gentry. Thus current best-selling fiction still carries the conception of a 'natural' hierarchy, the importance of reputation and of deference to the good gentleman, along with a hatred of exploitation and an ideology of justice in which law is perceived as the guardian of *all* English*men*. It would be quite wrong to see this genre as a repudiation of bourgeois thought and society, but the constant allusion to the myth of gentry paternalism in the novels supplies the missing framework in which money-making has its place. Thus social conflicts and unemployment are posed within an interpretative context which incorporates class critiques of both the agrarian and the industrial interests. The rigidities of the gentry-managed social structure, especially in the rejection of romantic marriage, provoke a critique of aspects of the landowning class, while the periodic crisis, its effects heightened by the luxury of the exploitative industrialist, is, in these novels, the Achilles heel of the bourgeois order.

There is a connection, too, between genres and gender ideologies. For inscribed into the thriller and the romance are different ideas about power. In the thriller, the solitary hero's competitive superiority leads to his victory over the criminals. In the romance the reforming of the State is a task seized on by both hero and heroine, being dependent upon the moral reform of both rich and poor. The romance has the hegemonic mission of idealising the ruling class by neutralising the weaknesses of each fraction and infusing it with the respective strength of the other. The pursuit of exchange-value (the value-form in which profitability derives from the production and market exchange of commodities) is softened by reference to the universal rights of salvation, citizenship or welfare, exhorted by women.

In Victorian conceptions of domestic ideology, women, particularly, were to be trained as such moral custodians: exemplary figures in the home for servants, children and neighbours. Thus in practice women may have spent all the money their husbands made and rigorously fortified class barriers, but in principle the cultural commitment to social unity was their responsibility.[32]

Romances and sagas spring from this consciousness. They mimic the earlier 'bourgeois anti-capitalism' of the 1840s. Terry Lovell has argued lucidly that it was this perspective which structured the novel, as the writers became more distanced than earlier from the social forces driving a market economy. It allowed the novel as a popular form to achieve a critical reputation with the traditional intelligentsia.[33] By elaborating a gentry world-view within their novels, she contends, some women writers were able to break through the habitual confinement of the female tradition within a 'woman-to-woman' discourse, so as to speak to the masters of factories within a 'woman-to-man' discourse. For this influence, cultural capital was not the sole prerequisite: women writers were qualified also by the peculiar sensitivity to suffering which the female authorial voice can claim. Thus as the victims of a historically unprecedented degree of female dependency, these writers gained partial imaginative access to the suffering of the industrial proletariat. Their contradictory social location exposed them to working-class protest: their cultural capital directed them towards resolutions furnished by paternalist capitalism.[34] Many romances and sagas today are still shaped by this tradition.

In conclusion, then, the deep structure of the genre is organised around two extremes, with a transcendent hero and heroine at the end. The 'extremes' vary, giving each novel its colour, but are typified at one pole by villainous figures from an oppressive ruling class – either 'patrician-banditti' or ruthless industrialists, coercive in their command of labour or violent towards women – and at the other pole by resentful agitators or sabotaging workers.[35] The heroic couple mediate between them. In the British gentry–bourgeois romance (Holt, Gaskin), the protagonists of the market are tamed by their insertion into the harmonious order of a gentry-led rural society. By contrast, in the American myth of writers such as Krantz, the aristocracy acquires harsher connotations of amoral hedonism rather than paternal authority and can only be purified by exposure to the discipline of the work ethic and the rigours of rationalisation. A similar exaltation of bourgeois principles is found in the Yorkshire writer, Bradford, whose heroine flouts Mills and Boon rules by becoming the bearer of an entrepreneurial ethos.

Yet, however important the social mission of the gentry, women's fiction cannot be reduced simply to regressive fantasies of class harmony. For these novels are also about women's experience and how they should live. In this respect a great variety of images emerge in contemporary popular novels as to the fate of the male household 'constitutional monarchy'. Patriarchal principles are interrogated, restored, replaced and redefined: in the most innovative popular writing, there appear fantasies of revenge, flight and radical disenchantment.[36] If moral regulation through the monogamous lifelong marriage continues to provide the main recuperative closure of women's best-selling fiction, the less formulaic writers have steadily expanded within their narratives the register of rights to which women are entitled. Women's education, the expression of female sexuality, single motherhood, divorce and maternal custody of children have all been legitimised in the modern romance. Thus while by no means expressing the current demands of feminism, the older idioms of dependency and subordination have been steadily eroded by the most popular writers.

Part III
CULTURAL RECEPTION

6 *Cultural Consumption*

THEORETICAL CONTEXT: BOURDIEU'S THEORY OF CULTURE

It used to be assumed that the death of the author would trigger the birth of the reader. Yet the protracted labour of reception theory has still only resulted in the critic's imputation of meaning to texts.[1] Nevertheless, Pierre Bourdieu's works, *Distinction* and 'The production of belief', do contain an empirically founded theory of the readers themselves and their tastes, in which he argues that cultural consumption both intensifies and helps reproduce class inequalities.[2] My own work on women's uses of literacy is partly aimed at assessing, in Scotland, the impact of class on culture. But it is less pessimistic than Bourdieu's tragic cynicism. It suggests that disagreements over literary pleasure, and other conflicts in the terrain of cultural politics, have a more complex relationship to the readers' class position than Bourdieu contends. Bourdieu has exaggerated the significance of the class of origin in the response to culture, neglected the role of social mobility and prematurely dismissed all hopes of art as a weapon of emancipation.

Bourdieu wisely insists that the reception of literature is socially structured: one person's meat is another person's poison. The *pain* or pleasure generated by the text depends on how it is read, that is on the interpretative framework within which it is perceived. Hence he distinguishes four groups, those with 'legitimate' or 'consecrated' taste (high culture); those with popular culture; those with middlebrow taste, who know only the most accessible works of the masters; finally, the autodidacts (a variant of middlebrow taste), who have acquired their knowledge of high culture through the insecure route of self-education. Such groupings are basically determined by the polar opposition between legitimate and popular culture.

Decodings of art vary according to class, education and gender. Bourdieu stresses that much art and literature is indecipherable to those who do not have the intellectual 'route-maps' to chart its meaning and significance. For this reason, culture – including cultural criticism – has increasingly served to legitimate the power of the dominant class by comparison with the disinherited.

Such an ironic assessment of the meaning of culture does indeed contain a brilliant display of insight into class antagonisms, tearing the veil from the discreet charm of the cultural 'nobility', with their consecrated or legitimate taste.[3] Bourdieu sees the possession of such legitimate culture as partly a *quantifiable* product, defined by how much 'cultural capital', or education conferring approved cultural skills, is possessed. It is also partly a *qualitative* disposition or ethos, which he calls the 'aesthetic attitude'. The heart of this ethos, according to Bourdieu, is the negation of popular culture, with its taste for realism, its unquestioned moral and political judgements and its pleasure in renowned natural beauties (sunset, tropical paradise, etc.). In contrast, the inner meaning of the legitimate 'aesthetic attitude' is the principle of form or style. For the commitment to style creates the 'symbolic violence' with which popular culture is abhorred, a violence which is paradoxical given also the refusal implicit in the aesthetic attitude to take things *seriously*, that is, the insistence on a game-like detachment.

Such a focus on style is a consequence of the separation from routine social life undergone by all arts when they enjoy the fate of 'consecration', thus becoming part of the canonical group of writers and artists taught in universities. In this respect art is merely the most recent form of the separation of the sacred from the profane, everyday world, and art now inherits the legitimising role of its predecessor, religion.

Cultural capital derives from the disinterested, non-utilitarian 'investment' in legitimate works, metaphorical or literal. Yet it, too, turns out to be 'dripping in blood from every pore' as Marx said of economic capital. For its bearers are those with inherited wealth or old money and it is expressed through an aesthetic disposition or attitude,

> which tends to bracket off the nature and function of the object represented and to exclude any 'naive' reaction – horror at the horrible, desire for the desirable, pious reverence for the sacred – along with all purely ethical

responses, in order to concentrate solely on the *mode of representation [or form]*.[4] (my italics)

The aesthetic attitude is bred from wealth, material security, leisure and freedom from manual activities.

Bourdieu's analysis started from a simple empirical ambition: to describe the cultural inheritance, knowledge and taste of individuals in his French 1960s sample. In his explanation of the systematic differences he discovers, Bourdieu attacks the individualistic view that *anyone* can acquire 'culture' and 'style'. In a society where high culture has replaced the grace-dispensing role of traditional religion, the 'consecrated' element of cultural knowledge is the understanding of the formal techniques of artistic production and this is shown through his research to be the possession of a *minority*. Such a minority responds to the work of art as a 'timeless', non-utilitarian cultural product, cut off from life rather than profoundly engaged with events. For this minority, of course, an artist's worth is ranked according to his or her critical reputation rather than generated by high sales.[5]

Where are the institutional centres of these attitudes? The *museum* and the *school* are reappraised by Bourdieu as the modern churches of this new cult and those with legitimate culture are its spiritual aristocrats. Of course, some art forms are only partially or recently 'consecrated', such as jazz, film, or photography, but these can be classified as initially the work of dissidents from the legitimate arts or 'heresiarchs' who are later embraced by high culture. In fact, the essence of *this* aesthetic gaze – the mystery of mysteries – is that nothing in art is permanently sacred. Literary and artistic rules *change* and even works which flout conventional ideas of beauty, which distort or disrupt common sense or which attack the dominant class, can be recuperated or incorporated by that class, through its spiritual aristocrats. For by these means, the cultivated indicate their liberal tolerance, their freedom from bourgeois respectability, their aesthetic breadth.

Those culturally competent in this way of seeing are not chosen haphazardly. Such apparently random talents or 'gifts' of understanding derive in fact from their comfortable material situation within the dominant class. In the modern context there are two main transmission belts for such cultural competence: the home, where a taste for, say, classical music is imbibed with the milk at the mother's breast, and the school, where a programme of gradual education into the correct tastes and attitudes is offered to all, but curiously, only those already initiated prove receptive.[6]

Those without cultural capital remain in what Kant and Bourdieu call, provocatively, barbarism. Popular art embodies a 'naïve gaze', portraying such beautiful objects as snowy mountains and attractive young women, while excluding from artistic representation objects such as cabbages or butcher's shops, which they view as 'ugly' or 'meaningless'.[7] Popular readers look for a strong plot, with well-demarcated characters, concluding in a happy and logical ending. Melodrama is a paradigmatic case with a strong, clear morality or set of political principles. Yet Bourdieu's depiction of popular aesthetics finally lacks clarity, being muddied by the inclusion of too many apparently conflicting elements. For on this argument, popular consciousness is shaped simultaneously by a taste for glittering, sumptuous consumption (for example, gilt furniture), by pleasure in the subversion of the pretensions of the great (as in pub comedians), by a desire for ethical reaffirmation (as in melodramatic theatre) and by the luxury of the festivity. Bourdieu's only comment on this is that popular 'barbarism' binds individuals in solidarity, whereas consecrated taste is marked by individual uniqueness and originality. These qualities, in turn, are the prerequisites of later economic success.

However, his analysis of popular culture does not advance us very far. Working–class culture, at least in Britain, has incorporated its own *formal* attack on *form*.[8] Is there no French equivalent to punk – which implied calculated stylistic aggression against consecrated culture and against all expensive cultural forms – with its conspicuous 'bad taste' in safety-pinned noses, crude hair-dyes, and profane cheap synthetics? Bourdieu fails to see how such subversive, often non-verbal jokes about dominant culture validate the subordinate world-view, particularly by means of a subtle appeal to style.[9] If new and vivid images can be such an important ingredient of the politics of popular culture, Bourdieu's dichotomy between the aesthetic disposition and popular taste begins to be more difficult to sustain.

Yet, he argues convincingly that the working class live under the hegemonic rule of another culture, as if in a colonised society. Bourdieu also holds that it is impossible for the 'organic intellectuals' of the working class to break free entirely from the dominant ideas. This is partly because of material factors such as lack of money to buy books and lack of time to read. It is also due to the effect of ideology which gives higher status to the canonised writers and art-forms: 'If there is no popular art in the sense of the urban working class it is perhaps because this class knows no other hierarchies than the purely negative ones which are measured by distance from absolute poverty.'[10] To the working class, the key question is how protected is their survival from the ravages of poverty. Hence 'culture' (in the consecrated sense) is a hierarchical sign that they are not in the gutter. Its further use in signalling respectability or a labour aristocracy impairs its effectiveness for contesting bourgeois power.

This 'social psychoanalysis'[11] *does* succeed in penetrating the inner logic, or rather inner schizophrenia of class cultures. Bourdieu is right that high culture has the potential to serve as a new form of legitimating ideology, which stabilises bourgeois societies by means of the profound gulf between its bearers and those without education. However, Bourdieu's weakness is his failure to ground his theory of culture in a sufficiently historical and/or comparative perspective and in his conspicuous silence about social change. He has been read as defending popular culture as a colonised consciousness, against the mandarins' desire to separate art from life.[12] I do not think this is Bourdieu's position. Yet if it *is* his implicit meaning, Bourdieu's writings teach us only the futility of the struggle for liberation or change! His debunking cynicism about the use of high culture is refreshingly acerbic but it is also blind to those occasions in which different patterns of action and different uses of culture can emerge. In particular, he leaves no possibility for a political alliance between a radical intelligentsia, and the working class (together with women as the oppressed gender), in which a critical art and literature have a major role.[13]

Secondly, Bourdieu tells us very little about the content of popular culture. Less than Brecht, for example, who distinguished between a culture that increased the internalised oppression of the subordinate class and a popular culture such as that of his own theatrical tradition which used a variety of media to illuminate 'the way things really are'.

THE SCOTTISH STUDY

In my own research, I looked particularly at the consumers' motivations, that is, whether people searched for entertainment and fantasy alone or whether they enjoyed the knowledge acquired through realist forms. Early interviews revealed that further debates – such as that between modernism and critical realism – had little meaning to my respondents, so this issue has been ignored. However, the art/entertainment dichotomy separates 'art' from entertaining diversions which depend on a magical interference with reality, by substituting an ego-sustaining armoury in place of truth. It is this division of taste which most concerned me.

I then assessed to what extent popular literature possesses a 'condition for working-class knowledge' or feminist perception.[14] The traces of such an emancipatory discourse may lack complex clashes of ideas but still serve to distinguish these texts from forms of mass culture which are entirely permeated with the ideas of the dominant class and gender. The readership of such popular literature was explored.

Initially I classified cultural consumption in the reading-groups according to Bourdieu's categories. The criteria used were derived from literature only, whereas other art forms figure prominently in the French study. I also allocated women to groups by a less rigorous and intimidating method, for where Bourdieu examined the extent of knowledge, I have simply reported the respondents' stated preferences. On the basis of this information, as well as the more general deficiencies analysed above, I decided that Bourdieu's broad brushstrokes in the specific area of popular culture masked as much as they revealed. Thus in the final classification the category of 'barbarism' was rejected in favour of less ironic labels, designating, first, those whose taste was for patriarchal or 'formulaic' romance; second, those enjoying less formulaic, transgressive romance and family sagas, and, third, those inheriting a radical canon, hostile to romance. To these groups I added Bourdieu's original designation of legitimate and middlebrow groups, the latter distinguished from the former by its knowledge of 'minor works of major arts'.

There are then five readership groups:

1. Legitimate taste.
2. Middlebrow taste.
3. Radical canon of popular literature.
4. Non-formulaic, or less formulaic, uncanonised women's fiction: the 'Cookson' group.
5. Formulaic romantic fiction.

Altogether 115 women from the West of Scotland were interviewed in 1986–7, with 34 consenting to a second discussion after reading two novels I lent them. I recruited the women from various milieux, including nurseries, schools, libraries, a publishing firm, a pensioner's group and a Woman's Aid refuge. Approaches to the women for interviews varied, some respondents being selected for me by intermediaries, such as personnel officers or community workers, others encountered while browsing in public libraries or waiting in dole queues, and yet others volunteering after I had introduced the research in various groups. Those who stated that they read neither books nor magazines were excluded: of these, the majority were very young women and it is this group whose tastes have been least explored. Respondents were chosen to ensure an overall balance in the number of women under and over 40 years of age (categorised as under 23, 23–39, 40–60 and over 60 years), of middle and working class, of houseworkers and those in paid work. Educational levels, or cultural capital, varied sharply, from the tiny minority with higher education, to the much larger group who had left school without qualifications. However, despite the variety of sources for women participants, there were still certain categories that were under-represented. In particular, the views of older houseworkers married to professionals, businessmen and managers have been inadequately canvassed. It is also worth noting that the method used depended on an open communication of tastes and that the stigmatisation of certain genres of popular culture may have led to reported consumption slightly under-estimating actual consumption.

Each woman was asked to name her 'favourite' writers and whether there were any writers she disliked. In order to discover more precisely the women's preferences, I constructed a list of novelists with representative titles – avoiding the most familiar classics, such as *Jane Eyre* or *Oliver Twist* – so as to assess more easily the real cultural cleavages between women. Titles were necessary, since for many popular readers it was titles rather than authors which served as keys to memory. Catherine Cookson, Barbara Cartland, Colleen McCullough, Victoria Holt and Maisie Mosco were included as currently popular writers whose books belong to different subgenres.[15] There then followed a group of three contemporary writers occupying different ideological positions but all likely to be included in the future in university curricula: Marge Piercy, Doris Lessing and Margaret Drabble. Dead canonised writers were George Eliot (*Middlemarch* and *Mill on the Floss* specified), Thomas Hardy (*Jude the Obscure*) and Lewis Grassic Gibbon (*A Scots Quair*), with Robert Tressell's *The Ragged Trousered Philanthropists* as the most celebrated novel of the unofficial radical canon. Women were also asked their responses to various genres, including 'romantic fiction', a deliberately ambiguous designation which those with middlebrow or legitimate taste sometimes found puzzling ('Is *War and Peace* romantic fiction?' asked one reader, not without justification). I also included historical fiction, thrillers and detective stories, science fiction, and Mills and Boon novels. Those who reported a dislike of the genre of 'romantic fiction' were asked to give their reasons.

Such was the raw material from which I constituted the typology of women readers, identified in the text as 'groups' although such groups have no real collective existence, being merely artificial constructs from individuals' cultural preferences and artistic perceptions. Exact allocations of individuals to groups required coding decisions of considerable interpretative complexity and hence greater subjective scope than in more systematically ordered fields of social enquiry, such as mobility surveys. It also needs to be borne in mind that individuals sometimes inhabit a particular reading category only temporarily. Thus one young woman was interviewed three times. Initially she was part of the formulaic romance group as a Mills and Boon *aficionada*, at the second interview she distanced herself, commenting on their loss of allure for her; finally, newly separated and a full-time wage earner, she became a convert to realism, emphatically disdaining the fantasies of the romantic writers she had once enjoyed.

Introducing the groups: cultural attitudes and their social parameters

Legitimate culture

The criteria adopted to measure legitimate culture was knowledge of writers who represented the official literary culture of modern Britain as designated by their inclusion on the curriculum of the school or university. Familiarity with these texts is viewed by Bourdieu as the possession of *cultural capital*.

No attempt was made to *define* the acquisition of legitimate culture in terms of an attachment to the 'aesthetic attitude', or the consideration of art in terms of form or beauty alone. Instead I decided to assess *empirically how often* readers' knowledge of legitimate culture led to the adoption of a formalist aesthetic attitude, in which questions of style are central, as opposed to the ideas or politics of the texts.

Table 6.1 The range of reading

	Legitimate	M'brow	'Cookson'	Romantic	Radical
Knows modern writers such as: Margaret Drabble Marge Piercy Doris Lessing	20(77%)	6(38%)	6(14%)	0	0
Knows at least two earlier writers: George Eliot Thomas Hardy Robert Tressell Grassic Gibbon	26(100%)	7(44%)	13(31%)	1(4%)	3(60%)
Knows novels by both groups of writers	20(77%)	2(13%)	1(2%)	0	0
Number interviewed	26	16	42	26	5

Although I used a range of criteria to allocate individuals to groups, the list of writers known and enjoyed by them can be used as indicators of women's reading. Care should be taken not to make too much of this: any such list has to be arbitrary if questions are not to be tedious and it may not reflect the extent of reading in any area. However, the divergence between the categories of readers is brought out very clearly in Table 6.1, which was the basis for the classification of individuals into groups. Readers were asked about their preferences in such a way as to reveal their knowledge. However, it should be noted that those with 'legitimate taste' also read writers who are not yet included in the curriculum, who are developing new forms or using established forms in a new context: for example, black women writers such as Maya Angelou, Toni Bambara and Alice Walker. It is also worth reporting the relative infrequency of modernist writers on their lists, although Marcel Proust, Thomas Mann, D.H. Lawrence, Salman Rushdie, Herman Hesse, Harold Pinter, Paul Scott, Primo Levi and Margaret Atwood were among those mentioned by one or two readers.

Pleasure in legitimate works is most often linked to disdain for romantic fiction and the expression of a sense of pollution by it. For example, one woman asked to read Marie Joseph's formulaic story, *Lisa Logan*, exploded: '"It's the epitome of all I hate! It's so badly written I felt depressed, in a black mood, the whole time I was reading it."'

However, legitimate culture does not automatically bestow a visceral intolerance towards contemporary romantic fiction. A minority who had acquired a disposition favourable to 'serious fiction' occasionally read a Mills and Boon novel.[16] They confessed these private, behind-the-scenes departures from legitimate taste as I imagine Kinsey's respondents must have yielded up their perversions for scientific scrutiny, fully aware of the pejorative connotations of such consumption in the perspective of the intelligentsia. The more profound their sense of inner distinction or election, the more legitimate their usual diet, the more these women neutralized their deviance. They exonerated their occasional incursions into commercial culture with reference to illness, fatigue or the need for light reading on holiday or when travelling. Yet condescension towards the formulaic romantic novel was not a monopoly of the legitimate cultural group, for such denigration emerged strongly amongst many of the 'Cookson' and radical canon groups. These dismissals were framed with reference to the youth, senility, ignorance or traditionalist femininity displayed by romantic fiction devotees.

So deeply entrenched are high cultural fortifications against the besieging barbarian forces of downmarket kitsch that only two of those possessing legitimate taste were prepared to flaunt their omnivorous reading. In this respect, the claims of postmodernist theorists that both high and popular culture are consumed today by the same groups are wide of the mark. Symptomatically, the two women concerned subtly subverted official cultural taboos by singing the praises of romantic fiction precisely as the narcotic antidote to modern angst or depression. They stressed that romances comforted them through the appeal of their nursery-rhyme moral certainties, with their reassuring cadences of uniform structure and the dependable excitement of the strong plot. Their opinions are perhaps also a key to the aesthetic views of those women with a predilection for such fiction, who were not always articulate about the reasons for their enjoyment of the romantic novels they read so avidly.

It was also notable that the few legitimate readers who still occasionally turn to Mills and Boon have working-class origins and are in professional or administrative work within the public sector. In this respect, they lend some support to Scott Lash and John

Urry's view of the distinctively catholic postmodernist tastes of the new service class, who alternate between popular and high culture.[17] Moreover, while the traditional romance was generally held in disdain by legitimate readers, the quasi-feminist romance, by writers such as Barbara Taylor Bradford, Shirley Conran or Judith Krantz was less contaminating, and might be chosen for holiday reading.

As the traditional romance genre is the bearer of women's duties to love and fulfil their social obligations within the sphere of the family, it is hardly surprising that the 'emancipated' women so often repudiated it. This latter group was most evident in the 'legitimate' category. Within the formulaic romance, the quest for independence is conflated with greed for wealth, luxury and an overblown id: small wonder, then, that for these women shifting from modern literary fiction to such a genre disturbs the fragile economy of the psyche.

The middlebrow culture

Middlebrow readers displayed a deference to legitimate culture and a pleasure in being associated with it. But without higher education in youth, the route to its acquisition was long and hard: hence there occurred the substitution of easier works for the heavier ones, a process which Bourdieu calls 'allodoxia'.[18] Many of these readers, and those of the 'Cookson' group, had promised themselves that they would undertake this more difficult reading at a later date: ' "I'm going to read all the classics when I retire", ' commented one middle-aged clerk in a characteristic declaration.

New imitations of well-established legitimate culture were popular amongst the middlebrow group. The success of *The Country Diary of an Edwardian Lady* exemplifies this phenomenon, in which respectability was linked both to reproduction of the old and to images of natural harmony. It can be connected, too, to the deference to the dominant class within middlebrow novels, a characteristic noted by Queenie Leavis in the inter-war period and still evident in the literature favoured by this group.[19]

However, although the middlebrow mainstream can be categorised by its 'cultural goodwill', there are difficulties in allocating some middlebrow individuals to the group. Such women offered examples of writers whom they have read as prescribed authors (Balzac, Jane Austen, Tolstoy), but they also quoted best-selling

popular texts, for example Dennis Wheatley's thrillers and Mar-
guerite Steen's and Judith Krantz's romances. This suggests that
genre fiction or romanticised biography offers the most lasting
memories of unparalleled literary pleasure. Such oscillation between
dutiful conformity to a culture associated with authority and a guilty
pleasure in best-selling works is one mark of the petty-bourgeois
middlebrow group, who, like the radical public, constantly
lamented lack of time for reading.

Yet, on closer inspection, the middlebrow classification is an
umbrella over mutually indifferent readerships. One quite divergent
element is the category of thriller devotees, which I have placed
under this heading. Such women appreciated particularly female
writers such as Agatha Christie, P.D. James and Emma Latham.
They also enjoyed certain male writers like Dashiel Hammett,
although other best-selling male authors, most notably, Ian
Fleming, failed to elicit any praise from the women interviewed.
The group of thriller readers were least in awe of 'highbrows'.
Another quite distinct category liked the fantasy epics of the Stephen
Donaldson type, while several youngers readers referred to science
fiction, especially Isaac Asimov, Ray Bradbury, Frank Herbert and
Anne McCaffrey. A third type, particularly widespread amongst
older women, possessed a 'negative aesthetic of respectability'
revolving around the excision of swear words and the maintenance
of a discreet silence about sexuality. These readers often preferred
nineteenth- and early twentieth-century novels and were happiest
with a fiction that was only partially secularised. Such ascetic values
served to cut them off from writers of currently popular family
romances. However, their social world-view was remarkably
congruent with those underpinning the family romances, especially
their work ethic, their celebration of women's invisible labour and
their longing for a rural community.

Middlebrow readers of this type are not in tune with the modern
world. They live out their lives in a spirit of nostalgia, feeling a
sense of loss and lack of control as dominant structures of feeling. In
brief, the middlebrow group presents a longing to be cultured but a
profound realisation of their inadequate means.

Radical canon of popular literature

Although they are unlike the women with legitimate culture in
lacking the formal education in which older elements of culture have

been prescribed, readers of the radical canon treasure the 'unconsecrated' radical pantheon of socialist or working-class writers. Emile Zola's *Germinal*, Lewis Jones's *Cwmardy* and *We Live*, Jack London's *The Iron Heel*, Lewis Grassic Gibbons's *A Scots Quair* are the texts of the labour movement, which have circulated by word of mouth recommendation for decades amongst groups of both women and men. Some of these novels are, or have been until the 1970s, totally excluded from academic culture, such as *The Ragged Trousered Philanthropists* – 'the painters' bible'. Yet others such as Zola or Grassic Gibbon have been belatedly recognised by legitimate culture. However, although the discovery of these novels often gives the working-class public a pleasure in reading which is not merely 'entertainment', their long hours of work limited the frequency and range of their self-education. Moreover, even where the radical canon was the cultural core of their world, other reading, purely for pleasure, was done as well. Thrillers or Catherine Cookson's novels were most often reported in this context. Thus individuals often possess catholic tastes and a wide stock of knowledge which floods irrepressibly out of any typology adopted for classification.

This group was particularly hostile to the reliance of other lower-class women on the escapist dreams offered by the romance. 'They'd do better organising, than reading that rubbish and crying their eyes out,' said one such reader. 'What do you need fantasy for if you are going to change the world?' asked another.

Non-formulaic but uncanonised women's fiction: the 'Cookson' group

As we have seen, Bourdieu's popular aesthetic is a mixture of sensual 'spectacular delights' and works structured by political or ethical imperatives. 'Cookson' readers had no higher education but were sufficiently perspicacious to require elements of realism rather than social myths within their novels. They wished to educate themselves when they read. However, pleasure in fantasies of individual happiness, especially a vision of well-deserved material success, were still important redemptive elements for these women. Thus most of them saw reading as primarily about light entertainment and only secondly about instruction. Nevertheless, as can be seen from Table 6.1, thirteen of them, just under a third, had read some of the English and Scottish classics. These readers showed a sophistication about the formulaic novel which was absent among the majority of the romantic fiction group. However, they looked for historical novels in particular and were unhappy with realist novels about the present, especially those written from a critical perspective. They also rejected naturalist novels revealing only the surface of working-class existence, many readers criticising the absence of strong plots or the inadequate development of characters. Although it was not uncommon for either the 'Cookson' readers or middlebrow readers to have some acquaintance with British canonised novels, especially those of the Brontës, Dickens and Hardy, they were happiest reading both recycled versions of old romances or the family romances of Colleen McCullough, Catherine Cookson and Barbara Taylor Bradford in which the heroine displayed strength and independence as well as acquiring the inevitable material success. From these often highly articulate popular readers emerged a popular canon: writers who were considered to be of very good quality, but selected independently of the judgements of those with consecrated taste.

Analysis of the favourite writers of the readers of popular culture shows that the authors who most often appear are: Catherine Cookson, who elicited nineteen spontaneous commendations; Virginia Andrews, mentioned by seven women; Barbara Taylor Bradford, with six references, Agatha Christie, with five, Christine Marion Fraser, with four, and Margaret Thompson Davis, with three. If these were mentioned spontaneously as the favourite writers of these groups, a category of 'anathematised writers' might also be constructed. Although specific writers were disliked by individuals and although women were mostly repelled by the science fiction and horror genres, only one woman writer elicited constant disapprobation. This was Barbara Cartland, concerning whom one distillery-worker asked, bitterly: 'What does she know about us, or care?' As well as this respondent, from the radical category, eleven of the 'Cookson' group and three from the romantic fiction group emphasised their antagonism to the values represented by Cartland.

The 'Cookson' group, which was distinguished by its greater readiness to accept new ideas and its more developed cultural range, was also unlike the romantic fiction group in being able to name the writers whom they preferred. In contrast, the relative lack of importance in making analytical judgements about their reading is indicated by the fact that as many as a quarter of the romantic fiction group *could not recall which writers they disliked.* The 'Cookson' group, that is, the individuals who preferred the more modern

Table 6.2 Class and reading preference

Class	Women's occupation	Total occupations	Legitim.	M'brow	'Cookson'	Romantic	Radical
1	1	2(2%)	1	1	0	0	0
2	23	25(22%)	15	3	4	2	1
3 Non manual	40	41(36%)	6	10	16	8	1
3 Man- ual	10	16(14%)	3	1	6	6	0
4	5	7(6%)	0	0	5	2	0
5	23	24(21%)	1	1	11	8	3
Total	102	115	26	16	42	26	5

Notes   *Women have been classified by their positions in the labour-market; where these are not known or they are students or houseworkers, they have been classified by their husband's work, or (where single) their father's work. The Registrar-General's categories of (paid) work are used.*

popular women writers, appeared to have been much more selective, for only four out of the thirty-nine who answered this question were unable to give the names of disapproved writers.

The formulaic romance group

This group was distinguished from others by their degree of unqualified commitment to romantic love stories as a genre. They all replied in the affirmative when asked whether they liked either Mills and Boon or romantic love stories. However, even these readers parodied a type of sentimental story which they considered only suitable for young girls, using terms like 'lovey dovey' or 'mushy' to indicate their disgust. As we shall see, many of these women stressed their preference for *fiction* and, in particular, for a novel world constructed around idealised principles. The romantic fiction category wanted stories that were moulded closely to their fantasy needs rather than to the realist depiction of specific social types. They consciously linked romance reading to the harrowing or enervating experiences they had had during the day: reading at night was an equivalent to a strong drink. Given this overwhelming need for relief through fantasy it is not surprising that this group was less selective about their reading; their intense commitment was to romance as a genre rather than to distinctive creative writers. This has led in at least one library in the West of Scotland to the development of an elaborate hieroglyphics amongst the readers. In order to eliminate the undesirable potential for re-reading, each reader resorted to her own mark – a flower, initials, etc. under the lending slip, as a permanent tally of her use.

Class and reading preference: the class origins and destiny of each reading group

To what extent are the cultural groups class-determined? Or, to put it in Bourdieu's terms, how far are we witnessing one part of a transformation process in which economic capital is converted into cultural capital, later to be converted back into economic capital in the form of educational credentials for high-income job advancement? Working with the imperfect Registrar-General's occupational codes for class, both expected and unexpected relationships emerge. As might be anticipated, a major gulf in the women's occupations existed as between the romantic fiction group at one pole and the legitimate culture group at the other, the former possessing a higher class position than that of the popular culture groups and the middlebrow being closer to the higher class positions of the legitimate culture group. The 'Cookson' or non-formulaic romance category, together with the tiny radical canon, were constituted partly by the cleaners and factory workers who dominated the formulaic romance group, partly by a greater proportion of clerical workers, sales workers and primary school teachers. These groupings were reproduced constantly in response to my questions, suggesting that beneath the shifting and brilliant kaleidoscope of individual attitudes were stable and deep-rooted differences in social experience and world-views. The association between relatively high class position and legitimate culture on the one hand and low class position and formulaic fictional choice on the other hand seems to suggest that Bourdieu is correct to argue that the real determinate basis for culture is the closeness or distance from material necessity, or from the urgent practical matters of everyday life.

However, the matter is not quite as simple as it first appears. Within this legitimate culture group were women who have or have had working-class jobs and who left school at the earliest opportunity, women who lacked the educational achievements and class comforts normally associated with the enjoyment of legitimate works. For example, an elderly print worker talked of her voracious reading of Russian classic novels and a Marks and Spencer sales assistant in her late fifties, as the mother of nine commented that she had always had romantic fiction banned from her house. Her own reading was nineteenth-century English and Russian novels, particularly those recommended in her sons' booklists as they trained to be teachers. The disparate social locations of a *minority* of individuals with legitimate culture needs to be acknowledged, although overall the pattern is the predictable one.

The romantic fiction group was composed of the greatest number of women from semi- and unskilled labour (classes 4 and 5) and only two lower professionals, nurses, whose categorisation in these instances as class 2 was less a mark of great professional expertise than the outcome of poor coding rules. As many as 48 per cent of the romantic fiction group appear formally to be 'non-manual' because of their preponderance in shop assistant and secretarial work, however only one-fifth of their husbands were in non-manual jobs. As far as could be judged from the interviews, their identities were working class. There is a stark difference between these women and those of the legitimate culture group, with one member in class 1, fourteen of their members in class 2, 91 per cent in the non-manual categories and with 78 per cent of their partners similarly non-manual. Of the women with legitimate culture 15 or 58 per cent had higher education but only four (15 per cent) of the next closest group possessing middlebrow or petty-bourgeois taste, and none of the popular culture groupings.

In general the Scottish study replicates Bourdieu's findings that class plays a key role in creating the disposition or 'habitus' in which to master legitimate literature. Class positions distributed the decision of the *arena* within which to read, the propensity to return to literature for education as against immediate entertainment, the delight in fantasy.[20] Put another way, class determined the nature of the social contract of readers with writers. To a lesser extent, their material distance from privation also influenced their hostility to romantic fiction. Indeed, as more women remain in the labour market, I would expect this class cleavage to increase. The community of women at home, which was, in the nineteenth century, the social base of the patriarchal romance, will be progressively eroded. It is for these reasons that I am sceptical of Peter Mann's conclusions that formulaic romance reading is 'that much better than what might be called the "mass" taste' and that amongst its readers are 'a fair number of reasonably well-educated women'.[21] There is a diametrical difference of opinion between Mann and Bourdieu. As the empirical evidence for Mann's conclusion is distinctly weak, his study cannot pose a serious challenge to the alternative view that class is a major determinant of romance-reading.[22]

In one respect the Scottish legitimate culture group can be distinguished sharply from Bourdieu's similar French group; that is, in the character of their social class origins. In France, this group was from professional and large employer/top manager backgrounds: only in their case did the academic demands of the school possess an affinity with the aspirations, ideas and concepts of their parents. In Scotland, however, the origins of the twenty-six women with legitimate culture were more diverse, with ten having working-class backgrounds. Surprisingly, in this respect their origins were more diverse than that of the middlebrow women. Nor were the working-class fathers of the legitimate group all from the labour aristocracy – they included a porter, two labourers, two factory workers (unskilled), a forestry worker, a chauffeur and a boilermaker. Thus just under a half of the fathers of those with legitimate culture were non-manual workers, in comparison with the more comfortably placed two-thirds of fathers from the middlebrow-group fathers. The greatest contrast is, then, between the middlebrow and the romantic-fiction group, in which only two of the twenty-three fathers had non-manual jobs, or the radical canon group, in which only one of the five fathers was non-manual.

How are we to interpret the surprisingly diverse class origins of those with legitimate culture? One possible explanation would be that the results are an artificial consequence of differences in methodology rather than any real break in the circuit proposed by Bourdieu: 'economic capital produces cultural capital, which is transformed in turn into economic capital.' By selecting questions referring to literature rather than photography and painting, and by reliance on the claims to knowledge rather than tests of knowledge, my results may have expanded the category of sophisticated readers beyond the number that would have been yielded by the French approach. It is also true that my respondents were gathered more from the dominated fraction of the dominant class, that is, because of their gender and the disproportionately few older women in this group, they were in a relatively low position on the professional or administrative career ladders. This is matched by their tendency to prefer recent writers, valued for charting areas of experience hitherto unexplored in literature.

A more likely explanation, in my view, is that the transformation of economic capital into legitimate culture is not such a simple mechanism of conversion as Bourdieu's theory suggests. In other words, to amend his image of 'the aristocracy' of taste, in Scotland, at least, there is also a *nouveau riche* cultural group whose possession of legitimate culture derives entirely from school. The growth of this class fraction corresponds to the specific conjuncture of post-war late capitalism until about 1973. The increase in these lower-class recruits to middle-class positions represents a variation of the 'general law of capital accumulation', which in periods of capital expansion allows a thrusting, upwardly mobile fragment of the working class to enter the milieu of the employers. In this case, the expansion of the middle class can be viewed as a result of the state's expansion of the welfare sector, as well as the growth of private services.[23] This is a political mechanism permitting the stabilisation of the dominant class: a counter-tendency to the process of the economic destruction of the bourgeoisie.[24]

What we are witnessing in this educational rise of the daughters of working-class men and women is a growth of the intermediate stratum. This stratum, cut off from the immense economic power and wealth of the bourgeoisie, has nevertheless acquired a level of economic comfort and security lacked by their parents.

This has been called the development of the 'new services' occupations, classified as class 2, and requiring educational credentials for entry. If this is right, then Bourdieu has over-simplified the nature and effect of the 'symbolic violence' he claims is employed in school by the denial of working-class culture. Social mobility is mentioned in the French study only briefly, and then only in the context of the inflation of educational credentials, explained as part of the strategy of the dominant class.[25] My research supports findings suggesting that, in situations of high employment, some working-class children find their desire to learn and the availability of good jobs triumphs over any disillusionment. Furthermore, the strong Scottish meritocratic ethos in the education system introduces a countervailing element to the conservative cultural trend of secondary school education, which serves the reproduction of social inequality. It thus operates so as to permit a *small* stream of lower-class children up the academic escalator.

How is this possible? Two cases can illustrate the trajectories involved. Thus one of the legitimate culture women, a young community worker of Irish descent, the daughter of an unemployed labourer, said that she attributed her 'reasonably successful' career to the Irish emphasis on education, which was particularly marked in her own family. Other factors had also aided her mobility: the absence of brothers, the consequent channelling of family resources to her sisters and herself; attendance at a single-sex Catholic school intent on training 'young ladies' and – perhaps most important – the

temporary suspension in the early 1970s of her father's fatalism
about the future, owing to his experience of constant work. In such
circumstances, too, intellectual improvement and the creation of a
new educated 'elite' lost their earlier negative connotations for the
local working class, normally fearful of any forces disruptive of
group solidarity.

Each individual's trajectory no doubt varies. Another young
woman, a secondary teacher of English, had come from a family in
which improvement of life chances had occurred in two phases.
First, her father had moved from manual work to a union official's
job and secondly she herself had been upwardly mobile through the
use of educational credentials.

Finally, a small group of women had been forced to leave school
at the lowest legal age to contribute to family income, but had
developed a preference for the serious novels of legitimate culture
rather than formulaic fiction. Such women had acquired an inner
confidence about their own intelligence, confirmed by requests from
their teachers to stay on, but had been blocked by their position in
the class structure. They later developed their own education when
they had sufficient leisure opportunities. The Marks and Spencer's
shop assistant, referred to earlier, was interviewed when she was re-
reading Dostoevsky's *The Idiot*. She commented:

> If I'm going learn something from it then I'll try it. Some
> people are not interested in learning – that doesn't mean to
> say they are stupid, but they just want something to relieve
> the drabness and give a wee bit of pleasure for an hour or
> two.'

Her husband had started at 14 as an apprentice joiner and was now a
construction manager in a firm operating on large contracts. They
had, she said, always wanted to 'better' themselves, materially and
through education.

> We've always had lots of books in the house. Do you
> remember the stalls in the Barrows where you could get
> poetry books for sixpence or a shilling? When we didn't have
> more than twopence we used to spend it on books. My
> husband and I were one-offs. How did we get this idea?
> There was something in the individual that wanted this
> education. Also, looking back I can remember thinking 'some
> day I'll get to the other side of that railway wall!' I left school
> at twelve and started out as a labourer in a biscuit factory,

later I became a dressmaker. I had eleven children, nine lived, and as they got older they used to bring their books in and we'd discuss them. It's difficult to keep on reading as you're learning your children, but later Frank, who was training to be a teacher, introduced me to Russian novels. . . .[26]

Another four women had also become 'autodidacts'. These respondents had been strongly influenced by the labour movement in which they or their families had been closely involved. One representative of this category is a shorthand-typist, an ex-shop assistant, now serving on a Family Panel, whose husband moved from skilled working class to management work. Her reading was sparked off by her socialist grandfather, who challenged her Catholic cosmology with his Darwinian views on evolution, and by her husband, who was thrown out of his family home for atheism. A major influence on their lives was their local Communist party branch in the 1940s. She commented wryly:

I'm getting into poetry gradually – Sappho for example. I've read Homer's *Odyssey* twice, I like Greek myths, Robert Graves's *I Claudius*. . . . I'm very fond of Shakespeare, and of some modern writers, Graham Greene and George Orwell, for example. I like to re-read several times to absorb the critical views of the writers.

A lab technician had a father who was a strong ILP man, and the solitary ferryman on the Finnieston ferry. He introduced her to the anarchist theory of Guy Aldred and to the novels of Upton Sinclair, Jack London, Howard Spring, Howard Fast, Robert Tressell, Ethel Mannin and Grassic Gibbon. This was her way in to the wide range of writers she currently reads, including Jane Austen, Simone de Beauvoir, Guy McCrone and Marge Piercy.

Another ex-shop assistant who became a manageress, had her intellectual development fostered by both her own family and by her husband. The education of women had been important for her parents, her grandmother having attended the classes of John MacLean, the Scottish socialist and teacher of political economy, who died from his treatment in jail as a conscientious objector in the First World War. She herself regards '*all* books [as] a form of escapism for everyone' but would never use romantic fiction such as Mills and Boon:

I agree that's what the reader wants but it's got nothing to do

> with my image of life. . . . They are just pure fantasy . . .
> which gives them a sense that life would be wonderful for
> them . . . you pick up such books and gain nothing from
> them.

She feeds her own desire for 'enlightenment' from the news and her
reading, although she added 'I don't think stories give you hope . . .
I don't think anything gives you hope.'

Five of the six 'autodidacts' interviewed had been influenced
strongly by the various radical traditions inherited within their
families, to the service of which these women actively place their
energies. None of them, in addition, had known great poverty. A
generation gap is obvious: those who went to school before the
Second World War valued education and felt that class, or, more
strongly, social injustice, had deprived them of further schooling;
younger women had to overcome working-class anti-intellec-
tualism. While the latter had initially protected them from
internalising the modern 'bourgeois' or dominant class view
equating personal worth with academic achievement, these particular people had also been exposed to countervailing perspectives.
Chief among these were the immigrant's respect for literacy, or the
radical slogan 'knowledge is power'. Through these routes the
young women could maintain their distance from the anti-
educational elements of the peer group.

The romantic fiction readers lack both knowledge of high culture
and economic capital. Class and the dependency of women are
linked together in the romantic fiction category but within two
sharply defined subgroups in which the act of reading has different
meanings. The first group of women could be said to exist on a
precarious cliff in which they are constantly threatened with the
removal of the attributes of individualism (such as the right to
financial decision-making and to independence of movement), or to
be thrown into a pit of servility and insecurity. More than any other
group of women they were dogged by crises: the sudden deaths in
their forties and fifties of their husbands, nervous breakdown lasting
for years at a time, traumatic marriages in which they were the
victims of battering, absentee husbands, long-term unemployment.
They were additionally exposed, as women, to charges of
intellectual inferiority. If not physically vulnerable, then, they lacked
confidence: their conversation was punctuated by self-criticisms of
stupidity or ignorance. As I shall show, these women represented a
particularly privatised group, cut off from involvement in public
political issues and unable to see a solution to their grievances. Such

grievances seemed all the more hopeless from their experience of the sacrifices made by their men in working-class employment. Acutely aware of poverty, the greatest number were nevertheless limited in their capacity to understand the class structure by the coexistence of fatalism with an individualist vision of society. Representative individuals can be chosen to illustrate these points.

A cook who had been unemployed for several years was an avid reader of Mills and Boon, as well as of Agatha Christie. She was medically unfit for work and looked much older than her 31 years. Heart failures resulting from constitutional weakness had allowed her husband to gain the legal custody of her children after divorce. 'I have a friend', she said, 'who has 296 Mills and Boon and she passes them on to me. My friend was thinking of setting up a second-hand bookshop. All Mills and Boon are good but each is completely different from the others. . . . I tried *War and Peace* once, but shut it half-way through – oh my goodness. I couldnae understand it.' She also produced one of the clearest statements I was given of the wrongs of women: 'We should have better jobs for women. They should have better pay and the right to speak; women are often just told to "shut up".'

A girl of 19, the daughter of a migrant Asian market trader, had been unemployed since leaving school three years ago. She oscillated between anorexic self-punishment and blithe optimism that she was 'on the road to success' and would soon acquire the good clerical job for which her commercial skills qualified her. The alternative to unemployment was the familiar sales work within the shops of the Indian community, where pay was £50 for as much as seven days' work a week. She read Mills and Boon and Enid Blyton, recalling that *Fiddler on the Roof* had been the one book that had made an impact on her. 'Mills and Boon is just to relax your mind, a pastime . . . the truth is covered up in almost any book I've read.'

An ex-nurse, Jane Bishop, who had left school at 15, commented: 'I'm not very bright.' One of the two lower professionals in this group, she recently separated from her husband, an optician, after a long and unhappy marriage. She is now in her early forties.

I wasn't allowed any friends – I think I would have had more liberty in jail than with my husband. I was a nurse before I married but there were pressures on me not to take a job although we had no children. I couldn't have a job because we moved around. He just wanted someone to cook and clean and run after him: a second mother, not a wife! I've settled down since I left him (I was down to six stone). The doctors said I wasn't fit to work and might not be able to cope even with the Refuge [Women's Aid Refuge]): now it's my name on the rent book and on the front door.

She read romances, especially when married '[maybe] it was to compensate for what I *wasn't* getting in the marriage.' She still enjoyed Mills and Boon, Silhouette and other romantic fiction, as well as 'mysteries' by P.D. James, Dick Francis and Frederick Forsyth. Reading mainly in bed at night, Jane preferred a formulaic novel with a happy ending: 'unhappy endings don't make me sleepy.'

In sharp contrast, another group of formulaic romance readers were working women, with husbands in skilled or lower managerial jobs, who felt their lives to be well under control. These women had low occupational aspirations, stable jobs, a strong family consciousness and happy marriages: although not without their problems, the desire for more *freedom* was alien to them. They were also better off financially than their parents and economically secure; experiences which perhaps prompted them to define British society as free from deep-rooted conflicts of interest. Within this perspective, romantic fiction was valued both for its epic qualities and for its reassertion of their assumptions of how things 'ought to be'. The hero represented a positive, exemplary figure, a modern counterpart of the idealised nobleman of feudal epics. Reading the romance had a redemptive effect not dissimilar to the ritual of daily prayers. These women were not looking for art but for the fiction embodying community values, or a version of them.[27] This group is typified in the person of Jeanette Mason whose portrait appears in the Appendix.

Some of the multiple deprivations found in the first romantic fiction category similarly affected the 'Cookson' group or the non-formulaic romance readers, to be offset by a stronger *culture of resistance* in their own families. Thus experiences of material and family crises had pushed these women, too, into depression and nervous breakdown on occasion, leading them into the spasmodic search for the immediate magical escapes bestowed by romance or thrillers. At other periods, their suffering receded, allowing them a greater freedom. One objective, then, was to develop their understanding of the world through reading novels. Whereas the genre romantic fiction readers, looking back from old age, would stress the hard lives they have had, for these women the intermittent character of money worries or ill health gave them, in their more stable periods, the material and psychological basis to explore ideas

– for instance the history of Glasgow (as in the novels of Jan Webster), Cornish tin mining via Susan Howatch, the Irish potato famine through the stories of E.V. Thompson. Even here, however, there was a positive evaluation of fantasy escapes, as in the much greater tolerance of happy endings, or 'not too much reality' as one reader put it. It becomes clear now what sustains Cookson's recipe of demystification plus fairy-tale ending. It is the uneasy coexistence of a desire for knowledge as well as the more sharply felt search for oblivion, the latter requiring a pursuit of illusion to rekindle the flames of hope. In contrast, the greater secularisation of thought and the more comfortable material lives of the legitimate culture group endowed them with sufficient psychological reserves to accept realism, even cast in those modernist forms dominated by angst and despair. Of course, all fiction offers a *form* of enjoyable escape by educating the reader about a world which is not his or her own, but the vast majority of readers of modern best-selling women's fiction disliked realism unembellished by any of the traditional figures of hope. In contrast, a majority of middle-class women with legitimate culture said they could face depressing novels even if they were themselves depressed. I am suggesting, then, that class shapes the pattern of needs to be satisfied in the personal leisure/pleasure economy so that the search for magical escapes via fantasy is more often found in the most exploited or oppressed groups.

There is a paradox here that I have found throughout these interviews: those with the worst lives, who were most in need of the knowledge conveyed in literature, were least likely to have access to it. Those with the most comfortable lives enjoyed the insights of realism needed by others.

If class has this vital role I am attributing to it in determining the taste for types of fiction, what of the largely working-class readership for the radical canon? Such women turn to socialist literature in general and working-class novels in particular. These are, of course, realist works and thus include a bleak analysis of deprivation, mass cyclical unemployment and the resort to fascism. However, they also developed from the problematic hero of middle-class novels a collective, positive hero (the working class itself) which is the embodiment of their hopes for human transformation and whose leadership expresses the utopian potential for rational control. The readers of the radical canon rejected the nihilist assumptions informing much literary modernism, arguing instead for a less atomistic conception of society. Still imbued with the conclusion that humans can intervene to shape history, the novels they read were underpinned by the same world-views and hopes.

Thus the pessimistic gaze of realism was balanced for them by awareness of alternative possibilities, the individualistic fantasy of the romance replaced by the active role of the dominated class.

Take, for example, Marion Munro, 59, whose first job at 14 was in a chemist's shop. There she was influenced by an older man who told her 'remember: *use* your vote', instructed her on health and gave her books to read. 'Being at work I began to read and that became my university.' Later she became a machine operator at Rolls Royce and tells (with ironic tones) of how she had to argue for improved wages for the skilled women workers by comparing them with a group of unskilled male floor-sweepers! At this time, she participated in the production of a woman shop steward's play, which was taken to the local Palace of Arts in Glasgow and shown to 'all the workers'. Recently she had become interested in Indian philosophy and Green issues, although still an active socialist. She liked 'stories about the working class, especially by Zola – it sounded awfully cruel but it was a cruel hard world. *Germinal* [the account of a nine months' long miners' strike in France ending in defeat] is a particular favourite, also Lewis Grassic Gibbon . . . if you have time!'

Another member of this group (NUM canteen manageress, ex-sample) said, 'I was born a trade unionist!' She especially liked Tressell's *The Ragged Trousered Philanthropists*: 'That novel always confirms you in your socialism. I read books when I'm feeling depressed to remember how much people had to suffer to gain our basic rights, even going to jail. That gives me a boost.' She found Cookson and romantic fiction 'too repetitive'.

The middlebrow group had fewer educational achievements and lower occupational positions than the legitimate culture group, although their social origins were more often middle class.[28] They had no aspirations to what they termed 'highbrow taste', but they carefully distinguished their preferences from the profane enjoyment of Mills and Boon and other romantic fiction writers. A typical comment was made by a single woman of 58 who was an export checker on the shop-floor of Collins's publishing house: '*Pride and Prejudice* is a brilliant book. I'm trying to get my nieces onto the classics – don't start reading Mills and Boon!' However, although she liked *War and Peace* she comments that 'if I can't get in after two pages then I get rid of them!'. She enjoys cowboy stories and historical fiction as well as the nineteenth-century 'classics', although more detailed enquiry revealed she had read none of the works of George Eliot or Thomas Hardy. Clearly, for her, novels also serve important wish-fulfilment functions: 'I like some that start at the bottom and struggles – or maybe a doctor doing something brilliant I'd like to do . . . but I like something down to earth as well.'

It is useful to distinguish subgroups within the middlebrow category. Many women perceived literary culture as an area of timeless, universal, human values to be appreciated rather as nature might be enjoyed in a reserve within an urban industrial region. 'Culture' here has connotations of a *refuge* from actual life rather than as a shock to preconceptions.[29] Jane Smith typified these attitudes. She alternated between horror stories and the works of John Galsworthy, John Masefield and other representatives of the traditional English intelligentsia, whose writings valorise imperialism, elitism and old money. Another respondent, Marjorie Lindsay, was also peculiarly consistent in her use of culture as a retreat from modernity, apparent in both her impassioned defence of the traditional regulation of sexuality in fiction and the importance of an uncorrupted, purified language. Her perception was shaped by a sense of social and cultural decline from a more healthily religious epoch.

An assistant librarian showed another pattern of the middlebrow group, a sense of awe and respect towards Literature coupled with an immediate delight in older romantic fiction or readable biographies of bohemian artists: 'If you've read a lot of the classical novels, you demand more – many modern novels are just ephemeral. They must come up to a standard of plot or they don't involve me – for example *The Agony and the Ecstasy* does do this.' Her uses of literacy have to be linked also to her wider world-view, which was shaped by the experiences of an upwardly mobile father. Identifying with her father, this middle-aged woman exuded contempt for local working-class trade unionism, voicing instead a commitment to the market and to a rigorous work ethic. Moreover, in her case the oscillation between striving for 'culture' and enjoying spontaneously the pleasures of romantic fiction were linked to her tremendous ascetic struggle to achieve education for the sake of a career.

Many non-manual members of this group distinguished themselves from 'highbrows', but also distanced themselves from the readers of mere pulp fiction by emphasising their enjoyment of the neo-medieval epics of writers such as Stephen Donaldson or of the thriller as a form. Thriller writers were sometimes spontaneously evaluated in ideological terms: 'I like Dashiell Hammett because he has a social conscience,' commented one secretary. Within the middlebrow circle was a subgroup of readers such as this woman who explicitly mentioned both lack of money and lack of time as

precluding serious reading. These respondents viewed such deprivations as channelling their energies away from otherwise desirable
objectives, one of which was the consumption of expensive new
books by feminist publishers.

READING, PLEASURES AND BELIEF

Bourdieu has described cultural stratification as creating variations in
the predispositions adopted towards literature and other arts.
Developing these in a different direction from Bourdieu, the
respondents' divergent needs for realism, fantasy and utopia were
explored by including a series of questions about their views of the
purpose of literature. Of course there are underlying motivations
which are difficult to establish through interviews and may not be
adequately represented here, for example the view that the
possession of culture characterises a spiritual elite and that such
knowledge cannot be distributed universally.[30] However, by asking
whether readers liked a formula, enjoyed an imaginary world or
desired a record of direct experience, I was seeking to uncover what
lay behind emotional reactions and heterogeneous fictional preferences, to haul into the light of consciousness the readers' latent
preconceptions. Unprepared as many of the women were for this
line of enquiry, their answers *did* reveal the same lines of fissure in
opinion observed on earlier matters.

The romantic fiction and the legitimate group were consistently
polarised. The legitimate group searched in literature for the
underlying truth about people, and about their own society in
particular. A member of this group, a music teacher, threw out a
surprising comment which illustrated this: 'My son is much more
interested in football than in reading any books. I think you find out
so much about people from novels. I would rather he never played
an instrument than that he gave up reading.'

For the romantic fiction group, conversely, literature had the
status of *story-telling*. Their novels were clearly perceived as 'fiction',
an illusory reality still associated with the child-like pleasure of
simple forms. For its fans, the traditional romance had the status of
mythology, divorced from their experience of late capitalism. Thus
the shell of fairy-tale form was still intact and preserved the charm
of wish fulfilment, while the duty of representation of reality was
conferred uniquely on television and newspapers.[31] It is true that the

Table 6.3 Attitudes to literature

	Legitimate	M'brow	Reading group 'Cookson'	Romantic	Radical	Total
Like to read novels about 'how things really are'?						
Yes	24(93%)	8(50%)	28(67%)	8(31%)	5(100%)	73(63%)
Sometimes, also likes fantasy	2(8%)	1(6%)	1(2%)	0	0	4(3%)
No	0	5(31%)	9(21%)	15(58%)	0	29(25%)
No answer	0	2(13%)	4(10%)	3(12%)	0	9(8%)
						115
Reasons for reading						
Interest in critical ideas of writer[1]	15(56%)	5(31%)	12(29%)	0	3(60%)	35(30%)
Distraction or pleasure[2]	0	1(6%)	4(10%)	10(38%)	0	15(13%)
Distraction or pleasure[3]	9(35%)	7(44%)	15(36%)	7(27%)	1(20%)	39(34%)
Interest in a record of lived experience[1]	16(62%)	7(44%)	28(67%)	9(35%)	4(80%)	64(56%)
Interest in an imaginary world of harmony[1]	9(35%)	5(31%)	7(17%)	9(35%)	1(20%)	31(17%)
						184
Enjoyment of a formula in romantic novels and family sagas						
Pleasure in a formula	0	4(25%)	16(38%)	20(77%)	0	40(35%)
Dislike of a formula	23(88%)	9(56%)	17(40%)	3(12%)	5(100)	57(50%)
Structure important, *not* romantic formula/other	2(8%)	1(6%)	3(7%)	0	0	6(5%)
No answer	1(4%)	2(13%)	6(14%)	3(12%)	0	12(10%)
						115

Notes
1 *Either sole reason stated or given with other reasons.*
2 *Sole reason.*
3 *Combined with other reasons.*

romantic fiction group were still prone to make deprecating comments: 'That's too far-fetched,' which shared some qualities of the legitimate distaste for unrealistic fantasy. Yet their primary investment was in fiction as a technology of 'coping'. Between these two groups, with their incompatible choices of realism and fantasy, the other readers lived out various intermediary positions.

I asked the question: 'Do you like books or stories about how things really are?', an enquiry which purposely left ambiguous the definition of reality. The legitimate group all replied affirmatively. Despite the powerful norm of realism in literary theory (or perhaps unaware of it), the majority of romantic fiction readers did not want realism (58 per cent; 15). Such a response emerged clearly in the interview with a retired cook, who joked about her constant reading ('I shall die with a book in my hands!'). She wanted her novels to be light, 'entertaining' stories, instancing the writing of Victoria Holt, Jeffrey Archer and Sydney Sheldon. Similarly, another romantic fiction reader declared innocently: 'I prefer to think about happy things.'

Interestingly, the 'Cookson' group was much closer to the legitimate public on this question, with 67 per cent (28) turning to the novels for realism. The greater retreatism of the middlebrow group was mirrored in their *lesser* preference for 'things as they really are' in comparison with the 'Cookson' readership (50 per cent versus 67 per cent). Unsurprisingly, the radical canon group were all champions of a realist aesthetic.

The romantic fiction readers did not mistake their best-selling formula fiction for realism. Very few were 'cultural dopes'. Only eight readers, a small fraction of this group, said that the romantic novels or *People's Friend* fiction that they enjoyed revealed images of social reality. These particular women demonstrated both profound conservatism and patriarchal preconceptions: their everyday discourse harmonised with the fictional discourse of much romance.

When asked if they would like to read more stories about ordinary people and their problems, such as unemployment or housing, the same stark polarisation emerged, with 70 per cent (19) of the legitimate group reacting positively.[32] Only half of the romantic fiction group said this would appeal to them, while almost as many, eleven, turned their backs on realism. A typical negative reply stated a reluctance to read a novel for 'what you can find in newspapers' or a more deep-rooted aversion to representations of conflict or alienation.

This can also be linked to the enjoyment of a formulaic structure, a concept which had to be explained to many readers. While it is commonplace for critics to differentiate between 'serious' and genre fiction, in which the latter are distinguished in terms of uniform narrative or ideological structures, other readers' reactions to formulaic devices have not been mapped clearly.[33] I asked: 'Do you like books to be written to a formula? This may include a good twist at the end. For example, a heroine is introduced, has plenty of adventures and ends up getting her man.'

None of the legitimate group enjoyed the romantic formula. Indeed, twenty-three (85 per cent) actively disliked it, for the question often elicited a nauseated disgust. Yet the romantic fiction readers reversed this, twenty, or 77 per cent, linking their pleasure to such a mythic narrative structure and the play of stereotypes. As on other issues, the 'Cookson' group straddled the two camps evenly, while middlebrow taste was closer to the negative recoil of those with legitimate culture. The middlebrow response was summed up by a primary teacher: 'I love the Brontës, Jane Austen and the classics, but I usually read modern writers. I had read about six Cooksons and six Wilbur Smiths, but after that I had worked out their formula. I gave them up because they were too predictable.' Interestingly, the positive thriller formula was much more acceptable than the romantic formula, especially in the latter two groups.

Implicit in the formulaic structure are certain conceptions of heroism. Leading male protagonists are overwhelmingly either gentry, businessmen or professionals. Readers were asked whether the publishers' view that this is what they wanted was accurate. Again, reactions varied according to the readership group. Twenty of the romantic fiction group preferred such heroes and only one disliked them. On the other hand, the legitimate group responded much more negatively: ten disliked such heroes and only four liked them.[34] Asked whether 'ordinary people' could be heroes, the same constellation of group responses emerged, with a majority of romantic fiction readers stating that they *disliked* such heroes (nine against; seven for), whereas all the legitimate group answered affirmatively.

This matter is less trivial than it first appears. Although the romance can be interpreted as a parable of unalienated society, it is instructive that so many of the lower-class readers of popular fiction could accept only members of the dominant class as candidates for idealisation. Implicitly, this suggests that the good fortune of such heroes is deserved. This assumption is part of the architecture of conservative fantasy, although precisely how such fantasies and images effect political actions is a notoriously complex question.

Do readers like happy outcomes? Predictably, the kaleidoscope of opinion crystallised into similar patterns in answer to this question. Only one of the twenty-six legitimate readers and ten (24 per cent) of the 'Cookson' readers answered affirmatively, in comparison with fourteen (53 per cent) of the romantic fiction group. If Kermode is right in regarding the happy ending of the Victorian novel as a sign of trust in the social order or a belief in progress, the readership for formulaic fiction still retained such social optimism.[35] Their preferred genre displayed recycled elements of the Victorian novel. Such readers were distanced from the pessimism of many forms of modernism.

Finally, my respondents were given four possible rationales for reading fiction and were asked to consider how many described their own motives. The proffered reasons were: 'distraction and pleasure from reading', interest in 'a record of lived experience', pleasure in 'an imagined world of harmony with a happy ending' and a concern for 'the critical ideas of the writers'. This question acted as an accurate barometer of all the 'cultural indications' elicited by earlier questions. Once again, the predilection of the formulaic fiction group was for novels as distraction or pleasure. *They could not conceive of an interest in the critical ideas of writers.* Yet as many as fifteen (56 per cent) of the legitimate group chose this as at least one of the reasons why they read, along with a smaller proportion (12 or 28 per cent) of the 'Cookson' group. Other women, from the various popular culture groups, made disarmingly self-deprecating comments about their capacity to understand critical ideas: 'Interest in the writers' critical ideas? Oh no, that's far beyond me!' (secretary, 40–60, 'Cookson' group.)

It is possible that popular readers might have enjoyed social criticism without recognising it in these terms: telling against this interpretation, however, was the fact that even interest in literature as a record of lived experience seemed to vary. Only nine of the twenty-six romantic-fiction readers mentioned a concern for fiction which embodied such experience. For the legitimate, 'Cookson' and radical groups, however, this was a key role for novelists – and was related to their perception that they could write a novel about their *own* personal experiences. Indeed, these readers responded positively and with great warmth to this account of their reasons for reading. In contrast such an interest in realism was not viewed as important by the middlebrow readers, many of whom self-consciously pursued 'fictions': only a minority of this group had any commitment to the representation of lived experience.

In conclusion, while bearing in mind all Brecht wrote about drama for pleasure as the means of extending people's ideas, interviews do bear out the momentous significance of the disposition towards 'instruction' or serious art, rather than 'entertainment'.

For 30 per cent of the readers – the proportion sharply varying in the different reader groups – the role of the writer as bearing witness to the truth and acting as a critical, dissident or even prophetic figure, is unknown or devalued. In addition, the novel as a form in which experience can be encoded for a contemporary or later public is unimportant for large numbers of popular readers. Thus for many of the working-class and middle-class women who are members of the world of best-selling fiction, the ideological universe is closely stitched up and unified. Such readers must bear any discontents they have as individual deprivations, shared at most with others in their immediate communities. They remain unaware of a tradition of opposition or dissent in literature. As I shall show, too, the majority remain in ignorance of the historical moments when working-class resistance and demands for popular rights have been most concerted and formidable.

What were the other defences of escapism made by readers of romantic fiction? This section aims to recover and clarify the meanings of romantic fiction in the perspectives of its readers. The needs of popular readers for imaginary alternatives to their present narrow and unsatisfactory lives led to a temporary refuge in the world as a magical garden. The belief in miracles may have lost its revealed, theologically ratified basis but human needs produce brief suspensions of disenchantment. Such miraculous subversions of social laws can produce outcomes embodying the suppressed hopes of daily existence, an elaborated sigh of 'If only. . .'.

First, then, a number of women referred to the vicarious sexual pleasures of the romance. An elderly cleaner listened tolerantly while other women around her criticised the genre: 'Well' she said, producing a large pile of Mills and Boon novels, 'when I go off to my bed alone, I like to take these with me!'. An unemployed girl of 19, of Indian origin, qualified her commitment to the Mills and Boon genre by saying 'Yes, I do like them, but you never read them when you've got a man of your own.'

Publishers of formulaic fiction issue precise instruction to writers on their representations of sexuality, some colour-coding their products so the consumer can tell immediately the degree of eroticism promised.[36] *Aficionados* pointed with irony to the recent narrative strategies used to permit the liberalisation of the genre, yet also to the rapid sating of the public for 'bodice-rippers'. Romantic fiction, to use Roland Barthes' terms, provides pleasure rather than bliss, that is to say, its images of desire must succumb to social regulation.[37] However, even within this genre, the emerging diversity of formulae reveals shifts in need between different categories of women, as for example, houseworkers and paid workers, older and younger generations.

Secondly, the magazines and romances provided fantasies of power and plenty. Within these fantasies, the wishful images of sexually attractive heroes are to be unadulterated by alien traces of mundane reality. One of the romantic fiction group, Margaret MacKenzie, also a cleaner, had been through a disastrous period of physical assault from her first husband, an alcoholic who parcelled out his life between home and jail. Her comments on magazine romance in which a young girl marries an *impecunious* fruit farmer revealed her conception of a proper hero: 'You can't have a hero who is a fruit farmer! He should be someone like a millionaire businessman and the heroine should be his secretary.' This emphasis on the material plenitude summoned up by the proper ending of a romantic story was sharply at variance with the attention to non-material issues in much minority cultural criticism of the bourgeois epoch.

The association of the hero with the status conceptions of the dominant class was also made crystal clear by Jill Wheelwright. She belonged to the 'Cookson' group and enjoyed detective stories and horror stories, while her favourite writers included Victoria Holt, Colleen McCullough, Susan Howatch and John Masefield:

> I enjoy . . . not too much reality. I accept that it's not real but I can get enough reality in everyday life. I like to enjoy what I read because there's enough that's depressing. I accept that the lowly shepherd is just as much a gentleman as the great man in his castle but that doesn't mean that I want to read about him.

A houseworker of 50, Jill is the wife of a dispatch clerk and the daughter of a policeman. She expressed great distaste for realist works, such as Joan Lingard's children's novels about the Northern Irish troubles.

Another woman spoke spontaneously of the attractions of a temporary release from the hard grind of housework, stressing the dream-like quality of the romance:

> As you get older you get more mellow. I can see it's awful nice to read a book where everything in the garden is rosy and everything just goes according to plan. Maybe for people without a job and in with children, it's a case of transference:

if you've got a low income and it's difficult to get an adequate diet . . . it takes you away from that planning out and managing you have to do – it's lovely to read about the sunny lands of Australia and up pops this wonderful man . . . it's like the women in my mother's day who went and wept over Errol Flynn – they forgot they had done a whole load of washing that day, in the outside wash house and the big stone boiler, with the whole thing ready for ironing later on. It was a wee bit fantasy island, and I think most people realise it's only a picture and not really living [. . . .] You would read them on holiday, like Mills and Boon, you'd read them on a train . . . my mother read *People's Friend* and *Women's Weekly*, not the lurid type – *Secrets* and *True Confessions*. Those had women like a gypsy woman with her bosoms showing – that was a sin and a traitor against the state – that was just not on, you know![38]

Two aspects of this perception of the escape are significant. First, although distancing herself by alternating between her own perspective and generalisations about others, the older woman nevertheless attributes a degree of choice and self-awareness to the readers of romantic fiction. Second, she helps us see that internalised filters of repression continued to operate in the magical release of the magazine story, as Freud explained in the case of dreams. Within some forms of patriarchal control, women's sexuality is so profoundly suppressed that it cannot even be liberated in fantasy.

The importance of 'the imaginary world' was stressed once again by another reader with working-class roots, the daughter of an Irish labourer:

When people's lives are very hard and physically exhausting, that's when you want escapism most – that's when I want soap operas on TV. You can read about the wealthy son of a landowner, about the corruption of money and the care of children, these are universal issues. It doesn't matter how much money you've got as long as you're a *good person*, for example, people think they're better than J.R.. Romantic fiction is often the only use women have for their imaginations . . . their sexual lives may be a disappointment, they're hankering after an attractive man: it's important to them, but they're not allowed to talk about it.

This woman was a community worker of 28. She had rejected

romantic fiction in her teens as 'nonsense . . . very boring and poorly constructed. If I like any romantic fiction I'd probably call it something else'. Particularly enjoying Jane Austen, George Eliot, Dostoevsky, Doris Lessing, Barbara Pym and Simone de Beauvoir, she was classified as possessing legitimate taste.

The status of the upper-class hero has also to be grasped within the miracle of escapist fiction, as a cypher of success. Although shared by many, this opinion was expressed most pithily by a divorced working-class mother, a member of the romantic fiction group. She was asked whether the publishers were right in assuming people prefer rich businessmen and gentry heroes:

> The readers want winners. I suppose I do, too. Everyone loves a winner: it gives you a sense of contentment – you say, 'well, it was easy for them, so there's a chance for me!' I wouldn't mind reading about ordinary people, someone who's loved, popular: you can be a winner in that way, too.

She preferred historical fiction, and stressed that she was an 'unadventurous reader'. It was noteworthy, however, that she commented, somewhat inconsistently in this context: 'Farewell to Arms sticks in your mind.'

A research assistant with higher education stressed the aesthetic appeal of modern romantic genre products in terms of the suspense and ultimate reassurance created by the strong plot and good characterisation, within a known framework:

> They have a good storyline, it doesn't take long to read them and you don't have to stop and savour the language all the time . . . there is a pleasure in knowing the girl is going to survive, not get killed off and that she'll finally end up with her man. The interest is in what happens to her in between'. . . . 'You can definitely distinguish between sales and quality. For example, Barbara Cartland sells more than Catharine Cookson but Cookson is much better. The snobbery of professional women towards these novels makes me defensive about them, defensive for the women who read them, who aren't stupid and could read the Doris Lessings but wouldn't want to. . . . 'Literature' novels often disturb people because she's living in this great house and all she's doing is moaning. For people who've not got much materially this is intensely annoying and some who have got good lives nevertheless find it irritating.'

The use of novels for fantasy purposes was *not* restricted to those pre-political or conservative women already mentioned. Cynicism or disaffection about contemporary British society may nourish a turn to fiction for the expression of desire. A community worker was asked whether she enjoyed reading about 'how things really are'. She replied:

> How things really are? I know how things really are, the job tells me. I like something that takes you away to Tahiti or somewhere, away from routine. You can say, oh! that's nice – [but] you do get a bit fed up with the aristocracy and the gentry – it's nicer to get an ordinary man: to get a bit of realism. Kitchen maids ending up with the gentry, it just doesn't happen! It would be better to have Joe Bloggs, labourer. But most women want an escape, though.

In her forties, her husband a draughtsman in Yarrow shipyards, she was a full-time worker with the unemployed. Conducted among her clients, this interview was a stark reminder of the miseries of recession. She had supported Militant Tendency for the last few years and had been reading Tony Benn's *Arguments for Socialism* with approval. Yet simultaneously she commented on her pleasure in Jean Plaidy: 'Jean Plaidy makes history very interesting – she's the Queen's favourite author and what's good enough for the Queen is good enough for me!' This reader was a woman of paradoxes, not just as a socialist and a royalist but also as a Militant supporter who felt that she had a special gift of communication and was a committed member of her local spiritualist church. She commented at the end of her interview: 'There's too little caring in this world.' Her literary taste included early Catherine Cookson and Doris Lessing novels, Pearl White, Margaret Mitchell's *Gone With the Wind* and John Jakes' *North and South*. A member of the 'Cookson' group, pleasure in escapism united her with her political antagonists.

A minority of the romance reading group and many of the 'Cookson' category required a balance between realism and fantasy. They *actively* sought to use their reading to compensate for their own formal educational deficiencies. I became increasingly aware how many women stressed this element of learning through fiction in which the genre elements of happy ending and contrived plot developments became merely formal elements subordinated to the novels' representation of history. The ideological message of the novel was of crucial importance for this group. For such readers, romantic literature had been a mere transient stage of the life cycle, before they discovered a literature that was somewhat more critical and less dependent on myth. A Renfrew woman made this point clearly:'

> I like to read about social history, social change, the Renaissance of learning. . . I used to read about the trade union movements . . . I was shocked to find out from one book recently that it took almost a hundred years to reduce the working week to forty hours . . . I've also read novels: Alastair MacLean's novels about the 'black gold' – the oil, books about the Highland Clearances. One author I did like was A.J. Cronin, *The Citadel*. I also liked *All This and Heaven Too*, *Papa Married a Mormon*, *The Grapes of Wrath*: I think it was to learn about other countries. . . . Mills and Boon are pleasant but you don't learn anything: books should be of educational value, even if it's just to know about another country.[39]

A retired cleaner had catholic tastes but emphasised her pleasure in historical fiction:

> I like the classics, like *Wuthering Heights*. I like *A Woman of Substance* and Mazo de la Roche . . . but my preference is historical fiction. Catherine Cookson is very down to earth and her books are very good. It's all about life as it was . . . she's outright about everything she says.

Cookson was the doyenne of this school of writers, highly esteemed for their historical analysis, of which Emma Blair, Jessica Stirling, Margaret Thompson Davis, Helen Forrester and Jan Webster were representative figures. These readers stressed the need to grasp the humiliations of subordinated and totally powerless groups, so that historical repetition might become impossible. This was expressed graphically by Elizabeth Kelly, a supervisor in a fire-station:

> I prefer to read authors who write about the 'other end': not the royalty, but how the other classes lived. Agnes Short comes to mind, what she writes is based on fact, her stories are set in the 1400s. Let's face it, living conditions today are about a thousand per cent better than they were in Dickens' day and I am interested in why they have improved. For example, I like E.V. Thompson who writes on tin mines in

Cornwall and how the different factions of a family go on from working in the tin mines, how they have improved.

She discussed *The Spoiled Earth* by Jessica Stirling, part of the 'social democratic' genre of family saga:

> Mirren [the heroine] remains constant to the miners throughout. She manipulates him [the coal owner] without him being aware of it, so that he won't evict a family or act in other ways like that. Let's face it, it's about the mine owners getting mince on their table instead of steak, so as to care for other people.[40]

This legitimation of a capitalism which conforms to the values of brotherhood, compassion and altruism was a constant theme of the readers:

> I like to read family sagas on holidays: stories about the pioneers going to America, the Plymouth fathers; trade unions in America. They're light and trivial but not quite to the degree that Dr Kildare is. At least they tell you about the backstreets of New York! I also like historical biography and read the old classics again – George Eliot, Dickens, Jane Austen.

A primary school teacher whose father had been a baker, she reiterated the views of many Cookson readers in avoiding contemporary realism:

> I think I like something with a bit of a bite – not mere romance – for example politics – 'trouble at t'mill'. But I don't know that I do want more books on 'how things really are'. I sometimes feel I've got my head in the sand, but just as I get upset hearing about wee children abused so I don't want to think about it. That's why I prefer books about things as they *were* and not things as they *are*.

Many respondents made similar comments about their preference for historical novels. See, for example, the Collins's worker who said 'I tend to look for something that's actually happened rather than something that's going to happen – maybe the industrial revolution. I was never a reader until I read [Winston Graham's]

Poldark series and they are more lower class than what they have these days.'[41] This same pursuit of historical realism coupled with inner resistance to the analogous pursuit of contemporary realism was evident in an ex-teacher's enthusiastic preference for entertaining reading:

> I like hysterical romances! I like a happy ending and I like them to be historical, such as Valerie Fitzgerald's *Zemindar*, about the Lucknow seige. . . . what I feel is lacking in James Bond is the background. . . . if you take books like the *Poldark* series, I feel I'm learning something about Cornwall from that.[42]

Lastly, a Collins's export clerk revealed her repugnance towards modern writing, which was bleakly dismissed as 'kitchen sink novels'. Yet she too expressed a great desire to learn about the past: 'We live in frightening times. I want to get away into a different world . . . perhaps that's why I like the historical novel. I'm interested in another age, how they lived, their different values.'[43] Whether her appetite was for truth or for mythology masquerading as history, my interviews were too blunt an instrument to reveal.

RADICALISM AND FEMINISM

Several questions elicited the reader's degree of class consciousness or individualism. Two, in particular, were important because they served to polarise women in terms consistent with broad Left and Right divisions. The responses should not be translated into the different context of party support nor be used as gauges of active commitment.

The initial question asked respondents to choose between models of social inequality in Britain at present. Three images were offered as alternatives: first, that Britain is made up of two main classes such that the more power one class has, the less power the other has (the 'class conflict' image); secondly, that British society is composed of individuals with different amounts of money, or thirdly, that society is made up of groups with different amounts of status. Of those answering, 57 per cent opted for the 'class conflict' image. This was a surprisingly high number in the light of earlier studies of consciousness.[44]

Table 6.4 Reading preference and views on politics and feminism★

Reading group	Political radical	Elements of radicalism	Not radical	Feminist	Elements of feminism	Traditional views on women
Legitimate (26)	16(64%)	4(16%)	5(20%)	19(73%)	2(8%)	5(19%)
M'brow (16)	4(25%)	2(13%)	10(63%)	6(38%)	3(19%)	7(44%)
'Cookson' (42)	9(23%)	13(33%)	18(45%)	14(34%)	10(24%)	17(41%)
Romantic (26)	3(11%)	3(11%)	20(78%)	3(13%)	10(38%)	13(50%)
Radical (5)	4(80%)	1(20%)	0	4(100%)	0	0
Total	36(32%)	23(21%)	53(47%)	46(41%)	25(22%)	42(37%)

★ Numbers and percentages are slightly divergent from reading group totals due to unclassifiable responses.

Women were next asked whether top positions were awarded on the basis of merit: 'People say that anyone can get to the top if they have ability and work hard. Would you agree or disagree with this?' Fifty-seven per cent dissented from this claim, the remainder justifying their agreement by citing illustrative individual cases of social mobility. Such individuals are not hard to find, especially, in Scotland where 36 per cent of the service class (class 1) had fathers who were working-class in comparison with 16 per cent in England. Nevertheless, the pessimism of the majority was better supported by recent research, which showed that only one child in fourteen from the Scottish working class made his or her way into the service class (class 1).[45]

Those disagreeing with this claim grounded their replies on two arguments. First, that *patronage* continues: 'Its who you know that counts, not what you can do.' Secondly, by the knock-on effects of the recession: 'Children don't try at school if there's not the end-product in jobs.' Interestingly, the respondents showed a touching faith in the 'democratic intellect', or the operation of meritocratic equality inside the school. The unequal class distribution of academically relevant knowledge was never once cited as a barrier to social mobility.

Yet even disenchantment appears from this study to be unevenly distributed. Disillusionment about the opportunities for class ascent were expressed by 70 per cent of classes 1 and 2 but only 40 per cent of class 4 and 44 per cent of class 5. A somewhat different pattern emerged with the 'class conflict' image which was chosen by a striking three-quarters of classes 1 and 2, by 63 per cent of class 5 but only by 47 per cent of routine non-manual, clerical and sales workers.[46]

Pleasure in reading legitimate books was linked to the adoption of the 'class conflict' view, which was held by 76 per cent of this group. Reading romances, on the other hand, was tied to a preference for the conception of society as a hierarchy of money or of status, only 39 per cent perceiving inequality in terms of antagonistic classes. The same pattern emerged on the social mobility question. Very high levels of disillusionment with the conception of modern Britain as an open, non-discriminatory society were displayed amongst those with legitimate taste (84 per cent), despite the fact that considerable numbers of this group had themselves experienced personal improvement. On this topic, the romantic fiction group were again much less disenchanted, since only 44 per cent (8) of this category expressed their disagreement with claims for the openness of modern Britain.[47]

Questions also probed women's commitment to dependence on men's earnings, their maintenance of the traditional gender responsibility for childcare and their rights to abortion. Feminist attitudes varied proportionately with class and education, but even more sharply with reading preferences. Feminist views were held by 73 per cent of the legitimate group and all the tiny radical canon sample, compared to only 13 per cent of the formulaic romantic fiction group, 38 per cent of the middlebrow and 34 per cent of the 'Cookson' readers.

Nobody upheld subordination to men, but traditional views of women's obligations were defended more frequently by women who read for entertainment – especially genre romance – while those with a taste for realism strongly supported women's rights as individuals. The accentuated experience of oppression by many formulaic fiction readers merely strengthened their belief in the ideal expressions of the traditional ordering of the private sphere. They turned to a 'good family story' for compensatory dreams, in which the deficiencies of their own family experience were magically rectified.

Since they lived in the West of Scotland, these women were also asked: 'What does the term "Red Clydeside" mean to you?' I had in mind the rent strike and the successful resistance to eviction during the First World War, the objection to conscription on the grounds of class internationalism and the development of a non-sectarian, non-sectionalist trade unionism especially from 1912–22.[48]

Table 6.5 Red Clydeside

	Legitimate	M'brow	'Cookson'	Romantic	Radical	Total
Approves Red Clydeside events	20(74%)	5(31%)	15(36%)	2(8%)	5(100%)	47(41%)
Disapproves	1(4%)	1(6%)	5(12%)	3(12%)	0	10(9%)
Means nothing to respondent	2(7%)	8(50%)	14(33%)	16(62%)	0	40(35%)
Knows about events: no judgement	2(7%)	0	1(2%)	0	0	3(3%)
No answer	1(4%)	2(13%)	7(17%)	5(19%)	0	15(13%)
						Total 115

Striking differences emerged in the degree of information about public life, many working-class women being totally unaware of the resonance of these events in the history of their own class ('Is it Jimmy Reid and the Upper Clyde Work-in?' asked one). Yet others invoked their personal connections with dramatic force ('Soldiers from all over the country in George Square! My grandfather put in jail!'). Ignorance was unevenly distributed amongst the readership groups, only two members of the legitimate group being uninformed on this topic and none of the radical canon, although as many as a third of the 'Cookson' group knew nothing. The most remarkable indication of alienation was furnished by the formulaic romance readers, almost two-thirds of whom (sixteen of the twenty-six) were unable to answer the question about Red Clydeside at all.[49]

Six areas of the interview related to the respondents' perspective on British society. When these answers were all assessed, so as to link them to an underlying world-view, definite associations appeared between the degree of political radicalism (of the Left) and the womens' reading preferences (see Table 6.4). This appears to be inexplicable simply in terms of the distribution of 'dominant' and 'radical' views in each class, for radical views were possessed slightly more frequently in the legitimate and radical canon groups than would be predicted by overall class correlations with such groups. Yet it is unlikely that a world-view is derived from reading alone. Rather, it seems more probable that a number of interlocking material and cultural experiences, such as autonomous work in a non-manual occupation, higher education and self-education within the labour movement, predisposed these women towards a taste for realism rather than fantasy. The reading-groups then operate as arenas or types of social contract with writers, into which entry is conditioned, first, by structural forces of class, age and education, second, by family cultures and, third, by choices reflecting deeper-rooted differences in personality. On this argument, reading merely *reinforces* the world-view to which the reader is drawn for other reasons. However, my evidence cannot rule out the conclusion that the type of literature consumed has some independent effect on ideas. On this view, art may indeed be a weapon for human emancipation, or, conversely, as in the arena of romantic fiction, literature may anaesthetise its readers' perceptions by dependence on stereotypes, dominant ideas and regressive myths.

DECODING A ROMANCE AND A REALIST TEXT

The second interview provided experimental documentation about the reception of literature. I chose two divergent examples of popular literature. In order to explore fully each woman's distinctive decoding, interpretation and evaluation, detailed quesions were posed about each novel. It should not be assumed that the reactions thus elicited were typical of normal reading patterns, for in this 'unnatural' exchange efforts might have been made which would not normally be repeated. Despite this caveat, the surprising variety of opinion gathered by this technique provides a new prism through which to reassess the general attitudes elicited earlier.

The two novels served to polarise responses since they were diametrically opposed in the type of pleasure or pain they generated. Both were organised around the life history of a strong female character. However, whereas the hope retained in the realist text was filtered through a tragic revelation of the costs of social transformation, the romance used realist devices mainly to heighten the final harmony between social order and individual happiness.

Agnes Smedley's *Daughter of Earth* (*Daughter*) (1929) belongs to the tradition of critical realism, invigorated by the use of powerful, painterly images.[50] Marie, its central protagonist, experiences as a child the impoverished nomadic agriculture of Missouri, with its domestic servitude for married women: 'Her tears,' she says of her mother, 'they embittered my life!' Her own escape through education is precarious, for 'We were of the class that had nothing and from whom everything was always taken away.' Marie becomes a teacher and a hawker of magazines. Her desertion of her brothers after her mother's death creates a slow-burning guilt within her that periodically flares up, destroying any sense of ease. Marriages to a Danish socialist and, later, an Indian nationalist are brief episodes of unalienated love. Each is cut short by her partners' insensitivity to her needs, especially for support after abortion and for acceptance as a political equal. Imprisoned during the First World War for her defence of the Indian anti-colonial movement, the bitter harvest of personal and political enmities afterwards precipitates a nervous breakdown. Marie remains indomitable despite her inner fragility and the novel ends as she travels to Europe to educate women about contraception.

Daughter of Earth has powerful lyrical passages, with a vivid intensity in its images of a Southern childhood. Pithy episodes reveal the destruction of confidence bred in those born 'on the wrong side of the tracks'. This artistic skill marks *Daughter* as more than a socialist–feminist genre product. It is also one of the few novels of working-class women's search for a love in which both partners retain their freedom, 'a love free from danger and subjection'.[51] Indeed, despite the impact of its first publication in 1929 its delineation of injuries of class and gender is still very much part of our contemporary structures of feeling.

The second text, Marie Joseph's *Lisa Logan* (1984) conforms to fairy-tale conventions with an initial period of social disorder delineated through the stock figures of the 1930s recession and Lisa's descent into poverty with the collapse of her family's shipbuilding firm.[52] The narrative traces her struggle to escape, as in *Daughter*, but unlike the latter, Lisa's ascent into the new bourgeoisie of the burgeoning consumer industries is an unalloyed triumph. From her reunion with her childhood sweetheart, Jonathan, a rich but compassionate building contractor, she gains money, love and respectability: a Northern Mary Quant has been substituted for the fairy-tale princess and Keynesian economics for the magic donor. Their union also reconstitutes the gender order. For through Jonathan's strength, Lisa can at last acknowledge the weakness and death of her father and put behind her the whole epoch of inter-war instability, with its shell-shocked men and marriages festering with adultery.

Joseph's text mystifies social relations, swinging between individualist accounts of her heroine's entrepreneurial virtuosity and genetic determinism (her 'Logan blood'). It is constructed through the use of highly standardised literary techniques. Thus the predictable form of the novel reinforces its thematic continuity with earlier myths of heroic ascent. These are still preserved intact in the kernel of the narrative beneath its surface feminism. In brief, if *Daughter* permits a test of readers' responses to realism, *Lisa Logan* exemplifies how women react to an 'escapist' fantasy.

Thirty-four women in the sample were interviewed on these two texts. With one exception, all the women from the legitimate culture group thought *Lisa Logan* a markedly inferior novel to *Daughter*, although one participant from this quarter stated that she would have chosen neither novel herself. This woman exuded a nauseated recoil from the romance: a reaction which Bourdieu stresses as a typical response to the transgression of a group's usual cultural choices.[53] The members of this group were united in their critical indictment of *Lisa Logan*, conveying through this their remoteness from the genre as a whole.

At first sight the romantic fiction group appeared simply to reverse these judgements. However, their responses to *Daughter* were less those of distaste than silence. This appeared to originate from a literal inability to read the book, or as they termed it, to 'concentrate' on it. Was there an element of political repugnance masked by this refusal? It is difficult to know: for the moment, my reluctant conclusion is that this text demanded greater skills of literacy than these women possessed.

The four middlebrow and eleven 'Cookson' representatives emerged as much more unpredictable in their judgements. However, two of these women liked both novels, while six showed a marked preference for the more difficult, realist text. These women, all lacking higher education, spoke of *Daughter* as though it had been a revelation, the only novel they knew which combined ideas of personal importance to them with fresh, vigorous writing.

The task now is to seek the social determinants of these divergent reactions. As I shall show, an occupational approach still leaves some puzzles in interpreting response. It is these difficulties we shall consider at the end.

Popular readers are often said to be concerned with content rather than form. The use of figurative language was predictably reported as a barrier to pleasure, even by some socially mobile members of the legitimate culture group. For popular audiences, the emphasis on the action of the plot – the skill of story-telling – is always at a premium, conferring a direct promise of happiness. Unfamiliar language risks the subversion of this promise by substituting for it an appeal to decorative, aesthetic qualities which divert the mind to the present and heighten awareness of the artist's own productive

Table 6.6 Second interview: subsample of 34

	Legitimate (12)	Middlebrow (4)	'Cookson' (11)	Romantic (6)	Radical (1)
Daughter of Earth (Smedley)					
Liked	8	2	6	1	0
Fairly favourable, but strong criticisms	3	0	0	0	0
Disliked	0	1	3	0	0
Returned unread/ couldn't read	0	1	1	4	1
Retained without comment	1	0	1	1	0
Lisa Logan (Joseph)					
Liked	0	2	8	2	0
Fairly favourable, but strong criticisms	2	0	1	0	0
Disliked	9	1	1	1	0
Returned unread	0	1	0	3	1
Retained without comment	1	0	1	0	0

role. This suspicion of images as middle-class formalism was articulated explicitly by a socially mobile member of the bourgeoisie, a partner in a bookshop I put this question to whom: 'Marie, the heroine of *Daughter of Earth*, refers to a dream in which she is holding a Chinese vase, which cracks spontaneously under her gaze. What aspects of her life provoke the use of this image?' She replied:

> The vase, these symbols appear too weak to convey the strength of emotions pervading the book, as though images overpower the mind. It is theatrical and theatricality sometimes seems to me middle class. The vase contrasts with descriptions of the desert which *are* tied up with how she felt! (bookshop owner, legitimate group, 23–39)

Another reader, a marginal member of the legitimate group, was similarly irritated with the interruption of the narrative of *Daughter* by the main protagonists' reflections. She proceeds to a fundamental objection to literature:

> I found it very difficult to read, she was . . . referring back as though there were things that hadn't been resolved and I got really fed up with her in the end. . . . I seemed to pick up her immense guilt, particularly for her brothers. . . . It didn't make for cheerful reading. I felt as though she might have been better having written it, but everyone else had to suffer who read it. (community worker, 23–39)

A retired cook, who had told me in the first interview that she read constantly, reported: 'I read it, but it was too heavy – I'll be honest with you! It was a good book, if you like serious reading. I prefer Marie Joseph. The other was too depressing.'

Not everyone with little education and from working-class origins shared this view of *Daughter*. In contrast, a miner's wife commented enthusiastically and spontaneously: 'It was like a visual aid to me. . . . I could see myself doing what the girl's mother did [she loses the will to live].' I shall return later to factors that override the difficulties presented by the Smedley novel to those without cultural capital.

The 'heaviness' to which the cook alluded may have derived in part from the more complex sentence structure in Smedley's novel than that in the romance. This complexity clearly created a clash between reading habits and social routines for my respondents. The majority of women read at night, before sleep. A novel that can only be assimilated easily when the reader feels fresh creates problems, especially for those not doing mental labour or professionally involved with cultural work. For many in my sample, there was a constant regret that this 'lack of time' prevented embarking on more demanding books. *Daughter* was one of this category. Unsuitable as a soporific yet demanding solitude, such a book conflicted with the social needs of a family, needs which could be satisfied with television. Reading, when a woman was alone, sometimes provoked a husband's irritation: 'I don't like to read at home during the day: my husband doesn't approve. He's not a reader himself, and he thinks I should be doing something else, being less anti-social.' (Ex-teacher aged 23–39, with a skilled manual background.)

Numerous respondents emphasised the difficulty of reading Smedley's novel. A primary-school teacher, quite sympathetic to the politics of the book, admitted that such a novel was hard going. Furthermore, the book undermined her propensity to 'block out' disturbing aspects of reality, a goal to which her other reading was tailored. She commented: 'It's pleasurable but upsetting at the same time – I wouldn't want to take it on holiday.' Thus the recoil from the formal difficulty of the text can be linked to my respondents' unease at the austerity of its social vision.

Open rejection of the realist text on the grounds of its politics was rare: only one reader, a secretary from the 'Cookson' group, mentioned this and then in conjunction with 'style'. *Lisa Logan*, however, provoked a more antagonistic response from those in the legitimate culture group, who stressed its over-simplified depiction of business success. Indeed, one respondent explicitly reversed the terms of the dominant culture by connoting Lisa with the 'selfish' pursuit of business wealth, and Marie with heroic struggle against oppression.

Surprisingly, even the non-radical readers of class 2 with legitimate taste spoke of *Daughter* in favourable political terms. In the absence of strong ideological antipathies and the personal possession of power, such women were, perhaps, influenced by the vigour of Smedley's writing to stress their opposition to American rural poverty and to exploitation:

> She doesn't say anything new about the class struggle. If you don't have money, power or other means of exchange as the rich have, you're exploited. The same *lack* of rules were there then. (Music teacher, 40–60.)
> You feel the woman is real, you feel for her. There are bits

> which pierce you to the heart. . . . clearly people like her
> family don't matter, they don't exist . . . just as Indians and
> Negroes are . . . bits of skin and bone to get jobs done so that
> people at the top can live comfortably . . . . (Houseworker,
> married to television director, 23–39.)

Both these responses drew on a set of images that had been notably submerged in the first interview, at which the teacher had long hesitated before settling on a class-conflict image of society and the second woman had rejected this view outright.

Smedley's text was assessed in unexpected and challenging ways by readers whose material circumstances had placed them close to the position of the heroine's family. One working-class pensioner observed acidly: 'She wasn't poor, as she said they were. They always had plenty of food on the table.'

Daughter provoked much more detailed comment, even among supporters, than did the romance. This was particularly evident concerning its complex feminism. The writer's depiction of conflicts and traumatic set-backs in the heroine's struggle for independence intensified the depressing aspect of the novel's impact by undermining a simplistic feminist reaction. For one reader, strongly committed to the women's movement, the presentation of such harsh choices led to a strange preference for the romance over the realist novel, although Smedley was seen as the better writer.

The political world-view of the readers conditioned how *Daughter* was appropriated, but in intricate ways. Despite the bleak passages registering breakdown and guilt, for many readers this book was not simply 'depressing realism' but also uplifting. That the heroine successfully escapes her surroundings, acquires education and uses this education for the emancipation of others, was a source of great optimism for these women. Marie represented a figure with whom they could identify. Typical of these readers was the miner's wife, aged 54, who linked the novel in a very concrete way to her own context:

> It was very relevant to now: a very good book that. . . . She
> was quite right [to remain childless and leave her brothers].
> Why should a woman tie herself down to a family? What's
> the point of having a family? There's nothing for the parents
> so what should there be for them [the children]?

She proceeded to relate the heroine's experience of a miners' strike to that of the British miners in the 1984–5 strike, which had resulted in the three men in her family becoming redundant and a shared sense of total futility. I asked her if she felt cheated of 'escape' when reading Smedley: 'No! I thoroughly enjoyed it. . . . I didn't find it depressing, not at all, in fact I found it uplifting, because it brought back what you experienced during the strike.'

An unemployed single parent, trained as a hairdresser, had commented on another occasion 'I think romances are to make us like the rich!' She was asked 'How much of *Daughter* is relevant to you now?':

> A lot of it: I am one of the poor classes as she was . . . my children don't go without shoes and we have food on the table but in the class system we're low! Also I [understood] how her feelings took over when she thought something really strongly but her knowledge and command of the language wouldn't allow her to speak it through. . . . It's only now I feel I could go into education. She's learning things but her confidence still goes . . . [t]o care for her brothers she would have had to give up her education and everything she wanted in life. . . . I really enjoyed it.

A woman in her early thirties, a solicitor's clerk, commented in similar vein: I've never read anything like this before. Now I'll look out for books that aren't just publishers' hype!'

A further woman who liked both novels, was a cleaner from the 'Cookson' group. *Daughter* impressed her much more deeply than did *Lisa Logan*. I asked her if *Daughter* shed any light on the needs that we have as women? 'It doesn't half! All the needs of women!' She admired the heroine's courage in 'escaping from the pit of poverty, trying to help others' but also the tragic costs of the heroine's will to freedom: 'In trying to get her independence, she actually lost her love.' Due to its greater realism, *Daughter* was actually preferable to novels that have a happy ending and to soap operas which just 'show their lives over again. They're not learning from it!' *Daughter* she would remember, *Lisa Logan* she would forget. This favourable response was particularly unexpected, for it was she who had originally recommended *Lisa Logan* to me.

Pleasure in *Daughter*'s subversion of ideologies of the family was also stressed by respondents with legitimate culture. A university teacher from Shetland voiced the dominant perception:

> An extraordinary book! I was fascinated by the woman. . . .
> A much more realistic portrayal of the lives of working-class

women [than in the romance], especially in the character of
the mother. A great fear of marriage – it made me think hard
about birth-control. . . . The novel took a historically
sensitive answer to women's predicaments.

Such a reaction was typical of most readers with legitimate culture.
   While political objections to the realist text were expressed only
on one occasion, this was not the case with ethical conflicts over
women's family and marital obligations. For a minority of readers,
the text provoked hostile and bitter responses, especially over the
dilemma between independence, including living for radical social
movements, and family commitments. Thus those with the
strongest family-centred, private commitments, women who had
rejected the morality of an individualistic choice of abortion or easy
divorce, were highly critical of the 'selfish' response of Marie in
Daughter. Against the grain of the text, such readers debunked the
pretensions of the heroine with reference to her precipitate marriages
and unacceptable abortions:

> There were all those rantings against marriage . . . then she
> marries after one week's acquaintance, hoping for an eternal
> soul-mate[. . . .] [The parting from her brothers was] the act
> of a selfish person. The abortion she never mentions again:
> she didn't feel too badly about that. I had very little sympathy
> with her towards the end [. . . .] she became neurotic and
> self-obsessed.

This comment was made by a music teacher, aged 23–39, a member
of the legitimate group who had earlier stated 'Abortion is pretty
close to murder in my book.' She still felt *Daughter* was a 'good
novel'.
   These arguments recurred:

> I would have . . . looked after the boys. It wasn't an
> entertaining novel, interesting and provocative but not
> entertaining, which is what I look for in novels these days. I
> found her irritating though still interesting at the end. . . . I
> have recommended the book to others though. (Ex-primary-
> teacher aged 23–39, 'Cookson' group.)

The capacity to read *Daughter* was clearly class-related. Nevertheless, once able to read it, the availability and evaluation of
feminist ideas was more influential than either their class position or

their family history in determining women's assessment of the book. One woman whose own experiences after her mother died resembled closely that of Marie's in *Daughter*, regretted that she had not escaped like her:

> She made me feel guilty. I'd not got out, the brothers needed me. My father relied on me to bail them out of gaol, get them out of hospital, write letters, certificate them. Her whole experience was harsher, more honest than mine. . . . In the wider world she can grasp why things are as they are, a grasp of reason. (Bookshop partner, legitimate group, 23–39.)

Contrary to Bourdieu's assertions, it is interesting that those with legitimate taste were anxious to discuss the novels in terms of their moral or political meanings.[54] For them, culture was not just a 'game' in which a spirit of seriousness was inapposite. Indeed, the respondents typically assessed the book in terms of the merits of its dominant character. This often excluded a wider conception of the author's politics and of the social structures determining action. Elizabeth Long's study of middle-class women's reading groups in America has shown that this psychological and moral approach is common to lay readers.[55] As she suggests, despite its blinkers, such reading does permit an expression of women's distinctive conception of morality through 'their members' deep relatedness and connectedness to the characters in the novels'.[56] For my legitimate readers, the novel was clearly important as a form of intellectual experiment through role-models.

For those who preferred the romance, the explicit reason was the reassuring pleasure in a familiar and benign world offered by the genre. 'At least you knew in *Lisa Logan* what the ending was going to be,' remarked one 18-year-old, a middlebrow reader, deprived of such consolation in *Daughter*. For such a reader, the realist novel compared poorly with other forms such as the medieval fantasy: 'It's bleak and uninteresting. I know about poverty in America already. It was boring.' Here the proletarian realist elements were read as a predictable formula. In contrast, Marie Joseph's skill in the romance in reuniting as lovers the childhood friends separated at the outset was highly valued. This respondent distinguished *Lisa Logan* from Mills and Boon novels by its better balance of the demands of innovation and melodramatic conformity.

Secondly, for many readers, the heroine of the realist text accumulated only knowledge, whereas the romance's accumulation of capital was of more absorbing fictional interest. Such women were from the 'Cookson' and formulaic romance groups. For them, the utopian content of the text derived from the dominant conception of social justice in which the acquisition of riches is legitimated by self-denial. They could identify all to easily with the minutiae of abstention. Moreover, they saw in success the transcending of class structure altogether, not its persistence: 'Inequality, the class structure, did come in *at the beginning* but not later on [my emphasis]. Having to work, Lisa Logan learned the other side of life, working hard, scrimping and saving, to keep your families. . . .' (Retired grocer's assistant, romantic fiction group.)

The seven women who preferred the romance unexpectedly answered in the affirmative to the question: 'Is this a good regional novel?'. Such women failed to notice the stereotypes, the 'cardboard characters' and implausible feats of heroic industry that bothered those with legitimate culture, who refused to inhabit the mythological landscape of the romance. Those with cultural capital resorted to the demands of absolute fidelity to life as a stick to beat the romance, as in one exasperated criticism: 'You can't run up three pairs of curtains in one evening!' (on the work ethic of the heroine). Yet the romance genre's readers know that this is one of a series of fictional devices which they justified in terms of an underlying fidelity to their view of essential reality. For the romance reader, the core of the story is its restoration of harmony between social practices and a set of ideal values: for the disenchanted possessor of legitimate art, these are merely the withered matrices of ideological thought.

The advocates of *Lisa Logan* valued highly the images of fulfilled desire that the novel offered, a discreet eroticism that produced the sexual pleasure clearly lacking in *Daughter*: 'We were told about the abortion, what about the conception?', commented the middlebrow reader, hostile to Smedley's text. Her expectation of sexual euphoria may not have been voiced by others in this interview, but it would be a mistake to assume therefore that her feelings were not shared. Worse, *Daughter* was criticised for totally flouting the romantic love ethic: *Lisa Logan* on the contrary, promises sensuality, love and a permanent relationship. To uncouple these was painful.

Those who had enjoyed the romance emerged principally from the group who had presented themselves as neither radical nor feminist. There were exceptions to this general pattern, though. Some disillusioned working-class women, whose cynicism was voiced in antagonistic class models, still found very little interest in a novel about self-education and social conflict, such as *Daughter*. Tiny narratives of personal success were more agreeable. Furthermore, the realistic materialism of these women was often interspersed with anecdotes of the unusual family members who had become affluent, in so far as they had joined the middle class. It can be conjectured that collective knowledge of these rare histories provided the pivot sustaining the fantasies of individual mobility which they liked in the romance.

We have already noted a significant number of readers who stressed their concern to hide distressing aspects of reality. Novels such as *Lisa Logan* block out these readers' sense of lack and are therefore satisfying. Future research may well demonstrate that they strengthen defence mechanisms which create the personality's sense of order and accommodation to reality.

In this experimental framework, the complex experiences of class constrain the readers without resulting in any simple homology between occupational position and the taste for the romance. I have already quoted the miner's wife who responded with spontaneous enthusiasm to Smedley. Against this case should be contrasted the negative response of another miner's wife. Both had been semi-skilled weavers in a carpet factory before marriage; both had been involved in community support for the miners' strike. However, the two women had contrasting social views: the second respondent being more privatised and unsure of her opinions, less consistent in her class model and anti-feminist; relevant also may have been the first woman's experience of dramatic family transition with a downwardly mobile father. Or again, take two cleaners, one from the respectable working class and politically radical, the second possessing a vision simultaneously more individualistic and fatalistic. The radical woman in each context preferred *Daughter* in marked opposition to their friends.

It is true that in general lower-middle-class and working-class women are cut off from literature except in genre form. Secondly, the majority of these lower-class women liked the romance; that is, they enjoyed a form in which the contradictions and confusion of society can be symbolically rectified. Further, the romance provides for its public an illusory feeling of wealth: it democratises luxury.

Yet for some readers outside the legitimate group and lacking higher education, a novel such as *Daughter* came with the quality of revelation to them. These women were unaware of rules about good and bad novels. Moreover, they would never have bought such a novel, being put off by the sober green cover, the oil reproduction of an 'ugly' woman and the subtitle 'Modern Classic'. Yet they were susceptible to the compelling qualities of the writing and the illumination of their own lives in *Daughter of Earth*. For this reason, the reading network, unified not by locality but by cultural consumption, may be a powerful instrument of a new conscious-ness.[57]

Post-modernist theorists have assumed too readily that earlier cultural divisions relating to class have collapsed in the wake of avant-garde modernism. In this respect Bourdieu is correct that the market for culture is deeply segmented and that economic capital (possessed over generations) provides the 'habitus', or situation plus dispositions, for legitimate taste. The Scottish research has shown, however, that this simple model has to be elaborated to take account of the presence of different routes to both cultural capital and legitimate taste. Most strikingly, I have drawn attention to a new stratum which possesses such educational resources and which is found mainly in public sector administrative and professional occupations. In the period of economic growth from the 1960s to the early 1970s, there emerged 'lasses o' pairts' – women who had working-class origins but whose schooling provided the route to relative success. Such a group had an ambivalent or ironic perspective on 'high culture', from which they were already distanced by the components of the Scottish *national* culture. Nevertheless, there was an immense gulf between this group and those working-class women who had been cut off from education, consequently moving in a world in which radical political and literary intellectuals had no impact.

Secondly, by distinguishing 'autodidacts' from those who pos-sessed cultural capital, Bourdieu risks making his thesis tautological. Instead of stressing simply the manipulation of social closure, by which the well-read working-class minority is excluded by a 'spiritual aristocracy' of the old ruling class, we might note their rejection of a cultural diet composed solely of popular thought. These women accumulated cultural capital instead through an arduous passage of self-education, sometimes participating at one remove in the scheduled learning opening up for their socially mobile children, sometimes fired by a political curiosity stoked by the labour movement. The democratic strand of bourgeois politics has perhaps helped sustain a wider access to knowledge in Scotland than in Bourdieu's France which, on his account, has preserved a more deeply entrenched minority culture and power despite its 200-year-old revolutionary tradition.

Thirdly, Bourdieu links class position to attitudes in a quite unproblematic manner. My study suggested that these correlations are not constant. The vast majority of Scottish women with cultural capital did not feel drawn to an aestheticist cultivation of form.

Rather, there was a consistent concern to address literature in terms of the moral or political criteria drawn from liberal/socialist humanism, transmitted through the schools in part as the Leavisite critical assault against a regressive and nostalgic elitism.

Finally, Bourdieu fails to observe popular culture with the same perception that he displays in unmasking the charades of the *grande bourgeoisie*, whose disinterested commitment to art provided a cloak of legitimacy over the naked preservation of power. He comments with enigmatic opacity that where popular culture is concerned 'Necessity imposes a taste for necessity or the resignation to the inevitable.'[58] This hardly does justice to the heterogeneous character of mass culture and the need to assess its character as ideology and utopia. I have focused particularly on the social constitutents of the readership for fantasy. The culture of women who read the most traditional or formulaic of romantic fantasies has been explored, showing that the larger group were seeking a transformation of reality through a half-disbelieved magical escape. Such women were highly fatalistic about the possibility of change and their discourse about class was grounded in a thoroughgoing cynical materialism. Paradoxically, the formulaic romance to which they turned was saturated in myths legitimating a (reformed) patriarchy and a united bourgeois-gentry class, recalling Bloch's observation that the 'long arm of capital' extends even to the 'holiday-hospital of nature'.[59] The romance is an alternative 'holiday-hospital' for women.

Conclusion

Much theoretical labour has been expended recently on analysis of the 'dominant ideology', those modes of thought (religious, racial or literary) which have permitted ruling classes to present their particular interests as the general interest of humanity. Because control based on coercion or material necessity is unstable, such classes have tried to win consent to their rule by rhetorical appeals to fundamental principles. A subsequent critique of this strand of Western Marxism has argued that in late capitalist societies, such class (and indeed patriarchal) ideology is irrelevant.[1]

It is true that some claims for the ideological sphere have been inflated and that modern societies can survive with lower levels of consensus than earlier modes of production.[2] However, as long as mass democracies are retained, the economically dominant class and their allies amongst the traditional professions must seek to exclude competing values in the battle for hearts and minds. To reject this is to risk a mechanical materialism which is fatally weakened in its opposition to idealism.[3]

Against such a new vulgar materialism, I want to argue that culture may be 'ordinary', as Raymond Williams emphasised, but it *is* important, not least because there is evidence of a connection between women's political or social world-view and their usual choice of literature outside the research setting. Reading the formulaic romance, I have indicated, is not randomly associated with women's other beliefs. On the contrary, it is linked to higher levels of political and gender conservatism, although the causal relationship between the two cannot be further clarified. My conclusion is that the formulaic fiction partly locks these women into collusion with dominant ideas – economic, patriarchal and racist – or, less strongly, it increases their lack of systematised resistance to them.

There has been a 'counter-hegemonic' popular literature, a culture of protest in which the democratic voice has been uppermost. Within the Chartist and industrial novel, writers from the 1850s onwards developed the middle-class form to portray the working class as a collective hero, while remaining sensitive to the oppression of women. Yet for all but a tiny minority, it has been a hidden resource, for this 'literature of labour' has lacked the popularity of the family saga and the romance. The vast majority of readers without higher education have either rejected or lacked access to such radical and feminist literature, as indeed to any critical realism or modernism.

How are we then to understand the role of romantic fiction for its readers? Are they motivated simply by false consciousness, as the cultural dope thesis suggests? Against this, I have shown that most readers do not confuse the genre with realism. Moreover, the development of the romance suggests its readers are not passive. Its paradises change, along with women's new material experiences and their greater exposure to the arenas of modernity. Such readers are still active and critical thinkers who repudiate writers too removed from their own image of society. Hence the shift towards new representations of working women. Moreover, I have shown that in Scotland certain writers are repudiated. For example, the link between Barbara Cartland's world-view and that of Thatcherism is both transparent to popular readers and the cause of Cartland's low reputation. The world of the dominant class she depicts is either seen as too alien to their experience or as the source of the poverty and social problems that harass them.[4] Jackie Collins's *Hollywood Wives* is also rigorously excluded: it transgresses too deeply their moral categories, destroying their careful resistance to passions perceived as animal-like or exploitative. Catherine Cookson, on the other hand, sustains the deep structure of the romance – the cross-class unity symbolised in marriage, the victory of the good ruling class – yet she pushes to the limit the romance as a vehicle for 'history from below'; hence her popularity. Thus there is evidence that lower-class readers *do select* those writers whose portrayals of the world both pinpoint some elements of their own alienation and whose hopes express their own aspirations.

There is a parallel with religion, to which the romance bears strong resemblance, despite its secular appearance. Religion is partially a projection of human capacities onto a god; by mystifying the real relations between humans it thus enhances their powerlessness or alienation. Yet religion is also the plane on which the masses express their true material and social needs.

Like religion, the romance distorts the structures of social reality, particularly in its gentry–patriarchal form. It cannot be seen simply as the site for ideology, however. For along with the architecture of conservative fantasy, the romance is also the 'heart of a heartless world', comforting in its familiar reassurance. Indeed, the interests of its lower-class readers have partially remoulded the inherited romance form. Similarly, working-class needs partially shaped the schismatic sectarian cultures of Paineite or Primitive Methodism, such that they, too, embraced uneasily both the new democratic aspirations of a 'chiliasm of the oppressed' and the stern inherited disciplines of time and labour.[5]

Thus the romance, like other artistic forms, also provides wish fulfilment. It offers an idealised vision of an unalienated, yet hierarchical society in which the normal laws of bourgeois society are miraculously suspended. In this imaginary universe, patriarchy fosters protective love and true nobility of mind justifies privilege, thus simultaneously defusing the historical dynamite of egalitarianism. Particularly to those enmeshed within the confines of kinship and still dependent economically on men, the formulaic romance survives as the 'dream-book' of the family.

Lacking access to radical writers, lower-class women have had their images of change colonised by the romance. It anaesthetises rather than defamiliarises contemporary reality. The traditional romance colludes with patriarchy, expressing its rhetoric not as fatalistic common sense but as ideal principles. In these female-centred texts, the moment of realism is superseded by the moment of aspiration. In this, the ideology of love no longer evokes its antithesis, the ideology of martyrdom, as in the collective experience of women. The social contract between female subjects and their constitutional monarchs ceases magically to be a contract of oppression. The romance represents a schizophrenic oscillation between realism and fantasy.

Appendix: The Consumers of Literature – Sample Interviews

MARY DENNISON: LEGITIMATE CULTURE GROUP

Mary lives in a tower block, the foyer so badly vandalised that the whole building appears uninhabited. She is 73 and retired from her printing job. On her bookshelf is a volume of Shakespeare along with a small collection of books, including Angela Tuckett's *History of the Scottish Trades Union Congress*, given for her services to the labour movement.

'My father worked all his life in a newsagent's: a dispatch clerk, I don't know whether you would say a skilled job'. Mary's comment about skill classifications is part of a wider scepticism about such designations. According to the Registrar General, such work is class 3 non-manual. 'My mother didn't work, except in printing when she was young. I am one of ten. Seven lived. My mother died at 56.

'I lived in the South Side, in Hutchesontown [Glasgow]. We were lucky in respect of poverty – my father was never idle: he wasnae a tradesman down the Clyde, fr'instance, that, when the slump came was out of work. *Because* he wasnae a tradesman, my father was the only one that worked up the stair. When I think of those who lived beside us, they had a much harder time. And *we* had a hard time. When it came to getting clothes it was very difficult . . . but there was a basic meal on the table. And that's where I find the community spirit really did operate in those days. Neighbours helped neighbours because of the close proximity of living together and seeing the poverty of those who lived by you.

'My younger sister and I went into the printing trade. Women werenae considered skilled in the printing trade . . . although I had a cousin up North with a full compositing apprenticeship. Where I was, women worked equally as hard as men, in many cases very intricate work, but they only got 50 per cent of the wages of men. We could only get a learnership . . . I was resentful that women werenae given equal pay.'

I asked her what were Glasgow's major problems? 'I'm no' a member of the SNP, but I do believe Scotland needs some sort of self-government. The problems all stem from decline: the *determined* decline of the major industries. One would think we were never going to use steel or coal again when we reach the great millennium, the year 2000, but we will need these. Pits are closing, the fate of Ravenscraig is in the balance. It's a deliberate policy, perhaps it's because we have a preponderance of Labour MPs in Scotland and this is one way of paying the Scottish people back . . . but this decline in industry is affecting all parts of the country, even Birmingham, and it used to be the Mecca of light industry [. . .] There are also other problems.' She talks about the poverty of old people and vandalism in high flats.

Asked about her image of society, Mary proposes a class-conflict view, although one in which a certain amount of upward mobility occurs. 'I would say that society hasn't changed one bit. We're still the ruling class and the working class. Or rather, there are three nations in this country: people on benefits, people in jobs and the wealthy, who are getting wealthier every day. . . .' She is in favour of women's economic independence, the right to choose an abortion, easy divorce. 'Women's position in Britain has advanced tremendously and I'm altogether glad of it. The wages a woman got in the printing industry wouldn't support her. We fought for differentials to be reduced which has helped women get the better situation they have now. We have a wee bit credit [*sic*].' Mary has always been single and spoke more vividly about the correlation between women and poorly paid work than any other respondent.

Cultural preferences

'I'm very fond o' reading and always have been, ever since I was a wee lassie. Sometimes, though, a book is a lot of crap. I'm not particularly partial to women writers, but I like Victoria Holt, Catherine Gaskin, Susan Howatch, Jessica Stirling, the novels about Ayrshire, not about the antique world. I liked Jan Webster's *Saturday City*. There was also a good book by a man, called *The Music Makers* – E.V. Thompson it was – it was marvellous. It's about the history of Ireland, the potato famine and the early political movement.

'I'm not very keen on romantic novels, although obviously a wee bit of romance comes into these. Mills and Boon's novels I'd read only occasionally, when I'm not feeling good.

'In my younger days I read the Russian stuff. Gorki: *Quiet flows the Don* and *The Don Flows Down to the Sea*. I liked the first of those particularly. *Dr Zhivago* I gave up after four pages because I couldn't keep track of the names. *Anna Karenina* I liked. In the thirties we had the Left Book Club.

'I have a partiality for American authors – Howard Fast, for example, was at one time active in the movement. Upton Sinclair's books were a real revelation about the exploitation that went on, particularly for the immigrants from the ethnic minorities who could only get factory jobs.' She also mentions with approval, the novels of C.P. Snow, John Braine's early works and Stan Barstow.

Mary then goes on to discuss the pursuit of knowledge and the pursuit of illusion: 'Yes, I like books about ordinary people and ordinary situations, not dream situations – although I have read this. There are times when you want to have a wee bit of escapism, because it's no' all that happy sometimes, the world. But then, we're living in it, so you must find out more about it and that's very pleasurable. I lived in a room and kitchen as a child and there was not much entertainment, so this was one thing you could do.' She goes on to distinguish between writers read for escapism alone, such as Victoria Holt (see Chapter 5), and others who were rejected because they used the romantic formula too obtrusively. Barbara Cartland was mentioned in the latter category: 'She lives in a different world.' On Catherine Cookson, she observes: 'I don't know whether she's apolitical. She's more interested in the struggles in a family or a street.' Other writers were appreciated for their class consciousness or their commitment to women's liberation.

At the end of the interview, she returned to Labour and Socialist politics in the West of Scotland: 'Of course I think favourably of "Red Clydeside". My grandmother instigated the rent strike in Govan! "Red Clydeside" took place in the First World War and I was involved in the movement afterwards, in the thirties.' She relates her experience as an electrician and shop steward in the Second World War, continuing: 'Later I became vice-president of the SOGAT branch and subsequently president in the 1960s.'

Bourdieu would probably have excluded Mary Dennison from his category of legitimate culture. She did not display an *aesthetic attitude* to culture, that is, emphasise the primacy of form over ethical or political ideas. Her difficulty in mastering novels such as Pasternak's *Dr Zhivago* may have been related to her political ambivalence to them. Although on the boundary between the legitimate group and the radical canon, I included her finally in the former category because of her wide range of 'legitimate' reading, which included Tolstoy, Sholokov and Snow. Precisely because she judged novels chiefly in terms of the realist and political criteria that Bourdieu links only to popular culture, her case indicated the existence of persistent tensions within the public for canonised works, tensions that Bourdieu himself underplays. Put crudely, these spring from whether literature is primarily perceived as demystification or as a form of entertainment based on the game-like play of textual strategies.

JEANETTE MASON: ROMANTIC FICTION GROUP

Jeanette is a secretary married to a telecommunications engineer, with one son. Her father was an engineering foreman and her mother a bank clerk, a 'very clever woman', who died young. Having herself had a stillbirth, she decided to have one child only and has been working full time since he started school. Recently, she has been promoted.

Despite an image of the social order composed of individuals differentiated by money alone, she argues that the lack of jobs closes off opportunities for many talented and hard-working people. Yet she also believes that *class inequality* is declining since clothes, accent and parental patronage now count for less: 'I'd like it to be that way and I think people will make it that way.'

For Jeanette, employers and workers ultimately possess common interests: 'I think you only need unions where there's very *bad* management. Otherwise people rely too much on them and leave union affairs to others who are more militant than they are.' When asked what the term 'Red Clydeside' means to her, she replies: 'Nothing – should I have heard of it?'

Jeanette considers women's time to be undervalued relative to men's and their opportunities for advancement fewer. Women should be financially independent: 'I wouldn't want to go to my husband and ask: "May I have a pound for a glass of wine?" ' If women want to work, there should be more nursery facilities and

teachers, or nannies employed privately, to allow them to do so.'
She is in favour of abortion on demand, especially if poverty would
otherwise prevent a proper upbringing – 'I'm sorry for the poor wee
mite whose family can't afford to keep it.' Divorce, on the other
hand should only be available on stringent grounds: 'I'm not in
favour of easy divorce . . . marriage is a partnership people should
be prepared to work at. It's too easy to split up. I have an extremely
happy marriage, so maybe this affects my views.'

Cultural preferences

'I read women's magazines when travelling, family sagas, which are
my favourites, Mills and Boon hospital series occasionally, when I
don't have anything else. I prefer romantic novels. I like a story, not
sheer kissing and sex . . . nor brutality and sex as in Mickey Spillane
and Harold Robbins – that's more for men! I like something with a
bit of bite in it: B.T. Bradford's *Woman of Substance*, Virginia
Andrews, for example . . . I don't mind Catherine Cookson,
Colleen McCullough or Barbara Cartland . . . I *do* like a formula –
yes! I'm a total romantic! I don't see novels as a form of escape
because I never feel the need to escape. I suppose I'm quite fortunate
. . . some people use books as an escape from their proper life . . .
but I feel I've got things under control. I'm quite happy with my life
and wouldn't want to change it. . . . I never use the word
"depressed" – "upset a little" never "depressed", that word's banned
in here. A good day is when I've made someone happy. I sometimes
feel I'm another Evelyn Home [a woman's magazine agony
aunt]. . . . 'I read for pure pleasure, something to pass the time. . . .
Women read novels so they don't have to think!'
    I asked her if she would like to read books or stories about 'how
things really are'. 'It depends – not if they're nasty things. I like to
read about nice, happy things not horrors, rapes, muggings,
murders. This *is* where the ostrich in me comes out. I know it goes
on in life but I don't want to read about it . . . people should live in
a world of harmony.' You like to read about an ideal world? 'Yes.'
A model for what your own should be? 'Yes.' She comments later:
'I'm not interested in the writers' critical ideas.'

This respondent is very well integrated socially, rejecting any hopes
or needs that she cannot realise. In general, she has a benign view of

contemporary Britain, based on her conception of a just market and traditional family life. The only obstacles to these are the persistent relics from an older order based on sex discrimination and patronage. The literature she chooses sustains these values: she reads so as to renew her conceptions of an ideal world, cast recognisably in the mould of the early theorists of economic individualism and predicated on a harmony between the genders. Her culture is of positive heroes and heroines who represent the qualities she esteems, just as feudal romances idealised aristocratic heroes and ethics. For her, it is *not* the role of literature to address questions of injustice, alienation or social disintegration.

MARJORIE LINDSAY: MIDDLEBROW GROUP

Marjorie Lindsay was trained as a clerical worker, becoming a comptometer operator until she had her first child. Her husband was also a clerk, but subsequently became a minister. She is in the 40–60 age-range, having two children, now grown up. One has a divinity degree and the other has trained to be a teacher. Her roots are on the boundary of the middle class, her mother having been a milliner and her father an analytical chemist. His early death led to economic insecurity in her childhood. Since marriage, her material situation has slightly improved.

She is content to stay at home, emphasising the amount of unofficial social work she does in the parish but defining herself as someone without ambition. 'I sat back and let the world go by . . . I could have got more if I hadn't thought "everything for a quiet life".'

In terms of class perspectives, her horizons are shaped by dominant social perceptions. She takes the view that society is made up of people differing in the amounts of money they possess, not of contesting classes. Upward mobility is the reward for effort and the right temperament. Nevertheless, resorting to a rhetoric of elitist conservatism, she also defines improved opportunities for working-class people as dangerously detrimental to high standards. However, she is nervous about party politics becoming too closely identified with organised class interests and reveals a fondness for earlier traditions of paternalism. She cites unemployment as the main problem in the West of Scotland, but her distance from the recession is perhaps indicated by her second priority: 'litter'. Furthermore, unemployment is, for Marjorie, beyond social control: 'I'm not criticising either the Government or political parties. It's a complex situation. SDP and Labour don't have the answers. Politicians are necessary but they should be less party-concerned and more people-concerned.'

In her view, the class structure has radically altered in the last ten years: 'I think perhaps we're going into a reverse situation. They [sic] don't have to speak clearly. You can get on if you're aggressive and make a lot of the fact that you come from a region. It's maybe always the case that people who were a bit ruthless got on. Low social class background is not much impediment. If you have ability or are ruthless you can get on although sometimes folk with ability and qualifications don't manage it. It's your character rather than where you are in the world. Although I must admit I'm a bit snobbish too – if the Queen dropped in and said "Hullo, Marjorie", I'd be delighted!'

'Women should not be dependent on men but in a partnership, each person contributing in their own right. . . . We should consider the other person rather than ourselves. It would be good if women had a certain amount of independence, yet that would cause more problems than it would solve because it would be too easy to opt out. . . . But I've never been in want of anything. I can't talk for people with problems and difficulties, desperate for money.'

She opposed policies such as a Government benefit for house-workers to enhance women's independence, and was also ambivalent about nurseries – 'A great idea for children but I'm not happy with the general concept of women happily plonking children and nipping off to work as a norm. . . . Family life is a great thing. If you make decisions to have children, then you should, as far as possible, be concerned and responsible for them. We must have a *caring* society. . . . Abortion on demand appals me: I would only agree to abortion where the life of the child/mother is in danger . . . life is very much sacred, we treat it so casually.'

Cultural preferences

'My favourite writers are Agatha Christie – very much enjoyed – . . . Ngaio Marsh, John Buchan, A.J. Cronin, Anne Stevenson, Madeleine Brent, Agnes Sly T. Turnball – she is American and writes with religious connotations, one or two are on the lives of ministers – Miss Read, Bill Knox, Robert MacLeod – adventure stories to do with police and fishery protection – Catherine Marshall – she married a minister and after his death wrote novels, romantic novels in a way. I also enjoy Guy MacCrone, *The Wax Fruit* trilogy, Helen McInnes – again the Glasgow connection! – M.M. Kaye, *The Shadow of the Moon* and *Far Pavilions*, Conan Doyle, Dorothy Sayers, Earl Stanley Gardner, *The Forsyte Saga*. I don't like any author who uses bad language and too much sex: this means most modern writers. I don't like pictures of degradation. For example, Catherine Cookson, she's a brilliant writer but I don't read her because I don't like her language. . . . She didn't have to use that language. . . . I didn't like her treatment of reality, although she is a graphic writer. She should write without blasphemy. . . . [But] Barbara Cartland is far too sugary.' The only other writer she had heard of on the interview list was Grassic Gibbon: 'Some of it was too raw. I like escapism, not the realities of life.'

I asked her if she thought it was well written. 'Yes, I felt the language worked well in relation to the area and the time. . . .' Do you like a formula in the books you read? 'Yes, definitely I like that. I hate it when the books don't work to pattern . . . that's part of the escapism. It's what you can't come to terms with in your own situation that you want to keep away from.'

Do you like novels that have at their centre ordinary people's problems, things as they *are*? 'It depends on the treatment. Let's have facts, OK, but sometimes they're exaggerated by the way folks treat them.' Do you like happy endings? 'Yes, let's have happy endings every time! But it would depend on the book and the content.'

This respondent reads about six novels a month, is a 'frivolous' reader, 'not a highbrow'. She never chooses Mills and Boon, but nor does she like books with 'too much reading'. She does not look for writers possessing critical views and is only interested in the record of experience a writer provides in so far as it is exemplary: she mentions as an example that Terry Waite would be a fit subject.

Marjorie's reading, then, is closely integrated into her Calvinist individualism and apolitical Christian social ethics. Thus she firmly maintains that 'some of the messes people get into are of their own making', citing extramarital laxness in Drumchapel – a post-war housing scheme – as an instance. She is strongly attached to the traditional division of labour, while accepting that women's talents should be used to the full. Avowedly escapist in inclination, she nevertheless holds to a view that conflict can be overcome by good intentions and resort to the 'facts' – a form of petty-bourgeois empiricism. Her reading is remarkably consistent in its support for her world-view, particularly in her carefully selected representations of desire and the preference for textual silences about sexuality. The strict linguistic classifications brought to bear on current writing suggest the avoidance both of contemporary realism and of any images of disruption, conflict and anomie. Thus her favourite writers do not so much *defamiliarise* as *refamiliarise* the world, deploying both racist or hierarchical categories and developing a 'law and order' rhetoric of criminal conspiracy.

CARMEN WARREN: RADICAL CANON

Carmen has become a full-time trade union organiser. The daughter of a skilled engineering worker and a skilled machinist, she left school at 16 to work as an office junior. Training on the job, she moved into computer programming and from there to work as a student welfare officer. In the age-range 23–39, she has a stable partner: they do not have children.

Political world-view

'I'm very much opposed to the 'American dream' phenomenon and the associated dangerous ideology that society can be organised on the basis of the success of individuals . . . . throughout this century there has been a recognition that this statement is not true: that there is an obligation on the part of the better-off through universal health and education systems to provide *for* people.' She adopts an image of class conflict in which wealth and poverty are becoming increasingly polarised: 'On the housing schemes [in Glasgow], in terms of unemployment and poverty, there is the gradual break-down of society in its acceptable form. There are problems of crime, alcohol abuse, and misuse of drugs, all of which can be entirely related to the tenants' economic position . . . You see a tremendous growth of fatalism – a disenchantment with politics . . . but signs, too, of vibrant community organisations.' She fears that a further term for Thatcher might lead to fascism.

The position of women

In her view, the financial position of women determines their access to other types of independence: 'It is only if we advocate that a woman has the right to be financially independent of her husband that there is a commitment to tackling the low pay in which women figure so prominently.' She is in favour of more good nurseries so that any woman can work without guilt, noting ironically: 'Beforehand, when we talked about full employment, we meant full *male* employment.

'I think we need to look again at our divorce laws, in which women are still to some extent the chattels of men.' She agrees with the right to abortion, commenting that this must be the woman's voluntary choice, given the forced sterilisation and abortion policies directed at American black women in the past.

Cultural preferences

I asked who her favourite writers were. 'I read the newspapers carefully everyday for this job so I don't read a great number of novels at night. When I do read, it tends to be books like *The Ragged Trousered Philanthropists*, or Angela Davis . . . the pulp would be Tom Sharpe because I fancied a good giggle. Novels are recommended by friends or in reviews and are usually political classics, for example Zola's *Germinal* . . . new writers like Maya Angelou . . . but I also like Shakespeare, although I find him difficult to read . . . and the trilogy, one of which was *Grey Granite* [by Lewis Grassic Gibbon]. I have also read Lewis Jones's brilliant *Cwmardy* and *We Live*, probably the only books to have moved me to tears. . . . I like novels about ordinary people and their problems, although there is quite a lot of emerging stuff around Glasgow and a risk of glamourising aspects, such as the treatment of gang warfare in *No Mean City*.'

Carmen also reads non-fictional works, mentioning John MacLean's *In the Rapids of Revolution*. In answer to the question about 'Red Clydeside', she raised issues about the periodisation of the events and the necessary distinctions between historical reality and the myths.

This respondent was among the most scathing in her dismissal of certain genres of popular literature: 'I don't *feel* the need to escape.'

At an earlier interview it was she who she had remarked on the subject of romantic fiction: 'If you're changing the world you don't need fantasy.'

Immersed in practical action, Carmen is one of the most consistent readers of the radical canon. Her choice of writer is conditioned principally by the recommendations of feminist or socialist friends and is relatively unaffected by current legitimate taste.

EDITH NEWBURY: LEGITIMATE TASTE

Edith is 59, the widow of a doctor. A teacher before her degree, she is now a bookshop assistant.

'My father owned a well-known shop in Glasgow. After he died there was nobody with whom I could talk about books: he loved books . . . literature. I was a teacher until I had my two boys, then went back when they were eight or nine, to remedial teaching. When they were older they said: "You would really like to go to university to get an Honours Degree, wouldn't you?" And so I did an English degree and later a whole year's evening course on Proust. I'm reading his letters at the moment. At the risk of sounding pretentious, for it is really sincere, every night when I went back to Proust I gave myself a treat. . . . After I graduated, I took on voluntary work and then this job in the bookshop.'

Political world-view

She hesitates at the over-simplification implicit in the question about *images of society*, then comments: 'I suppose its individuals with different amounts of money . . . although status is important, too. Class affects people's opportunities less than in the past and will recede in the future.' However, individuals with talent and industry cannot always get to the top: 'That doesn't always work: it depends on circumstances.'

I asked what the term 'Red Clydeside' meant to her. 'It was a socialist, working-class movement.' Do you approve? 'Oh, yes.'

The position of women

Edith states that she dislikes 'aggressive feminism'. Her attitudes are generally liberal, being in principle favourable to women's financial independence – 'That's probably a good idea' – to the right to abortion if wished and to more nurseries. However, she felt it was better not to have easy divorce: 'It should be possible to work at it.' For this reason, she is identified as possessing 'elements of feminism' in her views.

As is clear already, no doubt, Edith is happier answering questions about literature than about her views on society. In this area, she seems ill at ease or reticent, her stated opinions perhaps less adequate as a 'snapshot' of her ideas than is the case with other respondents. She has been classified as non-radical in her political sympathies.

Reading preferences

Edith intensely dislikes novels labelled romantic fiction, preferring books about people's relationships, in which a romantic element might be one aspect: 'Give me a good Russian novel any day! I like Anita Brookner, Jennifer Johnston. On a different level, I enjoy Proust, Tolstoy, Chekhov, Paul Scott . . . I liked *The Jewel and the Crown* very much, on television too, . . . Salman Rushdie: a wonderfully fertile imagination! Alice Munro: I liked her very good short stories . . . Rebecca West I read recently, haven't come across her before . . . Kim Chernin (*In My Mother's Room*, that's Virago). Maya Angelou . . . I enjoyed *I Know Why The Caged Bird Sings*; the second volume of autobiography rather less than the first. Alison Lurie, although she's not one of my favourite writers. Angela Carter – *Nights at the Circus*. David Lodge I like too and Howard Jacobson: these are very funny. Rosamund Lehmann I didn't enjoy very much.'

Asked about a range of specific authors, she has *not* read Cartland, Cookson, McCullough or Piercy, but liked Lessing's *Golden Notebook* and quite enjoyed Drabble. To questions about earlier writers, she comments 'I haven't read George Eliot for years, but thought *Middlemarch* very good . . . about Hardy I have mixed feelings. Tressell I read many years ago and can't remember it now.

A Scots' Quair, yes, I liked that. Asked whether she enjoys contemporary realism in general – 'things as they really are' – with ordinary people and their problems as the subject, she remarks: 'I don't want to read more novels about ordinary people, I don't like that type.' Do you like novels written to a formula? 'It never enters my head to look for novels that comply with a formula! I did try one novel like that, *Cain and Abel* (Jeffrey Archer): I hated its sentimental trashiness.'

She sees herself 'reading at different levels, for the story and for the social implications', selecting 'interest in a record of lived experience' and in 'the critical ideas of the writers' as accounts closest to her reading practices.

Edith can be allocated without hesitation to the group possessing legitimate taste. She comes closer than any other respondent to the 'aesthetic attitude' as defined by Bourdieu. Thus it is she who emphasises after reading *Lisa Logan*, the romance, that she 'felt depressed' by it, 'in a black mood'. Yet even in her case there are indications from her interest in the 'social implications' of literature that she also has political or ethical concerns, rather than the pure interest in literary form required by the aesthetic attitude.

ANNIE MCCRAE: ROMANTIC FICTION GROUP

Annie McCrae is in her 70s and 'loves reading'. She left school at 15, worked until her first child and then episodically after that. Her father was employed as a labourer in an iron foundry and her mother in factory and cleaning jobs. Although her husband was trained as a hairdresser, he later became a railway trackman. The following is an excerpt from a three-hour interview.

'Eighteen years ago I worked in [a whisky distillery] on a labelling machine . . . when I left school I worked in [a dry-cleaning firm]. I worked my way up from a message-girl to an ironer. That was a huge wage of £4-odd a week. That was a big wage . . . When I started at the whisky the wages were £3 5s a week. It was a family concern, now it's been taken over by [. . .]. I had loose eye muscles and double vision otherwise I would have stayed. It was a nice family business the way it was . . . they weren't concerned with the money coming in and just wanted to keep it the way it was. Then [. . .] made a bid for it. Oh! Changed days! New managers. Oh, I

got out just in time! It wasn't the same: it's all go-go-profit, business
. . . naturally, a different place taking over. [Before, the distillery-
owner] if you met him, he knew his workers, he kenned you all. He
got all his workers out one day, a cocktail thing for his daughter's
marriage . . . we collected, so it was lovely crystal glasses,
beautiful. . . . They made you feel spoke to an' that, real class, I
think, when people's like that. They know you're beneath them, but
they don't make you feel like that, you know. Yon peacocks out
. . . you stepped onto the lawn. . . .'

Political world-view

What are the West of Scotland's major problems in the 1980s? 'I
couldnae think o' that. I never think o' anything much, to tell you
the truth. I'm a right stupid cratter. I just jog along. Years ago, all
we thought about was, you just got your food: you didn't have time
to think about things. Years ago we were just struggling to survive
and you thought, politics and all thae kind o' things, what difference
could I make, however I thought? The working class never got a
chance, that was the way of it.'

What does the term 'Red Clydeside' mean to you? [Pause] 'I can
remember when the voting came along, They wouldnae miss
putting the vote in and all these meetings. And they talked, they
argued, it was great, it was exciting. The cars came and picked you
up. The excitement – it was like a holiday to all those kids. Now
nobody cares less.'

The position of women

Do you think women should be financially independent? 'You
know, I think they can get too much power . . . when women gets
a wee bit power, they're ruthless. Nowadays there's aye women
who gets good wages – although there's aye that wee bit against
them. Yet, actually, they're taking a man out of a job. See the old-
fashioned way, women got married and that was it . . . that was
you for the rest o' your life. If you get a job, you miss the best of
your babies, that's my personal opinion . . . I don't think that's
right leaving yon kids – that's precious that. No matter how good a
nanny you have, kids need you. I was more in the house, I was

enjoying playing with the kids. You can have good times wi' kids, you know.'

Reading preferences

'My favourite man is him that writes the cowboy books, Louis Amour . . . terrific writer – his grandfather was scalped by the Indians – he must have a good idea of what it was really like. Oh, I enjoy reading. . . . I like Catherine Cookson and a Glasgow girl, Christine Frazer. . . . I love a book that traces a family through the generations.' Do you like to read about any particular type of family, working-class, middle-class, aristocracy? 'A working-class family is more down-to-earth, but I've read quite a few about the others. It's interesting how they can slick each other out o' their inheritance, or one wee thing changes everybody's life.'

Do you like Mills and Boon novels? 'I like the books that are away in another country. It's no' just a book, you're learning and trying to understand it . . . the story, it's all lovey-dovey, stupid, she's aye got eyes like . . . glam . . . and he's got a fancy name, and they're aye rich. She's a typist, You know what's going to happen. But if it's got a story about another country, it makes it more interesting. Some of them are pretty good but some! I could write better myself! . . . I read Mickey Spillane. . . . I like that brash style. Sometimes I sit and read Mills and Boon and think, "Oh that's fine!" Other times I need something more solid and sensible.'

Family and class

She talked of her husband who 'couldn't be confined in the shop after he'd been in the war. He became a railway worker. You were lucky to get any work after the war. I said "You'll kill yourself." He stuck it out but it just about killed him. If you didn't keep it, what else are you going to get? But he was out in all that bad weather wi' asthma, then , finally, he got TB. My daughter woulnae go to church after her father's death, because she thought it was unfair.

'I get £36 a week pension. You've got to do everything on that. Not like kids who've only got to enjoy themselves.'

Classified as traditional in her views on feminism and on politics more generally, Annie McCrae showed an unusually deferential world-view. A clear affinity exists between her reading of romantic fiction or Westerns and her belief in a strict segregation of gender spheres, as well as very strong kinship ties.

FREDA CAMPBELL: 'COOKSON' GROUP

Freda, 59, works as a full-time cleaner, although she has had a variety of other jobs: a spray-painter in a factory, whisky inspector, fancy-box maker, a canteen assistant and a bus conductress. Her father was a stoker in the Navy, her mother a kilt-maker, later a garment-factory worker. 'My family was always treated as a little bit different in Possilpark. It was because we went to the library and didn't go to the pub. We were thought to be snobs. My mother always taught us to speak "proper": her father had been a company sergeant-major.

My father always wanted a boy. He gave me lots of boys' toys, boxing gloves, a wee gun. . . . Everywhere he went, I went too, wrestling, football, dog-racing and to the library. It was maybe because of him that I always read detective stories . . . McBain, Chandler, James Hadley Chase, Agatha Christie . . . although I don't like stories with 'Lord this and that' in them. I also read adventure stories, McLean, Fleming, Rider Haggard's *She*, Wilbur Smith. I hate romances, too sloppy and predictable. Seven out of the nine cleaners have read romances though, you ought to talk to them.'

Political world-view.

During the 1930s, her own family were not hungry, but many were: 'Things are going back to that – the poverty of the thirties, the hunger.' Her husband was a skilled engineer in the Post Office but has been unemployed for many years. She prefers the independence of working (she earns £61 a full-time week), yet is embittered by people on Social Security having cars and appearing to have a better life than she has: 'I sometimes think, as I am going out to my work on a dark, windy morning for 6 o'clock, I must be daft. All of them are lying in bed on Social Security!' Nevertheless sectional resentments do not undermine her sense of class power – 'You can do anything if you've got money – look at the Kennedies and that girl who died. Class has a great deal of impact, on individuals' opportunities. It's not true that if you work and have talent, you can always get on. You have to be there at the right time.'

She has always voted and opposes the other cleaners' cynicism about parties and unions – 'You're the union, and if you don't like it, you must change it.' She is a Scottish Nationalist, hoping for a society 'without unemployment, housing problems and dope – where all these things are reversed, where we are more sociable to one another, not getting one another's jobs. [Yet] . . . the young ones have had it too easy.'

What does the term 'Red Clydeside' mean to you? 'Men fighting for their principles, particularly for the right to work. . . . Not getting something for nothing, a Communist person believed you should work . . . it was stronger in the Second World War than the First. I generally approve.'

The position of women

She does not want to return to the 1930s and have women forced back into the home, although she also regrets children being given money and left on the streets. 'The best thing would be work nurseries, then a mother could stay in contact with the child.' She welcomes 'women's lib', despite jokes about it, approves of women's right to an abortion and disapproves of the Catholic Church's position on this.

Reading preferences (see above)

Freda has read English nineteenth-century novels, Dickens and the Brontës being named. She started Catherine Cookson by chance and then read her novels avidly: 'I like the details of how things were then. For example, how much of a struggle it was to be allowed to read.' She has never heard of Robert Tressell, Lewis Grassic Gibbon, Marge Piercy, Doris Lessing or Margaret Drabble. Her preferred contemporary writers are Virginia Andrews, Colleen McCullough, Barbara Taylor Bradford and Catherine Cookson, although Cookson has become disappointingly predictable. She reads between six and twenty-four novels a month. Lewis Jones's *Cwmardy* did not appeal to her, because the Welsh dialect was impenetrable, yet she liked *Daughter of Earth*.

Do you like realist novels: novels about things as they really are? 'Yes, but it's hard to define, isn't it? Different people define it differently. I like reality but I also like fantasies, fast-moving adventure stories: if you want to get away from everything, they're the ones to read. Things are getting so depressing, you don't want to read more about it. You're no' wanting to hear about someone else's sufferin'. . . . my son's unemployed; my nephew's unemployed; my son tried to commit suicide when his 5-year-old son died and his other child was diagnosed as having cystic fibrosis too. You've got so much hardship of your own, that it puts you off.' Hence her turning to the formula 'with a twist in the tail' and the preference, where possible, for a happy ending.

Classified as politically radical and a feminist, Freda has had no programme of self-education, like Mary Dennison, and indeed her views show why women turn to fantasy. However, as with many political activists, hers is a pattern in which reading is linked to political participation, to sobriety and clarity of speech in a culture of respectability. This both permits collective advance and confers on such individuals intrinsic benefits of self-esteem. This view was put more explicitly by another member of the sample: 'It's only if you have more knowledge that you are better.'

Notes

INTRODUCTION

1. Benjamin, W., *Illuminations* (London: Fontana, 1973), p. 184.
2. Bloch, E., *The Principle of Hope*, 3 vols., translated by N. and S. Plaice and S. Knight (Oxford: Blackwell, 1986, (1947)), vol. 1, p. 441.

CHAPTER 1

1. Gramsci has noted the inconsistencies within the 'artificial paradises' of popular literature. Gramsci, A., *Marxismo e Letteratura* (Rome: Riuniti, 1975), p. 155 (translated N. Paoletti, to whom I owe thanks).
2. The terms 'romance' and 'romantic fiction' are used interchangeably in this book.
3. Hegel, G.W.F., *Phenomenology of Spirit* (Oxford: Oxford University Press, 1977), pp. 116–18. De Beauvoir, S., *The Second Sex* (London: Jonathan Cape, 1953), p. 90, applied this model to gender, although in an ahistorical manner. Genovese has also commented that the slave's view of the oppressive slaveowner as a father-figure is not hard to understand, since the latter was the fount of all privileges, gifts and necessities. Cited in Thompson, E.P., 'Patrician society, plebeian culture', *Journal of Social History*, vol. 7, no. 4, summer 1974, pp. 382–405.
4. P. Corrigan and D. Sayer have pointed out that although the *class* exclusiveness in the meaning of 'the public' is often transparent, historically

the exclusion of females goes so deep as not to be thought worth indicating at all. . .women are understood as property, personally in relation to specific men. . .and more generally as social property. This has been the legitimate, approved, public expression of some 52% of the population . . . a term like schizophrenia catches some of its horror. (*The Great Arch* (Oxford: Blackwell, 1985), p. 134)

5. Murray, M., *Gender Relations and State Formation*, unpublished Ph.D., University of Glasgow, 1988, p. 80. I am grateful to Mary Murray for letting me see this excellent thesis before publication. French, M., *Beyond Power* (London: Jonathan Cape, 1985), p. 158.
6. Murray, *op.cit.*, pp. 179, 194.
7. *ibid.*, 115–18. She argues convincingly against MacFarlane that although under canon law there was free choice of spouse, this was absent *de facto*, since children could be married off before the age of consent, Parents were liable for damages if engagements were broken before age 12 and bequests in wills were often dependent on parental choice, even in the 1720s. This undermines MacFarlane's claim that romantic love was the basis of marriage in England from the twelfth century. Macfarlane, A., *Marriage and Love in England* (Oxford: Blackwell, 1986), pp. 330; 336.
8. French, *op.cit.*, p. 158; Murray *op.cit.*, p. 109.
9. Murray, *ibid.*, pp. 84, 309.
10. Middleton, C., 'The sexual division of labour in feudal England', *New Left Review*, nos. 113–14, January–April 1979, pp. 147–68, esp. pp. 166–7; French, *op.cit.*, p. 163.
11. Casey, K., 'The Cheshire cat. Reconstructing the experience of medieval women', in Carroll, B. (ed.) *Liberating Women's History* (Urbana: University of Illinois, 1976), pp. 227–32; Lewenhak, S., *Women and Work* (London: Fontana, 1980), pp. 132–3.
12. Middleton, *op.cit.*, pp. 56–159.
13. *ibid.*, p. 162.
14. Murray, *op. cit.*, p. 295. Punishment on such a sliding scale originated in Anglo-Saxon England, indicating that a class society, with its problems of inheritance, had already emerged from tribal society.
15. *ibid.*, p. 299.
16. Taylor, B., *Eve and the New Jerusalem* (London: Virago, 1983), p. 135.
17. Murray, *op. cit.*, pp. 200–1; Corrigan and Sayer, *op. cit.*, p. 36.
18. From a copious literature, see Cohn, N., *The Pursuit of the Millennium* (London: Mercury, 1962), pp. 165–76; p. 234.
19. Hill, C., *Society and Puritanism in Pre-Revolutionary England* (London: Panther, 1969), p. 432.
20. French, *op. cit.*, p. 160.
21. Clark, A., *Working Life of Women in the Seventeenth Century* (London: Routledge, 1982 (1919)), p. 196–7.
22. *ibid.*, pp. 156–7.
23. *ibid.*, pp. 196–7; Casey, *op. cit.*, p. 229.
24. *ibid.*, p. 229; French, p. 160, Clark, *op. cit.*, p.288; Larner, C., *Enemies of God* (London: Chatto and Windus, 1981), p. 125.
25. Clark, *op. cit.*, p. 86 and p. 305.
26. Murray, *op. cit.*, p. 110.

27. *ibid.*, p. 132, Corrigan and Sayer, *op. cit.*, p. 36, Stone, L., *Family, Sex and Marriage in England, 1500–1800* (Harmondsworth: Penguin, 1979), p. 136.

28. Branca, P., *Silent Sisterhood* (London: Croom Helm, 1975), p. 9.

29. Corrigan and Sayer, *op. cit.*, p. 36.

30. Branca, *op. cit.*, p. 8; Corrigan and Sayer, *op. cit.*, p. 37; Stone, *op. cit.*, p. 222.

31. Benjamin, W., *Illuminations* (London: Fontana, 1973), pp. 83–109. Bloch, M., *Feudal Society* (London: Routledge, 1962), p. 94.

32. Propp, V., *Morphology of the Folk-Tale* (Bloomington: Indiana University Press, 1968).

33. Levi-Strauss, C., 'La structure et la forme', *Cahiers de L'Institut de Science Economique Applique*, 99, Paris 1960, serie M, no. 7, pp. 25–33.

34. Meletinsky, E.M., 'Problème de la morphologie historique du conte populaire', *Semiotica*, II, 1970, no. 2, pp. 128–34.

35. Zipes, J., *Breaking the Magic Spell* (London: Heinemann, 1979).

36. Aarne, A., *The Types of the Folk-Tale* (Helsinki: Academia Scientiarum Fennica, 1964 (1928)).

37. Zipes, *op. cit.*, pp. 23–34.

38. *ibid.*, p. 160–82.

39. Ladurie, E.L., *Love, Death and Money in the Pays d'Oc* (Harmondsworth: Penguin, 1984), p. 42.

40. *ibid.*, pp. 141–2.

41. *ibid.*, p. 151.

42. *ibid.*, p. 37.

43. *ibid.*, p. 66.

44. *ibid.*, pp. 141–8.

45. *ibid.*, p. 312.

46. *ibid.*, p. 408, pp. 511–12.

47. *ibid.*, p. 153.

48. There is evidence that the romance is changing in the 1980s with the split in the experience of women. The imaginary unity sought in the resolution cannot accommodate simultaneously the desires of wage earners and houseworkers. Hence, the birth of a new series with working heroines in Mills and Boon, together with evidence of greater sensitivity to the women's individuated goals and needs. See Jones, A. R., 'Mills and Boon meets feminism', in Radford J. (ed.), *The Progress of Romance* (London: Routledge, 1986), pp. 195–221. The inner secularisation of the romance as a form is noted in Chapter 5, below.

49. Richardson, S., *Pamela*, Eaves, B., and Kimpel, B. (eds), (Boston: Houghton-Mifflin, 1971). I have restricted my scope to the plebeian narratives from which the form originated, omitting the influence on romantic novels such as *Pamela* of earlier English canonical writers, particularly Chaucer, Sidney, Spencer, Shakespeare and Milton.

50. Eagleton, T., *The Rape of Clarissa* (Oxford: Blackwell, 1982), p. 37.

51. Watt, I., *The Rise of the Novel* (Harmondsworth: Peregrine, 1963),

pp. 183, 189, 192; Laurenson, D. and Swingewood, A., *The Sociology of Literature* (London: MacGibbon and Kee, 1971), pp. 180–1; Eagleton, *op. cit.*, pp. 3, 9–10.

52. Watt, *op. cit.*, p. 172.

53. Christopher Hill refers to Richardson as a typical member of the rising bourgeoisie, in his movement from apprentice to successful employer with his own printing business: 'The social background to *Clarissa* is this developing bourgeois society' (*op. cit.*, p. 357).

54. Brenner, R., 'Agrarian class structure and economic development in pre-industrial Europe and the agrarian roots of European capitalism', in Aston, T.H. and Philbin, C.H.E. (eds), *The Brenner Debate* (Cambridge: Cambridge University Press, 1985), pp. 10–63, 213–327.

55. Thompson, E.P., *The Poverty of Theory* (London: Merlin, 1979), p. 48.

56. See Wood, N., *John Locke and Agrarian Capitalism* (Berkeley: University of California Press, 1984), p. 48.

57. Richardson, *op. cit.*, p. 371.

58. See Corrigan and Sayer, *op. cit.*, p. 192.

59. James, L., *Fiction for the Working Man* (Harmondsworth: Penguin, 1974), p. 116. See also his comment that the origin of the modern magazine story lay in the domestic romance, p. 134.

60. Dalziel, M., *Popular Fiction One Hundred Years Ago* (London: Cohen and West, 1957), p. 146.

61. Davidoff, L., and Hall, C., *Family Fortunes: Men and women of the English middle class, 1780–1850* (London: Hutchinson, 1987), p. 95. Taylor, *op. cit.*, pp. 125–7.

62. Taylor, *op. cit.*, p. 48.

63. Hill, *op. cit.*, p. 456. Hill's argument is that the patriarchalism of the Puritans, including the Levellers, was a transitional state between the feudal sense of kin community and the equal rights of men and women (p. 466). I would want to extend this to apply to the partially individuated consciousness of the heroine in the domestic romance.

64. Schucking, L., *The Puritan Family* (London: Routledge, 1969).

65. Taylor, *op. cit.*, p. 125.

66. The term 'moral disinfectant' is James's, *op. cit.*, p. 18, and the 'proletarianisation of the Enlightenment' is used by Taylor, *op. cit.*, p. 306.

67. James, *op. cit.*

68. Medick, H., 'Plebeian culture in the transition to capitalism', in Samuel, R. and Stedman Jones, G. (eds), *Culture, Ideology and Politics* (London: Routledge, 1980).

69. Mitchell, S., 'The forgotten women of the period: penny weekly magazines of the 1840s and 50s', in Vicinus, M. (ed.), *The Widening Sphere* (London: Methuen, 1980), pp. 29–51. The owner of *Family Herald* left £50,000; *London Journal* had £10,000 annual profit (in contrast James cited 25,000 circulation for *Howitt's Journal* and a lifespan of only six months for *Cooper's Journal* (James, *op. cit.*, pp. 147–9)). Mitchell viewed the popular family magazines as allowing women to define and justify a

new role after their loss of direct economic contribution. They valorised women's self-abasing service: 'The family magazine's vision of life purified and enobled a set of values which convinced the forgotten woman that she was important' (p. 51).
70. Mitchell, *op. cit.*, pp. 31, 33, 38.

CHAPTER 2

1. Balibar comments on the importance in this respect of A.L. Berquin's translations of Barbauld's English children's stories: Balibar, R., 'National language, education and literature', in Barker, F. (ed.), *Literature, Politics and Theory* (London: Methuen, 1986), pp. 126–47.
2. Altick, R.D., *The English Common Reader* (Chicago: University of Chicago Press, 1957), pp. 34, 41, 63–4; Thomas, K., 'The meaning of literacy in early modern England', in Bauman, G. (ed.), *The Written Word* (Oxford: Clarendon Press, 1986), p. 117.
3. Stern, M., *Publishers for Mass Entertainment in Nineteenth-Century America* (Boston, Mass.: G.K. Hall, 1980), p. ix; Mott, F.L., *Golden Multitudes* (New York: R.R. Bowker, 1947), p. 76. Mott dated the 'great revolution' in publishing from 1842 to 1845.
4. Stern, *op. cit.*, p. xv.
5. Hart, J.D., *The Popular Book* (New York: Oxford University Press, 1950), p. 96. The comparison with Smith is mine.
6. Gissing, G., *New Grub Street* (Harmondsworth: Penguin, 1968), p. 138.
7. Gramsci, A., *Marxismo e Letteratura* (Rome: Riuniti, 1975), p. 150; Forgacs, D. and Nowell-Smith, G. (eds.), *Antonio Gramsci: Selections from the Cultural Writings* (London: Lawrence and Wishart, 1985), p. 376.
8. Hart, *op. cit.*, p. 60.
9. *ibid.*, pp. 90, 154, 172. Mott's calculation of best sellers extends to those books with slow, steady sales, which would include Hawthorne's *The Scarlet Letter*.
10. Hart, *op. cit.*, on Grand and Tolstoy, p. 173; on Bellamy, pp. 169–72. Mott, *op. cit.*, on Grand, pp. 181–2; on Tolstoy, pp. 182–3; on Bellamy, pp. 168–70.
11. Mott, *ibid.*, p. 1; Hart, *op. cit.*, p. 120.
12. Stern, *op. cit.*, p. 45; Hart, *op. cit.*, p. 155.
13. When Alger's stories were priced as cheaply as dime novels, their popularity became immense, reaching 17 million between 1867 and 1910, See Mott, *op. cit.*, pp. 159–9.
14. Hart, *op. cit.*, p. 202. In view of the delayed mass readership for Alger (see note 13), it is important to note that production and distribution may have different rhythms.
15. *ibid.*, pp. 171–2, 220.
16. *ibid.*, p. 250.
17. *ibid.*, p. 263.

18. Kaplan, C., *Sea Changes: Culture and feminism* (London: Verso, 1986), p. 118.

19. James, L., *Fiction for the Working Man* (Harmondsworth: Penguin, 1974), p. 184.

20. Dalziel, M., *Popular Fiction One Hundred Years Ago* (London: Cohen and West, 1957), pp. 35–6; James, *op. cit.*, p. 194.

21. James, *op. cit.*, pp. 91–4.

22. *ibid.*, p. 126–7.

23. *ibid.*, pp. 217–223; Dalziel, *op. cit.*, pp. 14–16; 99.

24. Altick, *op. cit.*, pp. 290–1.

25. *ibid.*, p. 208–12; Suvin, D., 'The social addressees of Victorian fiction', *Literature and History*, vol. 8 (1), 1982, pp. 21, 38. Tolstoy was popular in America from 1885, *War and Peace* having been reprinted in 25 cent editions; Flaubert's *Madame Bovary* sold a million copies after a 25 cent edition; Mott, *op. cit.*, p. 248.

26. Gramsci, *op. cit.*, pp. 136–7; 152–4.

27. Eco, U., 'Rhetoric and ideology in Sue's *Les Mysteres de Paris*', *International Social Science Journal*, vol. xix, no. 4, 1967, Unesco.

28. Long, E., *The American Dream and the Popular Novel* (Boston and London: Routledge, 1985), p. 27.

29. Sutherland, J., *Bestsellers* (London: Routledge, 1981), p. 22.

30. Golding, P., *Creativity, Control and The Publishing Industry*, Conference Paper, University of Burgos, July 1979.

31. Curwen, P., *The U.K. Publishing Industry* (Oxford: Pergamon, 1981), p. 22; for the absence of any serious consideration of mergers, see pp. 16–22.

32. Radway, *Reading the Romance*, (Chapel Hill, University of Carolina Press, 1984), p. 39. It is worth noting that Mills and Boon have not always been restricted to domestic romance. A different genre of popular literature, Jack London's revolutionary novel, *The Iron Heel*, was first published by this firm in Britain.

33. Schifferin, A., 'Studying the Romantics', *New Society*, 27 November 1987, pp. 17–19.

34. Radway, *op. cit.*, p. 40.

35. Paizis, G., *The Contemporary Romantic Novel in France*, Ph.D. Thesis, University of London, 1986, p. 8.

36. Curwen, *op. cit.*, p. 36.

37. Gedin, P., *Literature in the Market Place* (London: Faber, 1977), p. 95.

38. McGuigan, J., *Writers and the Arts Council* (London: The Arts Council, 1981). Sutherland, J., *Fiction and the Fiction Industry* (London: Athlone Press, 1978).

39. Bourdieu, P., 'The production of belief', *Media, Culture and Society*, vol. 3, no. 2, July 1980, pp. 261–93.

40. Curwen, *op. cit.*, p. 10.

41. Curwen shows that fiction on the home market rose by 23 per cent between 1979 and 1980, p. 33.

42. Coser, L., Kadushin, C. and Powell, W., *Books: The culture and commerce of publishing* (New York: Basic Books, 1985), pp. 22–3.
43. Lane, M., *Books and Publishing: Commerce against culture* (Lexington, D.C. Heath, 1980), p. 128.
44. For a defence of this position, see Gans, H., *Popular and High Culture* (New York: Basic Books, 1974).
45. Their 'golden age ' covers the history of publishing to date, although Suvin, Lane and Sutherland point out the highly competitive nature of Victorian publishing, except where there was stable demand by circulating libraries. See Sutherland, J.A., *Victorian Novelists and Publishers* (London: The Athlone Press, 1976).
46. Lane, *op. cit.*, p. 127.
47. Coser *et al.*, *op. cit.*, p. 23.
48. Lane, *op. cit.*, pp. 127–8.
49. Coser *et al.*, *op. cit.*, p. 50.
50. *ibid.*, p. 358.
51. See second interview with the Scottish readers in Chapter 6.
52. Coser *et al.*, *op. cit.*, pp. 263–5.
53. Lane, *op. cit.*, p. 117.
54. This view is also held by Worpole, K., *Reading By Numbers* (London: Comedia, 1984), pp. 93, 107–8.
55. See Gramsci, *op. cit.*, Forgacs and Nowell-Smith, *op. cit.*
56. Gramsci, *op. cit.*, pp. 131–6.
57. Forgacs and Nowell-Smith, *op. cit.*, p. 349.
58. Gramsci, *op. cit.*, pp. 154–7. Eco has developed Gramsci's ideas on the superman, especially in his earlier work, see *The Role of The Reader* (London: Hutchinson, 1981), pp. 107–24.
59. Brecht, B., in Willett, J. (ed.), *Brecht on Theatre* (London: Eyre Methuen, 1978), pp. 89; 179.
60. Forgacs and Nowell-Smith, *op. cit.*, p. 357.
61. Gramsci, *op. cit.*, p. 155.
62. *ibid.*, p. 137.
63. Bloch, E., *The Principle of Hope*, 3 vols., translated by N. and S. Plaice and S. Knight (Oxford: Blackwell, 1986, (1947)).
64. Hudson, W., *The Philosophy of Ernst Bloch* (London: Macmillan, 1982); see also Lowy, M., 'Interview with Ernst Bloch', *New German Critique*, no. 9, fall 1976, pp. 35–46.
65. Bloch, *op. cit.*, vol. II, pp. 762–76.
66. *ibid.*, vol. I, p. 29.
67. *ibid.*, pp. 98–9.
68. *ibid.*, p. 97.
69. *ibid.*, p. 348. Following Said, Orientals should be included in this list; Said, E., *Orientalism* (Harmondsworth: Penguin, 1985).
70. Bloch, *op. cit.*, p. 351.
71. Bloch, E., *The Utopian Function of Art and Literature*, translated by Zipes,

J. and Mecklenberg, F. (Cambridge, Mass. and London: MIT Press, 1988), p. 184.

72. Haug, F., 'Daydreams', *New Left Review*, no. 162, March–April 1987, pp. 51–66.

73. This is true of Mulvey, L., 'Visual pleasure and narrative cinema', *Screen*, vol. 16., no. 3, 1975; Modleski, T., *Loving with a Vengeance* (London: Methuen, 1984) and, to a lesser extent, Radway, *op. cit.*

74. Denning, M., *Mechanic Accents: Dime novels and working-class culture in America* (London: Verso, 1987).

75. Symons, J., *Bloody Murder: From the detective story to the crime novel: A history* (London: Faber and Faber, 1972); Palmer, J., *Thrillers: genesis and structure of a popular genre* (London: E. Arnold, 1978); Mandel, E., *Delightful Murder: A social history of the crime story* (London: Pluto, 1974). See also Cawelti, J., *Adventure, Mystery and Romance: Formula stories as art and popular culture* (Chicago: University of Chicago Press, 1976).

76. Denning, M., *Cover Stories* (London: Routledge, 1987).

77. Williams, R., *Problems in Materialism and Culture* (London: Verso, 1980), pp. 196–213; Parrinder, P., *Science Fiction* (London: Methuen, 1980).

78. Leavis, Q.D., *Fiction and the Reading Public* (Harmondsworth: Penguin, 1979 (1932)).

79. Mulhern, F., *The Moment Of Scrutiny* (London: Verso NLB, 1979), p. 311.

80. *ibid.*, p. 152.

81. Leavis, Q.D., 'The discipline of letters', in Leavis, F.R. (ed.), *A Selection from Scrutiny* (Cambridge: Cambridge University Press, 1968), pp. 7–22.

82. Leavis, *Fiction*, p. 145.

83. *ibid.*, pp. 180 and 83.

84. *ibid.*, p. 63.

85. Freud, S., *New Introductory Lectures on Psychoanalysis* (Harmondsdworth: Penguin, 1973), pp. 145–69.

86. Williams used psychoanalytic terms within a historical framework in his revaluation of the fiction of 1848, see *Writing in Society* (London: Verso, no date), pp. 153–7; for his defence of the Freudian project, see *Problems in Materialism and Culture op. cit.*, pp. 103–22.

87. *The Uses of Literacy* (Harmondsworth: Penguin, 1958).

88. *ibid.*, p. 234.

89. *ibid.*, p. 101.

90. Eagleton, T., *Criticism and Ideology* (London: Verso NLB, 1976), p. 42.

91. *The Long Revolution* (Harmondsworth: Penguin, 1965),p. 73.

92. Tawney, R.H., *Religion and the Rise of Capitalism* (Harmondsworth: Penguin, 1948), p. 211–58.

93. Despite this, E.P. Thompson's criticism of Williams's anthropological model for reifying the 'whole way of life' of the working class has considerable justification. See *New Left Review*, no. 9, pp. 24–33, and no. 10, pp. 34–9, 1961.

94. Harrison, R., '*Shirley*: relations of reproduction and the ideology of

romance', in Centre for Contemporary Cultural Studies, *Women Take Issue* (London: Hutchinson, 1978).

95. Williams, *The Long Revolution*, *op. cit.*, p. 85; *The Country and the City* (London: Hogarth, 1985), p. 174; *Writing in Society*, *op. cit.*, pp. 150–65.

96. *Mary Barton* was written with a close knowledge of the autobiography of the radical weaver, Samuel Bamford.

97. See Bromley, R., 'Natural boundaries, the social function of popular fiction', *Red Letters*, no. 7, 1978, pp. 34–60; Bennett, T., *Formalism and Marxism* (London: Methuen, 1979), also 'Marxism and popular fiction', *Literature and History*, vol. 7, no. 2, autumn 1981, pp. 158–65; MacCabe, C., 'Realism and the cinema', *Screen*, vol. 15, no. 2, 1974, pp. 7–27. See also Sinfield, A., 'Four ways with a reactionary text', *Journal of Literature, Teaching and Politics*, vol. 1, no. 2, 1983, pp. 81–96. There are similarities between these approaches and the 'mechanical materialism' criticised by Williams in *Culture and Society* (Harmondsworth: Penguin, 1961), p. 266.

98. Sinfield, *op. cit.*, p. 81.

99. Eagleton, T., *Literary Theory* (Oxford: Blackwell, 1983), p. 214.

100. *ibid.*, p. 25.

101. Bromley, *op. cit.* For Bennett's response see Bennett, T., 'Marxism and popular fiction', *op. cit.*

102. Bennett also argued, contentiously, that through much of its history Marxist aesthetics has been complicit with bourgeois aesthetics. Marxist theorists have focused on the representation of a totality, the social typicality of characters and the illumination of historical contradictions through the clashing ideas of the protagonists. In my view, these are distinctive to Marxist aesthetics rather than 'bourgeois' conceptions of art. See my 'Marxist theories of the canon', *Cultural Studies*, vol. 1. no. 2, 1987, pp. 162–78.

103. Ryan, K., 'Towards a socialist criticism: reclaiming the canon', *Literature, Teaching and Politics*, no.3, 1984, p. 12.

104. For a pioneering assessment of the canon which seeks both to analyse the sociological implications of women's subordination in literature and to avoid a conspiracy theory of patriarchy, see Lovell, T., *Consuming Fiction* (London: Verso, 1987), pp. 130–2.

105. Eagleton, in *Literary Theory*, *op. cit.*, pp. 19–20, argues that this was the criterion with which a differentiated model of Literature was constructed in the eighteenth century. However, opposing views of literature were developed in the Romantic movement and Chartism. See James, *op. cit.*, pp.84–5; Thompson, E.P., *William Morris: From romantic to revolutionary* (London: Merlin, 1978), pp. 393–411; Foot, P., *Red Shelley* (London: Sedgwick and Jackson, 1981), pp. 207–8; 238–9.

106. Bloch, *op. cit.*, pp. 417–18. See also Raphael, M., *The Demands of Art* (London: Routledge, 1968), pp. 187, 201.

107. Such instances would be the important mediating roles played by Port Royal Jansenism in the case of the French *noblesse de robe* and Bloomsbury for the liberal wing of the British ruling class. Additionally, women

writers can be expected to experience class relations differently, due to their multiple exclusions.

108. Paizis, *op. cit.*, pp. 51–2.
109. *ibid.*, p. 156.
110. Jameson, F., 'Reification and utopia in mass culture', *Social Text*, no. 1, 1979, pp. 130–48; pp. 147–8.
111. Radway, *op. cit.*, p. 98.
112. *ibid.*, p. 221.
113. *ibid.*, p. 212.
114. *ibid.*, p. 221.

CHAPTER 3

1. Elsaesser, T., 'Tales of sound and fury', in (no ed.) *Melodrama in the Cinema* (Glasgow: Glasgow Film Theatre, 1977), reprinted in *Monogram, Brighton Film Review*, no. 4.
2. James, L., *Print and the People 1819–1851* (Harmondsworth: Penguin, 1976), p. 87. See also Basch, F., *Relative Creatures* (London: Allen Lane, 1974), pp. 227–8.
3. Kristeva, J., 'Ruins of a poetics', in Bann, S. and Bowlt, J.E. (eds), *Russian Formalism* (Edinburgh: Scottish Academic Press, 1973). In contrast, a third of 1980s *Woman* and *Woman's Own* stories are structured by the questioning forms and relativism characteristic of modernism, which has begun to percolate to sections of the mass market.
4. Jameson, F., 'Reification and utopia in mass culture', *Social Text*, no. 1, 1979, pp. 140–1.
5. Crowther, M.A., *The Workhouse System, 1834–1929* (London: Batsford, 1981), pp. 43, 233, 269. Crowther notes that penny novelettes and broadside ballads viewed workhouse inmates with pity and fear, p. 73. See also Taylor, B., *Eve and the New Jerusalem* (London: Virago, 1983), pp. 200–1.
6. The magazines sampled for the 1930s are listed below. It is impossible to include pre-war circulations for these magazines since the Thompson titles were not registered with the Audit Bureau of Circulations. However, their social distribution is unlikely to have differed markedly in the first major post-war analysis of representative magazines in *The Hulton Readership Survey*, compiled by Hobson, J.W. and Henry, M. (London: The Hulton Press, 1947). I also include the fuller data on the class distribution of women readers given by the Institute of Practitioners in Advertising, London, 1956. Impressionistic accounts confirming these results are those of Roberts, R., *The Classic Slum* (Manchester: Manchester University Press, 1971); Orwell, George, 'Boys' weeklies (1938)' in *Collected Essays, Journalism and Letters*, vol. 1 (Harmondsworth: Penguin, 1970) and Hoggart, Richard, *The Uses of Literacy* (Harmondsworth: Penguin, 1969).

Magazine	Date sampled	Publisher	No. of stories sampled
Women's Way	1929–30	D.C. Thompson	12; serial
Weekly Welcome	1929–30	D.C. Thompson	13; serial
Red Letter	1930	D.C. Thompson	13
Family Star	1934–5	D.C. Thompson	12
Home Chat	1929–30	Amalgamated Press	15; serial
The Oracle	1933–4	Amalgamated Press	13
My Weekly	1929–30	John Leng and Co.	13
People's Friend	1929–30	John Leng and Co.	14 (28 in total); serial
Lucky Star	1935–6	Newnes and Pearson	13
Silver Star	1937–8	C. Arthur Pearson	12
Family Herald	1929–30	J.T. Elvidge	12

Total of women's popular stories sampled: 160 (including 4 serials)

Hulton Readership Survey: percentages of each 'class' reading periodical, women, 1947

Magazine	AB	C	DE
People's Friend	★	4.2	5.7
Home Chat	3.8	3.1	3.4
Red Letter	★	★	6.2

National Readership Survey (IPA), women, 1956

Magazine	AB	C(i)	C(ii)	DE
People's Friend	4	5	6	6
Home Chat	4	6	5	4
Red Letter	1	2	5	7
Lucky Star	★	1	4	5
Silver Star	1	1	3	6
Oracle	★	1	2	3
True Romances	2	5	11	11

7. Clare, T., 'Whom God hath joined', *Weekly Welcome*, no. 1737, 29 June 1929, pp. 372–375.
8. Bennett, T., 'Hegemony, ideology, pleasure: Blackpool', in Bennett, T., Mercer, C. and Woollacott, J. (eds), *Popular Culture and Social Relations* (Milton Keynes: Open University Press, 1986), p. 141. Said, E. *Orientalism* (Harmondsworth: Penguin, 1985), p. 325.
9. On such dual elements, see Erlich, V., *Russian Formalism* (The Hague: Mouton, 1980 (1955)) and Matejka, L. and Pomorska, K. (eds), *Readings in Russian Poetics* (Cambridge, Mass. and London: MIT Press, 1971).
10. Hoggart, *op. cit.*, pp. 27–37. See also Steedman, C., *Landscape for a Good*

Woman (London: Virago, 1987), in which the author describes vividly her mother's difference from other working-class women in expressing her unacceptable desires for good things, pp. 8–9, 106–9.

11. Wheale, A., *Antigua Kiss* (London: Worldwide Romance, 1982), pp. 294, 319–20.

12. Basch, *op. cit.*, on the Madonna image, pp. xiii–17; on 'fallen' women, pp. 219, 249.

13. Sennett, R., *The Fall of Public Man* (Cambridge: Cambridge University Press, 1977) esp. pp. 177–82; 259.

14. Donzelot, J., *The Policing of Families* (London: Hutchinson, 1980), pp. 45–6.

15. Stone, L., *Family, Sex and Marriage in England, 1500–1800* (Harmondsworth: Penguin, 1979), pp. 388; 394–5. On this change, see also Scott, J.W. and Tilly, L.A., 'Women's work and the family in nineteenth-century Europe', in Amsden, A. (ed.), *The Economics of Women and Work* (Harmondsworth: Penguin, 1980), pp. 91–134; Lewis, J., *Women in England, 1870–1950* (Hemel Hempstead: Harvester Wheatsheaf, 1984), pp. 36–40.

16. Donzelot, *op. cit.*, p. 92; Taylor, *op. cit.*, p. 199–206.

17. A hedonistic world of consumption *is* an important element of the 1980s' 'feminist romance of modernity', in sharp contrast with the mild asceticism of 1930s' heroic figures; see Chapter 5.

18. 21 December 1929 to 22 March 1930, serialised, no author.

19. *The Oracle*, 2 June 1934, pp. 9–16, no author.

20. *ibid.*, p. 10.

21. *The Oracle*, 5 May 1934, pp. 2–10, no author; p. 9.

22. *The Oracle*, 2 June 1934, p. 13.

23. Young, J.M.D., 'Jenny's pirate partner', *Red Letter*, vol. 33, no. 2, 11 January 1930, pp. 39–41; p. 41.

24. *The Oracle*, 2 June 1934, p. 12.

25. The 'fallen woman' or whore was the 'other' of the Victorian canonised novels. A sympathetic portrayal was occasionally presented, but always linked to the character's early death. See Basch's illuminating discussion, particularly on Mrs Gaskell's *Ruth*, *op. cit.*, pp. 181–4, 246–51, 249.

26. *Silver Star*, 20 November 1937, pp. 2–15, 30, no author.

27. See Clarke, A., 'The politics of seduction in English popular culture, 1748–1848', in Radford, J. (ed.), *The Progress of Romance* (London: Routledge, 1986), pp. 47–62.

28. 'Her forgotten honeymoon', *Silver Star*, 2 April 1938; 'Secret wife', *Lucky Star*, 7 March 1936, no author.

29. See, for example, Jones, E., 'The wrongs of women', *Notes to the People* (London: Pavey, 1852; reprinted by Merlin, 1967), pp. 515–1012 (serialised).

30. Stone, *op. cit.*, 399–400.

31. Stone notes that by the eighteenth century the penalties for illegitimacy without paternal financial responsibility were severe, including loss of the

mother's work and confinement in the House of Correction. On the nineteenth century, see Taylor, *op. cit.*, pp. 200–1.

32. 'Steve West's secret', *Lucky Star*, 8 February 1936, no. 23, no author, p. 10.

33. Stone, *op. cit.*, pp. 35, 324 and 395. I am here extending an earlier argument against theories of popular literature reflecting society, see Fowler, B., 'True to me always: an analysis of magazine fiction', in Pawling, C. (ed.), *Popular Fiction and Social Change* (London: Macmillan, 1984), pp. 114–5.

34. The exception was Disraeli, see Basch, *op. cit.*, pp. 175, 187.

35. L.E.I. [*sic*], 'Caroline Anstruther', *Family Herald*, 6 November 1929.

36. Foucault, M., *Sexuality*, vol. 1 (London: Allen Lane, 1979), pp. 104–21.

37. 'Caroline Anstruther', *op. cit.*, p. 53. Compare this with Howard, J. C., 'A woman's job', *Tit-Bits*, 4 January 1930, pp. 12–13, which presents a business career for a woman as part of a 'world turned upside down'.

38. Cotroni, M., 'Mummy come back', *Red Letter*, no. 38, 20 September 1930, pp. 397–8; p. 398. See also Moore, E., 'The mother who ran away', *My Weekly*, no. 1045, 10 May 1935, pp. 561–3 and May, I., 'My wife needn't work!', *Woman's Way*, 29 September, pp. 10–11.

39. 'She took off her wedding-ring', *Lucky Star*, no. 6, 12 October 1935, no author, pp. 8–10.

40. *ibid.*, p. 8.

41. *ibid.*, p. 8.

42. *ibid.*, p. 7.

43. *ibid.*, p. 8.

44. 'Scandal ruined her life', *Lucky Star*, no. 30, 28 March 1936, no author, pp. 7–13: p. 8.

45. Gibbon, L.G., 'Smeddum', in Hendry, J.F. (ed.), *The Penguin Book of Scottish Short Stories* (Harmondsworth: Penguin, 1970); Larner, C. *Enemies of God* (London: Chatto and Windus, 1981), pp. 97–98.

46. Gilbert S. and Gubar, S., *The Madwoman in the Attic* (New Haven: Yale University Press, 1979).

47. Larner, *op. cit.*, p. 78.

48. 'Branded by Satan', *Lucky Star*, 2 May 1936, no author.

49. Propp, V. 'Fairy-tale transformations', in Matejka, M. and Pomorska, K. (eds), *op. cit.*, pp. 94–114.

50. 18 November 1933, no author, pp. 2–10; p. 2.

51. See Marx, K., *Capital* (Harmondsworth: Penuin, 1976), vol. 1, pp. 614–19. On the rationalisation of work by F.W. Taylor, see Braverman, H., *Labour and Monopoly Capital* (New York: Monthly Review Press, 1974).

52. See Wiener, M., *English Culture and the Decline of the Industrial Spirit* (Harmondsworth: Penguin, 1985 (1981)), p. 128.

53. *ibid.*, p. 130.

54. In Thompson, E.P., *The Poverty of Theory* (London: Merlin, 1979).

55. On the bourgeois public sphere, see Wolff J. and Seed, J., *The Culture of Capital: Art, power and the nineteenth-century middle class* (Manchester:

Manchester University Press, 1988); Corrigan, P. and Sayer, D., *The Great Arch* (Oxford: Blackwell, 1985), ch 6.

56. However, because these magazines are designed to entertain, the extreme asceticism characteristic of earlier Puritanism is absent.

57. In the Chartist novels, by contrast, property relations are exposed, while tramps and the unemployed were represented without stigmatisation; see, for example, Wheeler, T., 'Sunshine and shadows', *Northern Star*, 1 March 1949– 5 January 1850, and Jones, E. De Brassier, 'A democratic romance', *Notes to the People* (London: Pavey, 1851–2; reprinted by Merlin, 1967).

58. Phillips. S., 'Her dear ne'er-do-well', *Red Letter*, vol. 33, no. 6, 8 February 1930, p. 175.

59. 'True to him always', *The Oracle*, 7 April 1934, no author. p. 10–18, 24; p. 11.

60. *ibid.*, p. 15.

61. Rennie, B., *Weekly Welcome*, vol. XXX, no. 1733, 1 June 1929, pp. 241–3.

62. *ibid.*, p. 242.

63. By the 1970s, labour is no longer the central focus of people's lives in magazine fiction; the imperative of industriousness has lost its intensity. Heroes were almost twice as often referred to as 'hard working' in the 1930s as the 1970s (46 heroes in 160 stories, as against 23 heroes in the 142 1970s sample). However, the work ethic has not disappeared: 30 per cent of the 1970s stories (compared with 38 per cent of those of the 1930s) depict 'hard work' with positive connotations.

64. *Silver Star*, 20 November 1937, no author, pp. 2–15; 30.

65. *Lucky Star*, no. 10, 9 November 1935, no author, pp. 7–12.

66. See Veblen, T., *The Theory of the Leisure Class* (London: Allen and Unwin, 1925), p. 57.

67. Adorno, T., *Aesthetic Theory* (London: Routledge, 1984).

68. *The Oracle*, 23 September 1933, no author, pp. 2–8, 24, 26.

69. Denning, M., 'Cheap Stories: notes on popular fiction and working-class culture in nineteenth-century America', *History Workshop*, no. 22, autumn 1986, pp. 1–17. On the use of cryptoproletarian characters by Besant and other late Victorian writers, see Keating, P.J., *The Working Classes in Victorian Fiction* (London: Routledge, 1971), p. 98 and ch. 9.

70. Denning, *op. cit.*

71. Nelson, G.W., 'Just like the pictures', *Red Letter*, 4 October 1930.

72. Vawdrey, N., *Red Letter*, vol. 33, no. 14, 5 April 1930.

73. See, for example, 'Old sins will out', *Family Star*, 8 September 1934, no author, pp. 31–6.

74. The most powerful critiques of the objectivity of content analysis are in Cicourel, A., *Method and Measurement in Sociology* (Glencoe, NY: Free Press, 1973) and Bird, E., 'Aesthetic neutrality in the sociology of art', in Barrett, M., Corrigan, P., Kuhn, A. and Wolff, J., *Ideology and Cultural Production* (London: Croom Helm, 1979).

75. Williamson, J., *Decoding Advertisements* (London: Marion Boyars, 1978), see pp. 25–31.
76. Voloshinov, V.N., *Marxism and the Philosophy of Language* (New York: Seminar Press, 1973), ch. 2.
77. Macherey, P., *A Theory of Literary Production* (London: Routledge, 1978).

CHAPTER 4

1. See Public Lending Right Estimates of Public Library Borrowing, January to June 1983; July 1983 to July 1984 and July 1984 to July 1985. The first of these is in Sumsion, J., 'P.L.R.: an appraisal', *Library Association Record*, 88 (2), February 1986, pp. 71–2. Book sales are more difficult to establish. *The Sunday Times* and *The Bookseller* publish lists, the latter annually. These are far from satisfactory for researchers since they only reveal the order of the sales and not the precise quantities.
2. The term 'class compromise' is used in Beynon, H. and McMylor, P., 'Decisive power', in Beynon, H. (ed.), *Digging Deeper* (London: Verso, 1985) and in Hall, S., 'The great moving right show', in Hall, S. and Jacques, M., *The Politics of Thatcherism* (London: Lawrence and Wishart, 1983).
3. It is possible to distinguish between the atrophied forms of the romantic genre and those which employ genre elements in a more skilful and defamiliarising manner. The novels of the former category are written under her pseudonym, Catherine Marchant. See, for example, *The Fen Tiger* (London: Macdonald and Jane's, 1974).
4. Batsleer, J., Davies, T., O'Rourke, R. and Weedon, C., *Rewriting English* (London: Methuen, 1985), p. 92. They explicitly *deny* that Cookson has any significance as a historical writer:

This reversal of the common theme of history, allowing the usually marginalised female sphere to dominate, is extended in Catherine Cookson's work . . . In the *Mallen Trilogy* the history of the history books is only a signpost for the history of the family. . . Romance conventions eternalise and naturalise historical processes. (pp. 96–7)

5. Cookson, C., *Our Kate* (London: Corgi, 1974), p. 12.
6. *ibid.*, p. 16.
7. *ibid.*, p. 22.
8. *ibid.*, p. 192.
9. *ibid.*, p. 59.
10. BBC Television interview, August 1986.
11. British proletarian realism is represented in the works of Tressell, Gibbon, Jones, Greenwood and others.
12. On the Methodist strand of working-class culture, see Thompson, E.P., *The Making of the English Working Class* (Harmondsworth: Penguin, 1968;, pp. 385–469; Hobsbawm, E., 'Methodism and the threat of

revolution in Britain', *History Today*, vol. 7, 1957, pp. 115–24; Inglis, K., *Churches and the Working-Class in Victorian England* (London: Routledge, 1963); Currie, R., *Methodism Divided* (London: Faber and Faber, 1968), Hill, M., *A Sociology of Religion* (London: Heinemann, 1973); Moore, R.S., *Pitmen, Preachers and Politics* (Cambridge: Cambridge University Press, 1974); Douglas, D., *Pit Life in County Durham*, History Workshop Pamphlet, no. 6, 1972.

13. Moore, *op. cit.*, p. 37. Corrigan has argued that such late coercive elements as 'the feudal bonds of N.E. mineworkers [and the unfree character of N.E. women's domestic labour] should not be conceptualised as residuals from former modes of production . . . but as indicators of capitalism's expansion.' He has emphasised the resulting contradictions in forms of proletarian consciousness in the area, which is the concern of many Cookson novels ('Feudal relics or capitalist monuments', *Sociology*, vol. 11, no. 3, September 1977, pp. 435–63.

14. Moore *op. cit.*, p. 37.

15. Douglas, *op. cit.*, pp. 46–8. On conciliation agreements in a number of industries and their effects, see Potter, J.H., 'Wage bargaining under conciliation agreements, 1860–1914', *Economic History Review*, vol. 23, 1970, pp. 460–75.

16. Moore, *op. cit.*, p. 72 and 81–2. Not all the Methodist chapels served both employers and employees. Outside the Deerness valley in particular, the erection of both Wesleyan and Primitive chapels could be linked to the class difference in the two congregations. (Eldridge, J.E.T., personal communication.)

17. Moore, *op. cit.*, pp. 44–5 and pp. 182–5. However, Moore argues that the employers adopted a paternalist strategy from 1870–1900 (*ibid.*, pp. 78–92).

18. Cookson, C., *Maggie Rowan* (London: Macdonald, 1954; Corgi, 1979), p. 25.

19. *ibid.*, p. 30.

20. *ibid.*, p. 71.

21. Tillotson, K., *Novels of the Eighteen-Forties* (Oxford: Oxford University Press, 1954).

22. See *Kate Hannigan*, *Katie Mulholland* and *Tillie Trotter*, although not *The Round Tower*. I am grateful to Hugh Rae for the comparison with D.H. Lawrence.

23. See Byrne, D., 'The "Arab Riot" in South Shields: a race riot that never was', *Race and Class*, vol. xviii, no. 3, pp. 264–76.

24. Cookson, C., *Colour Blind* (London: Corgi, 1968), p. 15.

25. Bakhtin, M., in his *Rabelais and his world* (Cambridge, Mass.: MIT Press, 1968), examines the forms in which humour became a major conductor of ideological criticism: as in the types of parody used in carnivals and the comic debunking of authoritative figures by reference to their material bodies.

26. *Colour Blind*, *op. cit.*, p. 14.

27. *ibid.*, p. 254.
28. *ibid.*, p. 99.
29. Byrne, *op. cit.*, p. 276.
30. Joshua, H. and Wallace, T., with Booth H., *To Ride the Storm: The 1980 Bristol race riot and the state* (London: Heinemann, 1983), p. 15.
31. Byrne, *op. cit.*, p. 267.
32. This is not an argument for a reflection model in which it is assumed that literature must mirror minute details of industrial life: see the critique of this position in Eagleton, T., *Marxism and Literary Criticism* (London: Methuen, 1976).
33. Lukacs, G., *The Historical Novel* (Harmondsworth: Penguin, 1969). See the similar argument in Jameson, F., *Marxism and Form: Twentieth-century dialectical theories of literature* (Princeton: Princeton University Press, 1971), p. 286.
34. Cookson, C., *Katie Mulholland* (London: Corgi, 1967), p. 32.
35. Wilkinson, E., *The Town that was Murdered* (London: Gollancz, 1939), p. 39.
36. *ibid.*, pp. 39–40.
37. *ibid.*, p. 38.
38. *ibid.*, p. 22.
39. *Katie Mulholland*, *op. cit.*, p. 32.
40. *ibid.*, p. 402.
41. Showalter, E., *A Literature of their Own* (London: Virago, 1981), p. 150.
42. This phrase comes from Cookson's *The Mallen Streak* (London: Corgi, 1975). The ambivalence about literacy for the lower class is expressed in *The Girl* (London: Corgi, 1978): 'My, they'll have you so learned you won't look the side we're on, shortly' (p. 27).
43. Cookson, C., *The Mallen Girl* (London: Corgi, 1975); *Katie Mulholland, op. cit.*
44. Bloch, M., *Feudal Society* (London: Routledge, 1962), vol. 1, p. 94.
45. *The Girl, op. cit.*, p. 77.
46. A woman who had an illegitimate child could be whipped half-naked, because her child was a burden on the parish, see Macfarlane, A., *Marriage and Love in England: Modes of reproduction 1300–1840* (Oxford: Blackwell, 1986), p. 241.
47. *Colour Blind, op. cit.*, p. 15.
48. Foucault, M. *Discipline and Punish* (London: Penguin, 1979).
49. Showalter, *op. cit.*, pp. 19–32.
50. Clark, A., 'The politics of seduction in English popular culture', in Radford, J. (ed.), *The Progress of Romance* (London: Routledge, 1986), pp. 47–72.
51. *The Girl, op. cit.*, p. 79.
52. Murray, M., *Gender Relations and State Formation*, unpublished Ph.D., University of Glasgow, 1988.
53. *The Mallen Streak, op. cit.*, p. 91.
54. *ibid.*, p. 228. However, lest it be thought that her perception sustains a

distinctively feminist structure of thought, the alien 'other' of *Kate Hannigan* is a rich doctor's wife whose secret use of contraception both destroys the children wanted by her husband and facilitates her extra-marital sexual freedom.

55. The phrase is coined by Cawelti, J., *Adventure, Mystery and Romance* (Chicago: University of Chicago Press, 1976), p. 16.

56. Lane, T. and Roberts, K., *Strike at Pilkingtons* (London: Collins, 1971), p. 31.

57. *Katie Mulholland, op. cit.*, pp. 401.

58. Wilkinson, E., *op. cit.*, p. 171

59. Brown, R.K. and Brannen, P., 'Social relations and social perspectives among shipbuilding workers', *Sociology*, vol. 4. no. 1, January 1970, pp. 71–84, and no. 2. May 1970, pp. 197–211.

60. This patrician gentry used the law to criminalise as many as two hundred new capital offences against property. Yet since only half the number of offenders were actually executed, the patrician Theatre of the Law also revolved around the aristocracy's power to dispense mercy. Eighteenth-century gentry culture placed a premium on deference. This contributed to the continued importance of individuals' motives, whether of compassion, vengeance or judicial austerity. See Thompson, E.P., 'Patrician society, plebeian culture', *Journal of Social History*, vol. 7, no. 4, summer 1974, pp. 382–405; also Hay, D., 'Property, authority and the criminal law', in Hay, D. (ed.), *Albion's Fatal Tree* (Harmondsworth: Penguin, 1977), especially pp. 18, 22, 43, 48.

61. Moorhouse, H.F. and Chamberlain, C.W., 'Lower-class attitudes to property', *Sociology*, vol. 8, no. 3, September 1974, pp. 387–405; p. 400.

62. *Katie Mulholland, op. cit.*, p. 154.

63. See Jameson, F., *The Political Unconscious: Narrative as social symbolism* (New Haven: Yale University Press; London: Methuen, 1981). In this context, Cookson's novels should be seen as productive work on class ideology rather than a straightforward *reflection* of such ideology, see Eagleton, T., *Literature and Ideology* (London: Verso, 1981).

CHAPTER 5

1. Stirling, J., *The Spoiled Earth* trilogy (London: Hodder and Stoughton, 1974–7); Webster, J., *Saturday City* (London: Collins, 1978); see also Cookson (Chapter 4 above).

2. See Chapter 6 below.

3. Barrett notes this category in her classification of representations of women, *Women's Oppression Today* (London: Verso, 1980), pp. 109–10; Tompkins, J., *Sensational Designs, 1790–1860* (New York: Oxford University Press, 1985).

4. The term is Harold Macmillan's, but it describes also the politics of the romance.

5. On class conciliation, see Davies, T., 'Education, Ideology and Literature', in Bennett, T., Graham, M.C. and Mercer, C., *Culture, Ideology and Social Process* (London: Batsford, 1985).

6. On pastiche, see Jameson, F., 'The cultural logic of late capitalism', *New Left Review*, no. 144, 1984, pp. 53–92.

7. Tillotson, K., *Novels of the Eighteen-Forties* (Oxford: Oxford University Press, 1954), p. 117.

8. See Howatch, S., *Penmarric* (London: Pan, 1972); Stirling, *op. cit.*, and Cookson, *op. cit.*

9. Marx, K., and Engels, F., 'The holy family', *Collected Works*, vol. 4, (Moscow: Progress Publishers, 1975).

10. Although more overblown, such figures are the recognisable descendents of the heroines of the industrial novels of the 1840s. See T. Lovell's illuminating reading of *Mary Barton*, which stresses that its 'angle of vision' on industrial conflict was structured by female suffering (*Consuming Fiction*, London: Verso, 1987, pp. 87–8).

11. Howatch, *op. cit.*, p. 649.

12. Frisby, D., *Fragments of Modernity* (Cambridge: Polity, 1985), esp. pp. 14–20; Berman, M., *All that is Solid Melts into Air* (New York: Simon & Schuster; London: Verso, 1982), pp. 133, 145.

13. On images of shops and consumption in literature, see Bowlby, R., *Just Looking* (London: Methuen, 1985), esp. ch.5.

14. On the *flâneur*, see Benjamin, W., *Charles Baudelaire* (London: NLB, 1983 pp. 35–66); Wolff, J., 'The invisible *flâneuse*: women and the literature of modernity', *Theory, Culture and Society*, vol. 2, no. 3, 1985.

15. Wolff, *op. cit.*

16. For example, Emma, the heroine of Bradford's *Woman of Substance* (London: Bantam, 1987), siezes on the shortage of uniforms in the First World War to open her first textile factory.

17. Simmel, G., 'The Metropolis and mental life', in Wolff, K. (ed.), *The Sociology of Georg Simmel* (Glencoe, NY: Free Press, 1950), pp. 409–24; Benjamin, *op. cit.*, pp. 126–34.

18. On asceticism, see Marx, K., *Capital*, vol. 1, pp. 738–46; Weber, M., *The Protestant Ethic and the Spirit of Capitalism* (London: Allen and Unwin, 1962).

19. Bradford, *op. cit.* p. 422.

20. Marx, *op. cit.*, p. 742.

21. Conran, S., *Lace* (London: Sidgwick and Jackson, 1982); this novel, however, is neither on the PLR list of most loaned books, nor did my respondents count it among their 'popular canon'. For an interestingly rigorous account of the linguistic details of such transgressive romances, see the study of Krantz's *I'll Take Manhattan* in Wareing, S., *The Representation of Women in Fiction*, M.Litt. thesis, University of Strathclyde, 1988.

22. Conran, *op. cit.*, p. 485.

23. Virginia Andrews's, *Flowers in the Attic* trilogy (London: Fontana, 1980–81) should be mentioned, with its oscillation between 'the family as

paradise' and 'the family as nightmare'. The quasi-religious, quasi-anthropological mode of the Gothic novel, or *roman noir*, is invested with modern images. One reader, a philosophy graduate, emphasised that 'I couldn't peel my eyes off that book.' Her enjoyment was shared by working-class readers.

24. In Stirling, *op. cit.*, and Cookson's *Katie Mulholland* (London: Corgi, 1967), ideological crises over social injustice are displaced onto crises over legal injustice. In Stirling's *The Dark Pasture* justice prevails but in *Katie* the judiciary are depicted as the tool of the wealthy.

25. In *Capital*, Marx noted how an illusory realism about clan chiefs both facilitated the Scottish clearances and masked its character subsequently: 'But what clearing of estates really and properly signifies, we learn only in the Highlands of Scotland, the promised land of modern romantic novels' (Marx, *op. cit.*, p. 890).

26. Bromley, R., 'The gentry, bourgeois hegemony and popular fiction', *Literature and History*, vol. 7, no. 2, autumn 1981, pp. 166–83.

27. Palmer, J., *Thrillers: Genesis and structure of a popular genre* (London: E. Arnold, 1978).

28. See, especially, Anderson, P., 'The figures of descent', *New Left Review*, no. 161, January–February 1987.

29. Stone, L., quoted in Anderson, *op. cit.*, p. 28.

30. Anderson, *op. cit.*, p. 31.

31. *ibid.*, p. 41; see also Williams, R., *The Country and The City* (London: Hogarth, 1985).

32. Hall, C., 'The early formation of Victorian domestic religion', in Burman, S. (ed.), *Fit Work for Women* (London: Croom Helm, 1979); see also Lewis, J., *Women in England 1870–1950* (Hemel Hempstead: Harvester Wheatsheaf, 1984).

33. Lovell, T., *Consuming Fiction* (London: Verso, 1987), pp. 87–8.

34. *ibid.*, pp. 43 and 88.

35. In Wilbur Smith's South African romance, *Gold Mine* (London: Heinemann, 1970), the moral economy is saved both from the dehumanising labour control of an ex-Nazi director and from the declining syndrome of trust shown by alienated black workers. Its heroes are a conciliatory manager and a responsible native worker, the latter occupying the fictional space of the heroine.

36. See, for example, Binchy, M., *Light a Penny Candle* (London: Coronet, 1982) and McCullough, C., *An Indecent Obsession* (London: Macdonald, 1981).

CHAPTER 6

1. See, for example, Iser, W., *The Implied Reader* (Baltimore: John Hopkins University Press, 1974), p. xii. An exception to this general silence about how readers decode and evaluate texts is I.A. Richards's *Practical*

Criticism, published in 1929 (London: Kegan Paul, Trench and Trubner) which includes a detailed account of readers' responses to fourteen poems. Richards's purpose is to move from how people actually decode poems to the technical knowledge and practices that an intelligent critic should use. With respect to the first, he is concerned with the applied 'psychology' of the readers. He calls this a form of 'mental navigation' which stops short of the 'depth charge' of psychoanalysis. The untrained readers are shown how to decode or evaluate texts according to their perceptions of the poets' ideological views. Their own experience conditions their response to these. Richards's empirical enquiry thus confirmed his view that in poetry 'One man's meat is another man's poison.'

Despite its positivist presuppositions, this study is a useful starting-point for research on cultural reception, since it operates to *expose* the clash of opinions within 'the middle ground of ideologies'. Unfortunately, Richards does not show us whether or how *material position* affects responses to a poem. Even a rudimentary classification according to gender, occupation and age are absent: Richards's social perception is still too individualistic.

2. Bourdieu, P., *Distinction* (London: Routledge, 1984) and 'The production of belief', *Media , Culture and Society*, vol. 3, no. 2, July 1980, pp. 261–93.
3. Bourdieu, *Distinction, op. cit.*, p. 24.
4. *ibid.*, p. 54.
5. Bourdieu, 'Production of belief', *op. cit.*, pp. 262–3.
6. Bourdieu, *Distinction, op. cit.*, p. 13.
7. Bourdieu has not explained satisfactorily all his own findings. Thus a table on the aesthetic disposition by educational capital shows that the highest number of respondents who thought that cabbages could make an interesting subject for a photograph did indeed come from the most educated groups. However, he neglects to explain how respectively 67.5 per cent and 49 per cent of the two most educated groups found such a subject either meaningless or ugly.
8. The attack may have originated among petty-bourgeois art students, but it was taken up and amplified within the working class.
9. Hebdige, D., *Subculture: The meaning of style* (London: Methuen, 1979), pp. 44–5, 65–6. My example is taken from Hebdige's reading of punk style.
10. Bourdieu, *Distinction, op. cit.*, p. 395.
11. *ibid.*, p. 9.
12. See Garnham, N. and Williams, R. 'Pierre Bourdieu and the sociology of culture', *Media, Culture and Society*, vol. 3, no. 2, July 1980, pp. 209–23. This is a misreading of Bourdieu, who quotes Kraus ('If I have to choose between two evils, I choose neither' – *Distinction, op. cit.*, p. 466) to mean that *both* popular and legitimate culture are *distorted* forms within the class structures of late capitalism. The model is Schiller, whose criticism of

bourgeois alienation stresses its fragmentation of humans through their specialisation. Bourdieu's contrast between 'form' and 'function' (legitimate and popular culture) resembles Schiller's indictment of a society in which human personality is split into different social types: the speculative or analytical spirit which admires form, but in which imagination or sympathy is absent; the business spirit; the sensuous spirit of the uneducated people, limited entirely by their function. In Bourdieu's view, popular thought cannot generate an adequate aesthetic culture combining both the political or moral ideas of the lower class and an understanding of artistic forms. Similarly, legitimate culture is distorted by its exclusive preoccupation with style.

13.   In 'Production of belief' (*op. cit.*, p. 270) he interprets critical and visionary art as expressing only the transient interest in demystification on the part of young intellectuals and higher professionals before they acquire power. He neglects to examine the historical moments when such interests permitted a *fusion* of the radical intelligentsia with the working class, when artists expressed a people's hope for liberation or a class's aspirations for hegemony. Is the critical culture of French late capitalism totally different? For Bourdieu, oppositional art and literature is either deployed to destroy father figures or – at the point at which it has lost its contemporary urgency – *recuperated* as a status-adornment. Bourdieu's uniquely disenchanted perspective lacks even the emancipatory theory of his mentor, Schiller.

14.   Corrigan, P. and Willis, P., 'Cultural forms and class mediations', *Media, Culture and Society*, vol. 3, no. 2, July 1980, pp. 297–312.

15.   These writers are all among the most loaned authors from public libraries, according to Public Lending Right calculations. Mosco is high in specific areas such as Glasgow. The novels read before the second interview were Marie Joseph's *Lisa Logan* (London: Arrow, 1984), a well-loaned text on PLR figures, and Agnes Smedley's *Daughter of Earth* (London: Virago, 1977 (1929)), which does not appear in these statistics.

16.   Two in the sample; a further two interviewed outside it.

17.   Lash, S. and Urry J., *The End of Organized Capitalism* (Cambridge: Polity, 1987), pp. 244–7.

18.   Bourdieu, *Distinction, op. cit.*, p. 323.

19.   Leavis, Q.D., *Fiction and the Reading Public* (Harmondsworth: Penguin, 1979), pp. 64–5, 70.

20.   A further study should assess in more detail the degree to which various forms of popular art are permanently segregated from higher socio-economic classes. For example, tattooing as an art form is probably unrecognised outside the working class. At the other extreme, thrillers as a genre may approach 'mass' rather than class diffusion. The best-selling romance shows a different profile to the thriller genre, but is not yet as class-specific as tattooing.

21.   Mann, P., *The Romantic Novel: A study of reading habits* (London: Mills and Boon, 1969), p. 12.

22. Mann's own findings, presented as his Table 4, undermine his conclusions. Using an unexplained base line of 148, after coding a postal questionnaire reply from 2,788 Mills and Boon subscribers, he shows that 7 readers are 'schoolteachers or other professionals' and 37 are office-workers. He also wrongly claims that this shows 55 per cent are housewives, when in fact it is 55 out of 148. He states that 'it is clear that the [Mills and Boon] romance readers come greatly from women in office jobs and to a certain extent also from technical and professional occupations. The number in manual or shop jobs are not as great as might have been expected' (p. 5). While I would agree that a scattering of Mills and Boon readers is no doubt found throughout the female population, I would dispute that *these* figures show that the sample 'contains a fair number of reasonably well-educated women'. At the end Mann makes even bolder claims for the 'schoolteachers and other professionals', all 4.7 per cent of them: 'it is quite noteworthy how large a proportion are of the semi-professional or lower professional occupations' (p. 23). Not only does this amount to massaging the figures, but it ignores the serious objection, made by Swingewood, that a postal questionnaire to mail-order romance readers is likely to underestimate the proportion of working-class readers. See Swingewood, A., *The Myth of Mass Culture* (London: Macmillan, 1977), p. 136.
23. Payne, G., *Mobility and Change in Modern Society* (London: Macmillan, 1987), pp. 123, 127.
24. Goldthorpe, J.H., Llewellyn, C. and Payne, C., *Social Mobility and Class Structure* (Oxford: Clarendon, 1980), ch.1.
25. Bourdieu, *Distinction, op. cit.*, p. 137.
26. This respondent read popular modern writers (she referred to Walter Mackin), as well as nineteenth-century Russian and English novelists, and twentieth-century writers such as Grassic Gibbon. I have changed readers' names in order to preserve confidentiality.
27. This group's preferences are theorised by Ayn Rand, who has made the bizarre claim that the popular romance and the thrillers of writers such as Fleming and Spillane represent the real artistic achievements of the modern world! According to Rand, these texts are unacknowledged in the universities because of the decadent monopoly over art possessed by modernists, social critics and other spurious guardians of culture, who are intent on reflecting only the 'sewers'of modern life. See *The Romantic Manifesto* (New York: The World Publishing Company, 1969), especially ch. 5, pp. 81–111.
28. 56 per cent of the middlebrow group had middle-class fathers (44 per cent of them lower professionals). In comparison, only 46 per cent of the legitimate culture group had middle-class fathers and, of these, only 35 per cent were lower professionals.
29. Freud, S., 'The interest of psychoanalysis from the point of view of the science of aesthetics', in *Complete Works*, standard edn, vol. XIII (London: Hogarth, 1964), p. 188. See also Leavis, *op. cit.*, p. 70.

30. Bourdieu, *Distinction, op. cit.*, pp. 466–500, see also Simmel, G., *The Philosophy of Money* (London: Routledge, 1978), p. 440.

31. Benjamin refers to the moment of the First World War when experiences of the war and of inflation could no longer be encompassed within the community-based knowledge of the traditional story-teller, see *Illuminations* (London: Fontana, 1973), pp. 83–109.

32. Three of the legitimate readers stipulated additionally that their interest would be dependent on how well-written the novel was.

33. On formulae in popular fiction, see Eco, U., *The Role of the Reader* (London: Hutchinson, 1981), p. 162; Cawelti, J., *Adventure, Mystery and Romance* (Chicago: University of Chicago Press, 1976).

34. Again the middlebrow and 'Cookson' group were divided on this, while the radical canon readers responded as the legitimate readers had done.

35. On this, see Kermode, F., *The Sense of an Ending* (New York: Oxford University Press, 1967), p. 64.

36. Colour-coding is a Mills and Boon practice. Authors' instructions encode editorial expertise about market demand. Silhouette's rules discourage even images of black-haired heroines, see *Sunday Telegraph* Magazine, 1978. Magazine-story characters of the 1970s gained editorial approbation for being 'classless', while editors also explicitly avoided class as a theme: Ferguson, M., *Forever Feminine* (London: Heinemann, 1983), pp. 76; 116.

37. Barthes, R., *The Pleasure of the Text* (London: Cape, 1975).

38. The speaker is a manageress of 59, the widow of a commercial traveller. Her favourite writers were Cronin and Steinbeck. She was allocated to the 'Cookson' group.

39. See the manageress, note 38.

40. Aged 40–60, the respondent was single and a member of the 'Cookson' group.

41. An unskilled factory-worker of 39, this reader was a strong Scottish Nationalist; she, also, was allocated to the 'Cookson' group.

42. A houseworker, ex-primary teacher, 23–39, skilled manual background, 'Cookson'group.

43. An export clerk at Collins, aged 59, 'Cookson' group.

44. It should be remembered that the sample was small and not totally representative.

45. For Scotland, see Payne, *op. cit.*, p. 127, and for England, Goldthorpe, *op. cit.*, pp. 45–9. Goldthorpe argues persuasively both that absolute mobility has increased and that class inequalities have been unaltered in Britain. Economic growth can hide the persistence of inequality (p.252). The relative openness of the service class is compared with the medieval Catholic Church, which took the best brains of all classes into its top ranks in order to stabilise aristocratic rule (p. 67). In contrast, Bourdieu fails to accept the existence of upward mobility in France, for he emphasises the use of ever-changing 'closure' mechanisms on the part of the service class to exclude even qualified newcomers (p. 81). This argument is less compelling.

46. Lovenduski reports on the effect of gender on participation and voting. She cites Lafferty's research showing that women doing domestic labour, with an 'inbuilt' pressure to conservatism, are solely accountable for the noted sex differences, contrasting with this the findings of Dunleavy and Husbands, that *manual* housewives tend to be solidly committed to Labour and *non-manual* women, employed or not, tend to be more Conservative. See Lovenduski, J., *Women and European Politics* (Hemel Hempstead: Harvester Wheatsheaf, 1986), esp. pp. 132–3. Dunleavy and Husband's important study shows that gender difference ranks with other structural determinants of voting, such as work in the public or private sector, union membership, and the manual/non-manual divide, though it is weak on *theoretical* explanation of this. Such structural positions, they argue, create *differences in receptiveness to dominant ideas*, a model that is analogous to the one adopted in this chapter. See *British Democracy at the Crossroads* (London: Allen and Unwin, 1985), pp. 128–33.
47. The middlebrow group, like the formulaic readers, had a strong tendency to accept the meritocratic image of Britain, although they were more likely to adopt the 'class conflict' view than the romantic fiction group.
48. See Hinton, J., *The First Shop Stewards' Movement* (London: Allen and Unwin, 1973).
49. Significant numbers of men may also lack knowledge of the public sphere. See Siltanen, J. and Stanworth, M.'s title essay in their edited *The Politics of Private Woman and Public Man* (London: Hutchinson, 1984), pp. 185–208. My sample is of women only. Of course, the remoteness of these largely lower-class women from the public world derives partially from the sense that their voices are unimportant in that sphere. Powerlessness so permeates their self-perception that they have no interest in knowledge. On this, see Bourdieu, *Distinction*, *op. cit.*, ch. 8.
50. Smedley, A., *op. cit.*
51. *ibid.*, p. 120.
52. Joseph, M., *op. cit.*
53. Bourdieu, *Distinction*, *op. cit.*, p. 56.
54. *ibid.*, p. 54.
55. Long, E., 'Women reading and cultural authority', *American Quarterly*, vol. 38, no. 4, fall 1986, pp. 591–612.
56. *ibid.*, p. 611.
57. See also Williams, R.H., *Dream Worlds* (Berkeley: University of California Press, 1982), p. 376.
58. Bourdieu, *Distinction*, *op. cit.*, p. 380.
59. Bloch, E., *The Principle of Hope*, vol. 3, *op. cit.*, p. 907.

CONCLUSION

1. Abercrombie, N., Hill, S. and Turner, B., *The Dominant Ideology Thesis* (London: Allen and Unwin, 1980).

2. See Anderson's critique of the structuralist aggrandisement of the linguistic sphere, in *In the Tracks of Historical Materialism* (London: Verso, 1983), p. 64.
3. A similar point is made by Bottomore in his Foreword to Abercrombie *et al.*, *op. cit.*
4. Reading Cartland, or mention of her name, evoked a rage in lower-class Scottish women which paralleled their response to Thatcherism. Thus where reading provokes a strong sense of injustice, indignation can boil over, uncontained by the lid of ideology.
5. On Methodist development, see Thompson, E.P., *The Making of the English Working Class* (Harmondsworth: Penguin, 1968), chs. 2 and 11.

Select Bibliography

This list excludes general works in order to specialise on popular culture, the sociology of literature and Marxist-feminist accounts of ideology.

Abercrombie, N., Hill, S. and Turner, B., *The Dominant Ideology Thesis* (London: Allen and Unwin, 1980).

Adorno, T. *Aesthetic Theory* (London: Routledge, 1984).

Adorno, T. and Horkheimer, M., *Dialectic of Enlightenment* (London: Verso, 1979).

Altick, R.D. *The English Common Reader* (Chicago: University of Chicago Press, 1957).

Anderson, R., *The Purple Heart Throbs: The sub-literature of love* (London: Hodder, 1974).

Bakhtin, M., *Rabelais and his World* (Cambridge, Mass.: MIT Press, 1968).

Barrett, M., *Women's Oppression Today* (London: Verso, 1980), esp. ch. 3.

Barrett, M., 'Materialist aesthetics', *New Left Review*, no. 126, March–April 1981, pp. 86–93.

Barrett M., 'Max Raphael and the question of aesthetics', *New Left Review*, no. 161, January–February 1987, pp. 78–97.

Barthes, R., *The Pleasure of the Text*, trans. R. Miller (London: Cape, 1975).

Barthes, R., 'The Death Of The Author', in Caughie, J. (ed.), *Theories of Authorship* (London: Routledge, 1981), pp. 208–14.

Basch, F., *Relative Ceatures* (London: Allen Lane, 1974).

Batsleer, J., Davies, T., O'Rourke, R. and Weedon, C., *Rewriting English* (London: Methuen, 1985).

Bell, D., *The Cultural Contradictions of Capitalism* (London: Heinemann, 1976).

Benjamin, W., *Illuminations* (London: Fontana, 1973).

Bennett, T., *Formalism and Marxism* (London: Methuen, 1979).

Bennett, T., 'Marxism and popular fiction', *Literature and History*, vol. 7, no 2., autumn 1981, pp. 158–65.

Bennett, T., 'Hegemony, ideology, pleasure', in Bennett, T., Mercer, C.

and Wollacott, J., *Popular Culture and Social Relations* (Milton Keynes: Open University, 1986).

Berman, M., *All that is Solid Melts into Air* (London: Verso, 1982).

Berman, R.A., 'Writing for the book industry', *New German Critique*, no. 29, spring–summer 1983, pp. 39-56.

Bloch, E., *The Principle of Hope*, vols 1–3, translated by Plaice, N. and S., and Knight, S., (Oxford: Blackwell, 1986).

Bloch, E., *The Utopian Function of Art and Literature* (Cambridge, Mass.: MIT Press, 1988).

Bromley, R., 'Natural boundaries: the social function of popular fiction', *Red Letters*, no. 7, 1978, pp. 34–60.

Bromley, R., 'The gentry, bourgeois hegemony and popular fiction', *Literature and History*, vol. 7, no. 2, autumn 1981, pp. 166–83.

Cawelti, J., *Adventure, Mystery and Romance: Formula Stories as Art and Popular Culture* (Chicago: University of Chicago Press, 1976).

Clarke, A., 'The politics of seduction in English popular culture 1748–1848', in Radford, J. (ed.), *The Progress of Romance* (London: Routledge, 1986).

Clark, K., *The Soviet Novel* (Chicago: University of Chicago Press, 1981).

Cockburn, C., *Bestseller* (London: Sidgwick and Jackson, 1972).

Cookson, C., *Our Kate* (London: Corgi, 1974).

Corrigan, P. and Gillespie, V., *Class Struggle, Social Literacy and Idle Time* (London: Librarians for Social Change, 1978).

Corrigan, P. and Willis, P., 'Cultural forms and class mediations', *Media, Culture and Society*, vol. 3, no. 2, July 1980, pp. 297–312.

Craig, D. and Egan, M., 'Historicist criticism', in Widdowson, P. (ed.), *Rereading English* (London: Methuen, 1981).

Dalziel, M., *Popular Fiction One Hundred Years Ago* (London: Cohen and West, 1957).

Davidoff, L. and Hall C., *Family Fortunes: Men and women of the English middle class, 1780–1850* (London: Hutchinson, 1987).

Davies, T., 'Education, ideology and literature', in Bennett, T., Mercer, C. and Wollacott, J., *Culture, Ideology and Social Process* (London: Batsford, 1981).

Denning, M., 'Cheap stories: notes on popular fiction and working-class novels in nineteenth-century America', *History Workshop*, no. 22, autumn 1986, pp. 1–17.

Denning, M., *Mechanic Accents: Dime novels and working-class culture in America* (London: Verso, 1987).

Eagleton, T., *Criticism and Ideology* (London: Verso NLB, 1976).

Eagleton, T., *The Rape of Clarissa* (Oxford: Blackwell, 1982).

Eagleton, T., *Literary Theory* (Oxford: Blackwell, 1983).

Eco, U., *The Role of the Reader* (London: Hutchinson, 1981).

Ehrlich, V., *Russian Formalism* (The Hague: Mouton, 1980 (1955)).

Ewen E., *Immigrant Women in the Land of Dollars* (New York: Monthly Review Press, 1985).

Ewen, S., *Captains of Consciousness* (New York: McGraw-Hill, 1976).

Fachel, L.O. and Oliven, R.G., 'Class interpretations of a soap opera narrative: the case of the Brazilian novella, *Summer Sun*', *Theory, Culture and Society*, vol. 5, 1988, pp. 81–99.

Flora, C., 'Changes in women's status in women's magazine fiction', *Social Problems*, vol. 26, no. 5., June 1979, pp. 558–69.

Fowler, B., 'Marxist theories of the canon', *Cultural Studies*, vol. 1, no. 2, 1987, pp. 162–78.

Freud, S., 'The interest of psychoanalysis from the point of view of the science of aesthetics', in *Complete Works*, standard edn., vol. XIII (London: Hogarth, 1964).

Frisby. D., *Fragments of Modernity* (Cambridge: Polity, 1985).

Gans, H., *Popular and High Culture* (New York: Basic Books, 1974).

Garnham, N. and Williams, R., 'Pierre Bourdieu and the sociology of culture', *Media, Culture and Society*, vol. 3, no. 2, July 1980, pp. 209–23.

Gedin, P., *Literature in the Market Place* (London: Faber, 1977).

Gilbert, S. and Gubar, S., *The Madwoman in the Attic* (New Haven: Yale University Press, 1979).

Gramsci, A., *Marxismo e Letteratura* (Rome: Riuniti, 1975).

Grazia, V. de, *The Culture of Consent* (Cambridge: Cambridge University Press, 1981).

Hall, C., 'The early formation of Victorian domestic ideology', in Burman, S. (ed.), *Fit Work for Women* (London: Croom Helm, 1979).

Hall, S., 'Cultural studies: two paradigms', in Bennett, T., Mercer, C. and Wollacott, J. (eds), *Culture, Ideology and Social Process* (Milton Keynes: Open University Press, 1981).

Hall, S. and Whannel, P., *The Popular Arts* (London: Hutchinson, 1962).

Harrison R., '*Shirley*, relations of reproduction and the ideology of romance', in Centre for Contemporary Cultural Studies, *Women Take Issue* (London: Hutchinson, 1978).

Hart, J.D., *The Popular Book* (New York: Oxford University Press, 1950).

Haug, F., 'Daydreams', *New Left Review*, no. 162, March–April 1987, pp. 51–66.

Hebdige, D., *Subculture: The meaning of style* (London: Methuen, 1979).

Hill, C., *Society and Puritanism in Pre-Revolutionary England* (London: Panther, 1969).

Hill, J., 'Ideology and economy in the British cinema', in Barrett, M., Corrigan, P., Kuhn, A. and Wolff, J. (eds), *Ideology and Cultural Production* (London: Croom Helm, 1979), pp. 112–34.

Hoggart, R., *The Uses of Literacy* (Harmondsworth: Penguin, 1969).

Huyssen, A., 'Adorno in reverse', *New German Critique*, no. 29, spring/summer, 1983, pp. 8–38.

Iser, W., *The Implied Reader* (Baltimore: Johns Hopkins University Press, 1974).

Jacobus, M. (ed.), *Women Writing and Writing about Women* (London: Croom Helm, 1979).

James, L., *Fiction for the Working Man* (Harmondsworth: Penguin, 1974).

James, L., *Print and the People, 1819–1851* (Harmondsworth: Penguin, 1976).

Jameson, F., *Marxism and Form: Twentieth-century dialectical theories of literature* (Princeton: Princeton University Press, 1971).

Jameson, F., 'Reification and utopia in mass culture', *Social Text*, no. 1, 1979, pp. 130–48.

Jameson, F., *The Political Unconscious: Narrative as social symbolism* (London: Methuen, 1981).

Jones, A.R., 'Mills and Boon meets feminism', in Radford, J. (ed.), *The Progress of Romance* (London: Routledge, 1986).

Kaplan, C., *Sea Changes: Culture and feminism* (London: Verso, 1986).

Keating, P.J., *The Working Classes in Victorian Fiction* (London: Routledge, 1971).

Kermode, F., *The Sense of an Ending: Studies in the theory of fiction* (London: Oxford University Press, 1967).

Klapper, J., *The Effects of Mass Communication* (Glencoe, NY: Free Press, 1960).

Kristeva, J., 'Ruins of a poetics', in Bann, S. and Bowlt, J.E., *Russian Formalism* (Edinburgh: Scottish Academic Press, 1973).

Ladurie, E. L., *Love, Death and Money in the Pays d'Oc* (Harmondsworth: Penguin, 1984).

Lane, M., *Books and Publishing: Commerce against culture* (Lexington: D.C. Heath, 1980).

Lash, S. and Urry, J., *The End of Organized Capitalism* (Cambridge: Polity, 1987), esp. ch 9.

Laurenson, D. and Swingewood, A., *The Sociology of Literature* (London: MacGibbon anhd Kee, 1971).

Leavis, Q.D., *Fiction and the Reading Public* (Harmondsworth: Penguin, 1979).

Leenhardt, J., 'Towards a sociology of reading', in Suleiman, S. and Crosman, I., *The Reader in the Text* (Princeton: Princeton University Press, 1980).

Lévi-Strauss, C., 'La structure et la forme', *Cahiers de l'Institut de Science Economique Applique*, 99, Paris 1960, serie M, no. 7, pp. 25–33.

Long, E., 'Women reading and cultural authority', *American Quarterly*, vol. 38, no. 4, fall 1986, pp. 591–612.

Lovell, T., *Pictures of Reality* (London: BFI, 1980).

Lovell, T., *Consuming Fiction* (London, Verso, 1987).

Lukács, G., *The Historical Novel* (Harmondsworth: Penguin, 1969).

Lunn, E., *Marxism and Modernism* (London: Verso, 1987).

MacCabe, C., 'Realism and the cinema', *Screen,* vol. 15, no. 2, 1974, pp. 7–27.

McGuigan, J., *Writers and the Arts Council* (London: The Arts Council, 1981).

McRobbie, A., '*Jackie*, an ideology of adolescent femininity', in Waites B., Bennett, T. and Martin, C.G., *Popular Culture: Past and present* (London: Croom Helm, 1982), pp. 263–82.

Macherey, P., *A Theory of Literary Production* (London, Routledge, 1978).

Mandel, E., *Delightful Murder: A social history of the crime story* (London: Pluto, 1974).

Mann, P., *The Romantic Novel: A study of reading habits* (London: Mills and Boon, 1969).

Marx, K. and Engels, F., *Collected Works*, vol. 4 (Moscow: Progress Publishers, 1975).

Meletinski, E.M., 'Problème de la morphologie historique du conte populaire', *Semiotica*, II, 1970, no. 2, pp. 128–34.

Mitchell, S., *The Fallen Angel: Chastity, class and women's reading, 1835–80* (Bowling Green, Ohio: Bowling Green University Popular Press, 1981).

Modleski, T., *Loving with a Vengeance: Mass-produced fantasies for women* (London: Methuen, 1984).

Moers, E., *Literary Women* (New York: Doubleday, 1976; London: The Women's Press, 1986).

Mott, F.L. *Golden Multitudes* (New York: B.R. Bowker, 1947).

Mulhern, F., *The Moment of Scrutiny* (London: NLB, 1979).

Paizis, G., *The Contemporary Romantic Novel in France*, Ph.D. Thesis, University of London, 1986.

Palmer, J., *Thrillers: Genesis and structure of a popular genre* (London: E. Arnold, 1978).

Pawling, C., *Popular Fiction and Social Change* (London, Macmillan, 1984).

Peiss C., *Cheap Amusements: Working women and leisure in turn-of-the-century New York* (Philadelphia: Temple University Press, 1986).

Prawer, S., *Karl Marx and World Literature* (Oxford: Oxford University Press, 1976).

Propp, V., *Morphology of the Folk-Tale* (Bloomington: Indiana University Press, 1968).

Propp, V., 'Fairy-tale transformations', in Matejka, M. and Pomorska, K. (eds), *Readings in Russian Poetics* (Cambridge, Mass.: MIT Press, 1971).

Radford, J. (ed.), *The Progress of Romance* (London: Routledge, 1986).

Radway, J.A., *Reading the Romance* (Chapel Hill: University of Carolina Press, 1984).

Richards, I.A., *Practical Criticism* (London: Kegan Paul, Trench and Trubner, 1929).

Richardson, S., *'Pamela'*, in Kimpel B. and Eaves B. (eds), (Boston: Houghton-Mifflin, 1971).

Roberts H., 'Propaganda and ideology in women's fiiction', in Laurenson, D. (ed.), *The Sociology of Literature: Applied studies* (Keele: University Sociological Review Monograph, no. 6, 1978).

Rougemont D. de, *Love in the Western World* (Princeton; Princeton University Press, 1983).

Ryan, K., 'Towards a socialist criticism: Reclaiming the canon', *Literature, Teaching and Politics*, no. 3, 1984, pp. 2–18.

Said, E., *Orientalism* (Harmondsworth: Penguin, 1985).

Schucking, L., *The Puritan Family* (London: Routledge, 1969).

Schulte-Sasse, J., 'Towards a culture for the masses: the social psychological function of popular literature in Germany and the United States, 1880–1920', *New German Critique*, 29, spring–summer 1983, pp. 85–103.

Showalter, E., *The New Feminist Criticism* (London: Virago, 1980).

Showalter, E., *A Literature of their Own* (London: Virago, 1981).

Sinfield, A. 'Four ways with a reactionary text', *Journal of Literature, Teaching and Politics*, vol. 1, no. 2, 1983.

Stedman Jones, G., 'Working-class culture and working-class politics in London, 1870–1900', in Waite, B., Bennett, T. and Martin, C.G. (eds), *Popular Culture: Past and present* (London: Croom Helm, 1982).

Sutherland, J., *Fiction and the Fiction Industry* (London: The Athlone Press, 1978).

Sutherland, J., *Bestsellers* (London: Routledge, 1981).

Swingewood, A., *The Myth of Mass Culture* (London: Macmillan, 1977).

Thomas, K., 'The meaning of literacy', in Baumann, G. (ed.), *The Written Word* (Oxford: Clarendon, 1986), pp. 97–132.

Thompson, E.P., 'Review of Raymond Williams's *Long Revolution*', *New Left Review*, no. 8, March–April 1961, pp. 34–9; no. 9, May–June 1961, pp. 34–9.

Thompson, E.P., *The Making of the English Working Class* (Harmondsworth: Penguin, 1968).

Thompson, E.P., *The Poverty of Theory* (London: Merlin, 1979).

Tillotson, K., *Novels of the Eighteen-Forties* (Oxford: Oxford University Press, 1954).

Tompkins, J.P., *Sensational Designs: The cultural work of American fiction, 1790–1860* (New York: Oxford University Press, 1985).

Trommler, F., 'Working-class culture and modern mass culture', *New German Critique*, 29, spring–summer 1983, pp. 57–70.

Vicinus, M., *The Industrial Muse* (London: Croom Helm, 1974).

Vincent, D., *Bread, Knowledge and Freedom* (London: Europa, 1981).

Volosinov, *Marxism and the Philosophy of Language* (New York: Seminar Press, 1973).

Watt, I., *The Rise of the Novel* (Harmondsworth: Peregrine, 1963).

Webb, R.K. *The British Working-Class Reader, 1770–1848* (New York: Augustus Kelley, 1971, (1955)).

Wiener, M., *English Culture and the Decline of the Industrial Spirit* (Harmondsworth: Penguin, 1985).

Williams, R., *Communications* (Harmondsworth: Penguin, 1962).

Williams, R., *The Long Revolution* (Harmondsworth: Penguin, 1965).

Williams, R., *Problems in Materialism and Culture* (London: Verso, 1980).

Williams, R., *The Country and the City* (London: Hogarth, 1985).

Williams, R., *Writing in Society* (London: Verso, no date).

Worpole, K., *Dockers and Detectives* (London: Verso, 1983).

Worpole, K., *Reading by Numbers* (London: Comedia, 1984).

Wolff, J., 'The invisible *flâneuse*: women and the literature of modernity', *Theory, Culture and Society*, vol. 2, no. 3, 1985, pp. 37–47.

Wolff, J. and Seed, J. *The Culture of Capital: Art, power and the nineteenth-century middle class* (Manchester: Manchester University Press, 1988).

Wright, W., *Sixguns and Society. A structural study of the western* (Berkeley: University of California Press, 1975).

Zipes, J. *Breaking the Magic Spell* (London: Heinemann, 1979).

Index

legitimate group 124
  repudiated 135, 140, 184
  sexuality of 147
  working heroines 197
miners 78, 81, 88, 92, 165
Mitchell, Margaret *Gone With the Wind* 24, 151
Mitchell, S. 198
modernism 42, 52, 100, 139, 174
monogamy 54, 110
Moore, Robert 79
Moorhouse, H.F. 97
moral
  Methodists' values 78, 81
  obligations 34
  regulation 40
  virtue 57
More, Sir Thomas 33
Morris, Wiliam 33
Mosco, Maisie 121, 216
Munro, Alice 188
Munro, Marion (respondent) 140
Murray, Mary 196

Nairn, Tom 64
narrative structures 70
needs and reading preferences 139
Newbury, Edith (respondent) 187–9
Nietzsche, F. 31
night-dreams 1, 33–4
nostalgia 126
novelists *see* writers

objectivity in research 69–71
oppositional consciousness 55–6
oppositional culture 68
oppression
  and day-dreams 35
  women 13, 58
  working class 51, 119
Orwell, George 135
'other female' 57, 62–4, 65 *see also* villains

Paine, Tom 36
Paizis, George 26, 45–6
Paladin books 26
Palmer, Charles Mark 89, 95–6, 97
Pamela (Richardson) 2, 15–17, 46
Panther books 26
paradise *see* utopia
passive stories 34, 35
Pasternak, Boris 180
pastoral ideal 67
paternalism 7, 88, 96–7, 109
patriarchy 7, 8, 15, 53, 198
  control of sexuality 92–3, 94
  in Cookson 92–3, 94, 96

and deviance 57
and endings 101
family 39
in family magazines (1930s) 51
and feudalism 9–11, 13, 19
formula as 54
infraction of 59, 60
modern 44, 45, 46, 47, 110
reformed 9, 171
and romantic fiction 144, 175
and women's sexuality 149
patronage 21, 155
peasant 10
  novels 11, 13–15
    heroes 13
  see also feudal
penny issue romances 18, 19, 24–5, 198
People's Friend 51, 144, 149, 205
Perrault, Charles 12
Piercy, Marge 121, 123, 135, 188, 193
Pinter, Harold 123
Plaidy, Jean 151
poetry 39, 135, 215
politics 32, 71, 99
Poor Law 53, 58, 76
Pope, Alexander 23
popular culture group (Bourdieu) 115–16, 216
post modernism 26
poverty 55, 119, 137, 185
Powell, Enoch 82
power 109, 148, 219
  economic 105
  female 80
  inequalities 41
  language of 16, 44
  and punishment 92
  and sexuality 101
Prest, Thomas 24
primogeniture 9, 94
private sphere 8, 54, 101
  as females' 61–2
  and public 70, 71
  regulation of 1
proletarian novel 59
property rights 58, 62, 90, 212
Propp, Vladimir 12
protest
  culture of 42, 67, 174
  and popular culture 118
Protestant ethics 40–1, 63, 65–6
Proust, Marcel 123, 187, 188
public libraries 28, 129–30
  lending estimates 209, 216
public sphere 70, 71, 104
publishing 25–30
  crisis in 28–9